THE GHOST HUNTER'S STRANGEST CASES

THE GHOST HUNTER'S STRANGEST CASES

HANS HOLZER

BARNES & NOBLE
NEW YORK

Book design by Lundquist Design, New York

ISBN 0-7607-7863-9

Printed and bound in the United States of America

10 9 8 7 6 5 4 3 2 1

CONTENTS

INTRODUCTION

$\mathcal{I}$ ought to explain what ghosts are, even if you have read one of my previous books or have a ghost of your own perhaps. In my view, ghosts are the surviving emotional memories of people who have died tragically and are unaware of their own passing. A ghost is a split-off part of the personality remaining behind in the atmosphere of their previous existence, whether a home or place of work, but closely tied to the spot where their death occurred.

Ghosts do not travel, they do not follow people around, and rarely leave the immediate vicinity of their own tragedy. Once in awhile, ghosts roam a house from top to bottom, or may be observed in the garden or adjacent field. But they do not get on cars or buses, they do not appear at the other end of town: those are free spirits, able to reason for themselves and to attempt communication with the living.

In the mind of the casual observer, of course, ghosts and spirits are the same thing. Not so to the trained parapsychologist: ghosts are similar to psychotic human beings, incapable of reasoning for themselves or taking much action. Spirits, on the other hand, are the surviving personalities of all of us who pass through the door of death in a reasonably normal fashion. A spirit is capable of continuing a full existence in the next dimension, to think, reason, feel and act, while his unfortunate colleague, the ghost, could do none of those things. All he can do is repeat the final moments of his passing, the unfinished business, as it were, over and over until it becomes an obsession. In this benighted state he is incapable of much action and ghosts are therefore usually harmless. In the handful of cases where ghosts seem to have caused people to suffer, there was a relationship between the person and the ghost. In one case, someone slept in a bed in which someone else had been murdered and was mistaken, by the murderer, for the same individual. In another case, the murderer returned to the scene of his crime and was attacked by the person he had killed. But by and large ghosts do not attack people—there is little danger in observing them or having contact with them, *if* one is able to.

The majority of ghostly manifestations draw upon energy from the living to be able to penetrate our three-dimensional world. Other manifestations are subjective, especially where the receiver is psychic. In that case, the psychic person hears or sees the departed individual in his mind's eye only, while others cannot so observe it.

Where an objective manifestation takes place, and everyone present is capable of hearing or seeing it, energy drawn from the living is used by the entity to cause certain phenomena, such as an apparition, a voice phenomenon, or perhaps the movement of objects, the recreation of footsteps or doors opening by themselves, and other signs of a presence. When the manifestations become physical in nature and are capable of being observed by several individuals or recorded by machines, they are called Poltergeist phenomena, or noisy phenomena. Not every ghostly manifestation leads to that stage, but many do.

Ghosts, that is individuals unaware of their own passing or incapable of accepting the transition because of unfinished business, will generally make themselves known to living people at infrequent intervals. There is no sure way of knowing when or why some individuals make a post-mortem appearance and others do not. It seems to depend on the intensity of feeling, the residue of unresolved problems, which they have within their system at the time of death. Consequently, not everyone dying a violent death becomes a ghost; far from it.

A common misconception concerning ghosts is that they appear only at midnight, or, at any rate, only at night; or that they eventually fade away as time goes on. To begin with, ghosts are split-off parts of personality incapable of realizing the difference between day and night. They are always in residence, so to speak, and can be contacted by properly equipped mediums at all times. They may put in an appearance only at certain hours of the day or night, depending upon the atmosphere; for the fewer physical disturbances there are, the easier it is for them to communicate themselves to the outer world. They are dimly aware that there is something out there different from themselves, but their diminished reality does not permit them to fully grasp the situation. Consequently, a quiet moment, such as is more likely to be found at night than in the daytime, is the period when the majority of sightings are reported.

Some manifestations occur on the exact moment of the anniversary, because at that time the memory of the unhappy event is strongest. But that does not mean that the presence is absent at other times—merely less capable of manifestations. Since ghosts are not only expressions of human personality left behind in the physical atmosphere but no longer part of it, but are, in terms of physical science, electromagnetic fields uniquely impressed by the personality and memories of the departed one, they represent a certain energy imprint in the atmosphere and, as such, cannot simply fade into nothingness. Professor Albert Einstein has demonstrated that energy can never dissipate, only transmute into other forms. Ghosts do not fade away over the centuries; they are present for all eternity, so to say, unless someone makes contact with them through a trance medium and brings reality to them, allowing them to understand their predicament and thus free themselves from their self-imposed prison. The moment the mirror of truth is held up to a ghost, and he or she realizes that the problems they feel are insoluble are no longer important, they will be able to leave.

Frequently, the rescuer has to explain that the only way they can leave is by calling out to someone close to them in life—a loved one, or a friend, who will then come and take them away with them into the next stage of existence, where they should have gone long before. This is called the rescue circle and a rather delicate operation calling for the services of a trained psychical researcher and a good trance medium. Amateurs are warned not to attempt it, especially not when they're alone.

The cases in this book are from my files, which bulge with interesting experiences by ordinary people in all walks of life, and from all corners of the globe. The majority of the witnesses knew nothing about ghosts, nor did they seek out such phenomena. When they had the experiences described in these pages, they were taken by surprise; sometimes shocked, sometimes worried. They came to me for advice, because they could not obtain satisfactory counsel from ordinary sources, such as psychologists, psychiatrists, or their minister.

Small wonder, for such professionals are rarely equipped to deal with phenomena involving parapsychology. Perhaps in years to come they will be able to do so, but not now. In all cases, I advised the individuals not to be afraid of what might transpire in their presence, to take the phenomenon as part of human existence and to deal with it in a friendly, quiet way. For it is the worst one can do to become panicky in the presence of ghosts, since it will not help the ghost and cause the observer unnecessary anxiety. Never forget that those who are "hung up" between two phases of existence are in trouble, and not trouble-makers, and a compassionate gesture toward them may very well relieve their anxieties.

The people whose cases I tell of in these pages seek no publicity or notoriety; they have come to terms with the hauntings to which they were witness. In some cases, it has changed their outlook on life by showing them the reality of another world next door. In other cases what was once fear has turned into a better understanding of the nature of humanity; still other instances permitted the witnesses to the phenomena a better understanding of the current status of loved ones, and the reassuring feeling that they would meet again on the other side of the curtain.

When you read these pages, friends, remember that any of the phenomena described here could have happened to *you* or to your people, that there is nothing *supernatural* about any of this, and that in years to come we will deal with them as ordinary events, part and parcel of human experience.

VISITS AND VISITATIONS

People all over the world have moved into houses which seemed ordinary and pleasant, and spent years without ever encountering anything out of the ordinary. Then, one day, something happens to disturb their tranquility: a ghost appears, strange noises are heard, and a psychic presence makes itself known.

Why is it that phenomena occur at times long after someone moves into an affected house? Of course, there are just as many cases where the ominous presence is felt the very moment one steps across the threshold. But in cases where ghosts make their presence manifest long after the new tenants have moved in, certain conditions have not been right for such manifestations to take place at the beginning. For instance, it may involve the presence of youngsters in the household who furnish the energy for ghosts to appear. Or it may be that the shadowy entities remaining behind in the house are dimly aware of the new tenants, but wish to find out more about them before manifesting to them. Either way, once manifestations begin, the owner of the house has the choice of either ignoring them, fighting them, or coming to terms with them.

In many cases, unfortunately, people simply think that by ignoring the phenomena or trying hard to explain them by so-called natural causes, the matter can be solved. Ignoring problems never helps, in any area of life. When it comes to psychic phenomena, the phenomena may become worse, because even the most benighted ghost, barely aware of its predicament, will become more powerful, more restless, by being ignored.

Take Ms. A.M.B., for instance. She lived in central Illinois and was by training and profession a practical nurse, engaged in psychiatric work. If anything, she was able to distinguish psychosis from psychic activity. She had had ESP abilities ever since she could remember. Once, when she was twelve years old, she was playing in front of her house when she met what to her was an old man, inquiring about a certain widow living in the next block of the village. The young Ms. B. knew very well that the lady had become a widow due to her husband having been killed while working as a crossing guard during a blizzard the previous winter. She remembered the husband well, but the stranger did not resemble the deceased at all, so she assumed he was a relative inquiring about the dead man.

The stranger wanted to know where the widow had moved to. The twelve year old Ms. B. explained that the lady had gone to visit a sister somewhere in Missouri, due to the fact that her husband had been killed in an accident. At that, the stranger nodded; he knew of the accident, he said. "Let me help you," Ms. B. said to the stranger. "I'll point out to you where another sister of the widow lives, not more than two blocks away from here. Perhaps they can tell you which town in Missouri she is visiting." The stranger obliged her, and the two were walking along the front porch, toward the steps leading down into the street, still in conversation. At that moment, her mother appeared at the front door in back of her and demanded to know what she was talking about. The girl was surprised, and explained that the gentleman was merely asking where Mrs. C. had gone, and added, "I told him she went to Missouri." But the mother replied, in a surprised tone of voice, "What are you talking about? I don't see anyone." The young girl immediately pointed at the visitor, who by that time had had enough time to get to the steps, for the front porch was rather large.

But—to her shock—she saw no one there! Immediately the girl and her mother walked into the yard, looking about everywhere without finding any trace of the strange visitor. He had simply vanished the moment the young girl had turned around to answer her mother.

Mrs. M.R. was a housewife who lived in a medium-sized New England town. When she and I were in contact, her husband worked for the United States Post Office, and Mrs. R. took care of two of their three children, the oldest being already married and living away from home. She, too, had lived with the psychic world practically from the beginning. When she was only seven years old, she and her sister, two years her senior, were in bed, playing and whispering to each other in order not to wake up their parents, whose room was next to theirs. Suddenly, there appeared a misty figure at the door connecting the children's room with the living room. It drifted through the children's room and stopped at the door to the parents' room, facing the sleeping couple. The children both saw it: the figure seemed grayish-white and had some sort of cord around its waist. At that moment their father awoke and saw it too. Yelling out to it to go away, he awoke his wife. Even though the figure still stood in the doorway of their room, she could not see it. At that moment, the ghost just disappeared.

Although Mrs. R. had many dreams that later came true, she did not see a ghost again until she was twenty-three years old. At that time she had already given birth to her first child, and she and her husband were staying for a week at her mother's apartment. The child was still in the hospital, having been a premature baby, and Mrs. R. lay in bed, thinking about her child. At that moment there appeared at the door to the room a very tall, dark, hooded figure. Far from being afraid, she watched the figure glide into the room, come around the foot of the bed and toward her to her side. The room seemed filled with a soft glow, not unlike moonlight, even though the shades were down; the furniture could be seen plainly as if there were lights in the room. By now the visitor stood right next to the bed and Mrs. R. was able to look up into his face; but in the emptiness of the hood, where a face should be, there was nothing, absolutely nothing. Then, very slowly, the figure bent over her from its great height, and it was only when the empty hood was almost touching her face, that Mrs. R. cried out in a kind of muffled way. Apparently, her outcry had broken the spell, for the phantom disappeared as quickly as it had come. Whether there was any connection between the ghostly visitor she had seen as a child and the monk-like phantom who came to her many years later, Mrs. R. does not know. But it may well be that both were one and the same, perhaps sent to protect her or guide her in some way, from out of the distant past.

David H. was only seventeen years old and lived in Michigan. When he was eight he had his first encounter with a ghost. The house his parents lived in was more than a hundred years old, and rather on the large side. David slept in one of two main rooms on the upper floor of the house; the room next to it was unfurnished. One night he was lying in bed when he had a sudden urge to sit up, and as he did so he looked down the hall. All of a sudden he noticed a small shadow-like man jump down from the attic and run towards him. But instead of coming into his room, he turned down the stairs. David could see that he wore a small derby hat but what was even more fascinating was the fact that the figure walked about two inches above the floor! After the figure had disappeared, David thought it was all his imagination. A particularly bright eight-year-old, he was not easily taken in by fantasies or daydreams.

But the strange figure reappeared several times more, and eventually David came to the conclusion that it was real. He asked his parents whether he could swap rooms with them and they agreed to let him sleep downstairs. It was about that time that his mother told him that she had heard the old piano playing at night downstairs. She had thought that it was the cat climbing up on the keys, but one night the piano played in plain view of herself and one of her daughters, without even a trace of the cat in the room. There was also the sound of pages in a book being turned in the same area, although nobody had a book or turned any pages.

David settled down in his room on the lower floor and finally forgot all about his ghostly experiences. Shortly after, he heard a crunching noise on the stairs, as if someone were walking on them. He assumed it was his mother coming down the stairs to tell him to turn off his radio, but no one came.

As he grew older, he moved back upstairs, since the room on the ground floor had become too small for him. This proved to be somewhat of a strain for him: many times he would be lying in bed when someone would call his name. But there never was anyone there. Exasperated, the youngster spoke up, challenging the ghost to give some sign of his presence so that there could be communication between them. "If you can hear me, make a noise," David said to his ghost. At that very moment, the door to his room began to rattle without apparent cause. Still unconvinced, since the door had rattled before because of natural causes, David continued his monologue with, "If you are there, show yourself," and at that moment he heard a strange noise behind him. The door to his closet, which had been closed, was slowly opening. This wasn't very reassuring, even though it might represent some kind

5

of dialogue with the ghost.

Shortly thereafter, and in broad daylight, just as he had gotten home from school, David heard a very loud noise in the upper portion of the house: it sounded as if all their cats were tearing each other to pieces and the sound of a lot of coat hangers falling down augmented the bedlam. Quickly, David ran up the stairs—only to find neither cats nor fallen coat hangers. And to this day, David doesn't know who the strange visitor was.

Lana T. was one of seven children from eastern Missouri, who had ESP to a considerable extent. Three of her sisters also have this ability, so perhaps it runs in the family. When she contacted me, she was a housewife and she and her husband lived in a big city in central Missouri. Clairvoyant dreams and other verified incidents of ESP led to an interest in the much-maligned Ouija board, and she and her three sisters, Jean, Judy, and Tony, became veritable addicts of this little gadget. A close friend and her husband moved into a nearby house in the same community, without realizing that the house had become available due to the suicide of the previous owner.

Lana T.'s friend had come from another state, so the local facts were not well known to her. When the new owner discovered that her neighbor, Lana T., had psychic gifts and an interest in occult matters, she confided freely in her. It appeared that one of the bathrooms was always cold, regardless of the weather outside or the temperature in the rest of the house; a certain closet door would simply not stay closed; and the heat register was bound to rattle of its own volition. Objects would move from one place to another, without anyone having touched them. Footsteps were heard going up and down the hall, as if someone were pacing up and down. Once the new owner saw a whitish mist which dissolved immediately when she spoke to it.

Her husband, who published a local newspaper, would not

even discuss the matter, considering it foolish. But one night he woke up and informed her that he had just been touched by a cold, clammy hand. This was enough to drive the new owner to consult with her neighbor. Lana T. offered to try and find out who the disturbing ghost was. Together with one of her sisters, she sat herself down with her trusty Ouija board, and asked it to identify the disturbing entity in the house. Ouija board communication is slow and sometimes boring, but, in this instance, the instrument rapidly identified the communicator as a certain Ted. A chill went down Lana's spine, for Ted was the man who had committed suicide in her friend's house.

From then on, a veritable conversation ensued between Lana T. and the ghost, in which he explained that he was angry because the new owner had burned something of his. Lana asked what the new owner could do to satisfy him, and the angry ghost replied that she should destroy something of her own to make up for his loss—something white. When Lana described her conversation with the ghost to the new owner of the house, the lady was mystified. She could not recall having burned anything belonging to the former owner. Back to the Ouija board went Lana T. When she demanded that the ghost describe the item in question more fully, he replied, somewhat impatiently, that it had been white with green trim and had the letters SFCC on it. Lana returned to her neighbor with this additional information. This time she struck paydirt: shortly after the couple from out of state had moved into the house, the lady of the house had discovered an old golf cap in the top drawer of one of her closets, white with green trim and the initials of the country club, SFCC, on it! The cap had somehow bothered her, so she had tossed it into the trash can and the contents of the can were later burned. The ghost had told the truth. But how could she satisfy his strange whim in return? At that time she and her husband had considered buying a small, expensive white marble statue. They decided to forego this pleasure.

7

Perhaps their sacrifice of this "white" item would make up for the lost golf cap? Evidently it did—for the house quieted down, and the former occupant was not heard from again!

Mrs. Edith F. was the wife of a law enforcement officer in the west. Her husband put very little credence in anything "supernatural," but Mrs. F. knew otherwise. The house she and her family lived in was only about twelve years old, and fifteen years earlier, the area was still "in the country," although people may have lived there in a previous house. In fact, rumor had it that some old houses were torn down on the land where her house then stood. The series of odd incidents which convinced Mrs. F. of the reality of another dimension began in the summer of 1972.

At that time her nine-year-old son was in the basement family room, watching television. On the north wall of this large room there was a door leading to a storeroom. A rollaway bed had been put there for possible summer company, and the boy was in this particular bed, propped up with a large pillow. He had just finished a snack, and leaned up to brush the crumbs from under him, when he happened to look up and saw an old woman standing beside the bed, staring at him. He looked away from her for a moment, then returned his eyes onto her; she was still there. Frightened, he began to yell for his mother, at which the woman moved back towards the door. The door opened about two inches, and she quickly slid through it, as if she were two-dimensional.

By that time Mrs. F. arrived downstairs and found her son so frightened he could hardly talk. He described the visitor as very old, with black and gray hair parted in the middle, wearing a long black dress and a single pair of colored beads. Mrs. F. decided not to discuss it with her husband, who would only scoff at it, but decided to return to the basement with her twenty-year-old-daughter to see whether anything would occur in her presence. The two women stood on the spot where the boy had seen the ghost and asked her what she wanted of them. For a moment, nothing happened. Then, suddenly, Mrs. F. felt as though someone were lifting her right arm which turned tingly and raised up in front of her by its own volition! She broke out in goose pimples and quickly whirled around, running back upstairs.

For several days, she did not dare go back to the basement out of fear that the phenomenon might repeat itself. But on the fourth day, Mrs. F. could not hold back any longer; she had to know what the ghost wanted. Somehow she felt she would get it by writing. Again she went to the basement with her twenty-year-old daughter, said a prayer for protection from evil, and stood upright with paper and a pen in her right hand—why, she didn't really know, for she was *left*-handed. She asked aloud if there was anyone present, and the pen wrote, "Yes. You must watch out to woman," and then it drew an arrow toward the northern part of the room. Mrs. F. demanded to know what the ghost wanted, and in reply, the pen in her hand wrote, "Priest. Hear my confession." Mrs. F. demanded to know what her name was, and the ghost identified herself as Mary Arthur.

Still upset by it all, she telephoned the Reverend L.B., a Methodist minister, whom, she hoped, would have an open mind concerning occult phenomena. With her new information Mrs. F. and her daughter went to her minister friend, who decided to accompany the two women back to the house. He, too, stood in the basement and asked the ghost to give him a sign that she was present. A lamp, which they knew to be in good order, blinked on and off several times in response to their questions. Then, through automatic writing, the ghost informed them that she had died at age eighty-nine, had had nine children, and knew she had passed on in 1959. But the Methodist minister could not help her, she explained; it had to be a Catholic priest. The Reverend B. offered to talk to his Catholic colleague, but Mrs. F. suggested the ghost might find peace in nearby St. Agnes Church. On this note, the presence disappeared and was gone until the following Monday.

On that day, Mrs. F. was in the basement room, working on an ironing board. It was a very warm day, but suddenly she was startled by walking into a blast of icy air on the spot where the ghost had been originally observed by her son. Quickly she called for her daughter to join her and watch. After a moment, her daughter complained that her arm was being lifted the way her mother's had been before. She felt as if someone held it, and the arm felt tingly. Mrs. F. grabbed a pencil and paper from a nearby desk and gave it to her daughter. Her daughter then wrote "Mary" in exactly the same handwriting as Mrs. F. had originally. Then she handed the pencil and paper back to her mother, afraid to continue. So the mother continued the communication and the ghost wrote "Mary Arthur." Gradually, the reasons for her presence became clear. "Father, forgive me, for I have sinned," the ghost wrote, and demanded that the note be taken to a Roman Catholic priest. But Mrs. F. instead suggested that Mary call out to her loved ones to take her away from the place so she could find peace. "No, because of my sins," the ghost replied, and when Mrs. F. wanted to know what the sins consisted of, she simply said, "the marriage."

It was then that Mrs. F. learned that Mary had been born Catholic, had left the church and married a Lutheran and had had nine children with him. To her, this marriage was illegal, sinful. Eventually, the Roman Catholic clergy got into the act. But a special priest would have to be sent to exorcise Mary's sins. This did not sit well with Mrs. F., nor with her Methodist friend, neither of whom thought that Mary marrying outside her faith made her evil.

Time passed, and things seemed to quiet down in the basement. Then, on Labor Day of the same year, 1972, with her husband and son fast asleep in bed, Mrs. F. was in the kitchen canning tomatoes from their garden. Again she felt Mary's presence upstairs, a strange feeling that was hard to describe. Again, her right arm was tingling and her fingers felt as they did when Mary first wanted to write something through her. However, since the Roman Catholic clergy had been reluctant to enter the case, Mrs. F. determined to ignore her promptings. Here she was, washing tomatoes at her kitchen sink, when all of a sudden she heard a *plop!* behind her, turned around, and saw one of the tomatoes lying split open in the middle of the floor. Since she was the only person in the kitchen, there was no rational explanation for the fall of the tomato. Had it merely fallen off the counter, it would have gone straight down instead of jumping four feet away!

Quietly, Mrs. F. turned in the direction where she assumed her ghost lady was and reprimanded her for throwing the tomato. "They are saying special prayers at the church for you," she said, and asked Mary to go there and wait for her delivery.

Everything was quiet after that. About ten days later, a lamp in Mrs. F.'s living room blinked on and off four times as if the ghost were trying to tell her something. This time Mrs. F. did not feel the tingling sensation in her arm, and somehow felt that this was a farewell message. And after that time there were no more signs of Mary's presence. With the help of her minister friend, Mrs. F. was able to check the records of various funeral homes in the area. A Mary Arthur was buried in 1959.

Mrs. E. never had any interest in the occult nor experiences along ghostly lines until after her father died. It was a great loss to her and the family, since he had been a pillar of strength and had handled all their affairs. Shortly after he died, Mrs. E. was sitting in her mother's house and suddenly, without explanation, she found herself picking up a pen with her right hand, even though she too was left-handed. On the back of a used envelope she wrote the words, "Tell Mama to take that will to the lawyer." Her mother had added some postscripts to her father's will, but had not realized that these requests would not be honored unless and until they had been witnessed and notarized again by an attorney! Mrs. E.'s ghost was giving her good advice!

Jananne B. was an attractive twenty-five-year-old woman, who had truck with the unseen since she was very small. While she was visiting her aunt in New Jersey, she remembers clearly seeing a figure in the old carriage house. There was no one in the carriage house at the time. At age seventeen, Miss B. was spending a weekend with another aunt, also in New Jersey. Both women were occupying the same bed. In the middle of the night the young woman sat up in bed, waking up her aunt. There was a tall man in a brown suit standing next to the bed, she explained, and went on to describe his brown hair and handlebar moustache in great detail. Without saying a word, her aunt got up and brought out the family album. Leafing through it, Miss B. pointed at one particular picture: it was her great-grandfather. She had never seen pictures of him, nor of course ever met him. He had died in the very room and bed in which the two women were sleeping at the time.

When she was twenty-four years old, Jananne moved into what was formerly her brother's room, her brother having moved to his own apartment. The very first night she stayed in the room, she felt a presence, and couldn't sleep. Somehow the room had always been the stuffiest room in the house, but that night it was particularly cold. This upset her greatly since she had put in a great deal of time and effort to redecorate it to her taste. Somehow she managed to go to sleep that night, trying to forget or ignore her feelings. But, a few nights later she woke up in the middle of the night, feeling extremely cold. As she sat up in bed, she saw a woman out of the corner of her eye: the woman seemed middle-aged, with brown hair pulled back in a very plain bun, wearing a long, straight skirt and a white ruffled blouse with long sleeves and high collar.

Jananne did not experience a feeling of fear, for somehow she knew the spirit was friendly. The next morning just as she was about to wake up, she saw the name "Elly" being written on the wall above her shelves. There were other lines around the name, but before she could make them out, the vision faded. Since she keeps a dream log, recording all unusual dreams, she immediately wrote this incident down, before she could forget it. She also told her mother about the incidents. Time passed, and several months later a local psychic came to the house to do a reading for the family, using her bedroom to work in.

The psychic described the entity in the room precisely the way Jananne had seen it. By then Jananne B. was not the only one to be aware of the ghost. Various friends also heard footsteps overhead while sitting in a room directly underneath hers, and had seen the lights dim of their own volition. Because of the ghostly presence, Jananne's room was unusually cold, and she frequently complained about it. Another time, when she remarked how cold it was, the door to the outdoor widow's walk flew wide open and her bedroom door shut of its own volition.

This happened a number of times, making the room even colder. On several occasions, Miss B. came home to find her bedroom door tightly shut, and very hard to open. Once inside, she noticed that her bedspread was on the floor, propped up against the outside door from the inside. No one could have placed it there except from inside the room—and the room had been locked.

Soon enough Miss B. realized that she had to get used to sharing her room with the strange lady. Once her mind was made up to accept her as a companion, the phenomenon became less annoying. A short time later, she decided to take some random pictures of the room, to see whether anything unusual would show up on them. Only the available room light was used, no flash light or electrical lighting. Two of the pictures came back from the laboratory with a white mist on them, one of them showing the letters Elly indistinctly, but nevertheless apparent beyond the shadow of a doubt. Miss B. showed the photographs to her brother, a professional photographer, and to some of his friends. They agreed that double exposure or light leaks were out; the white mist appears to be blotchy, almost like smoke, whereas light leaks would tend to be uniform.

Jananne realizes that Elly was able to manifest for her only because she was psychic. If she needed any further proof of her ability in this respect, it was furnished to her a month later when a friend took her to a certain lady's trailer home for dinner. Jananne's friend asked her to dress lightly because it was always warm there, he said.

But when they arrived at the trailer, it was unusually cold inside. They were having a quiet conversation after dinner, sitting on the couch, when Miss B. looked up and saw the figure of a very sad young man standing in the entrance to the hallway. His head was bowed, and he seemed very lost. Since the hostess had turned out to be rather on the nervous side, Jananne decided not to tell her about the apparition. But on the way home, she informed her friend what she had seen, describing the man in every detail. Her friend swallowed hard, then informed her that the husband of their hostess had disappeared shortly after returning from Vietnam. Three months later his body was found in the woods; he had committed suicide.

Dorothy Mark-Moore was twelve years old when her Aunt Mary bought a house in Green Brook, New Jersey. The house was on Washington Street and the year was 1933. All the members of the family had retired for the night, and it was rather a warm night at that, so Dorothy thought she'd roll up her pajama legs, and go sleep like that. She awoke in the early hours of the morning with a start and looked around the room. It so happened that it was a moonlit night so she could make out very clearly if there happened to be an intruder in the room.

As she looked toward the window, she saw a woman walk in, return to the window, look out of it and then turn toward her. Frightened, Dorothy pretended to be asleep for a moment, but then she opened her eyes again and to her amazement saw a nun standing there, looking at her from head to foot. Then the nun came over and moved her hand onto her legs. But when the nun touched Dorothy's legs, it felt "like an old dried-out piece of wood."

The ghostly nun was then close enough to the bed for Dorothy to make out a ring on her hand and beads around her waist, with a large cross dangling at the end of it. The woman appeared to be in her thirties, and seemed quite solid. Suddenly Dorothy realized she was looking at a ghost. She shot up and looked straight into the nun's face. For a moment, girl and ghost stared at each other. Then the nun's face softened as she walked away from Dorothy and vanished into the wall.

Four years later the ghostly nun returned. This time Dorothy was asleep in another bedroom of the same house and it was around seven o'clock in the morning. All of a sudden, Dorothy heard loud organ music and sat up in bed to find out where it came from. The music became so loud she could not stand it and fell back onto the pillows. It felt as if an invisible hand were holding her down. At that moment, the nun entered the room, with a gentleman in his forties, with dark hair and brown eyes, wearing a dark blue serge suit. Dorothy was petrified with fear, especially as the organ music increased to an almost ear-splitting level. Looking at the two apparitions, she noticed that they were reciting the Lord's Prayer, from the movement of their lips. As they did so, the music became less loud, and the two figures slowly walked towards the door. As they left the room, the music stopped abruptly. At that moment, Dorothy seemed to snap out of her trance state, sat up in bed and quickly grabbed all her clothes, running to the bathroom and locking herself in. When she had regained her composure, she made some inquiries about the house and learned that a gentle-man of that description had killed himself in the very bathroom into which she had locked herself, some fifty years before.

It was a warm weekend in June of 1971, and a group of New Jersey college students decided to throw a party at a place known as "The Farmhouse," which had been rented for the occasion. Most of the young people were between nineteen and twenty-two years of age, and as the party progressed, the spirits were high. Sometime that evening, a boy named Arthur D., son of a policeman, crashed the party and a fight ensued. According to local newspapers, the fight was part of the shindig, but according to others, the boy was ejected and lay in wait to get even with those who had turned him down. But as a result of the fighting, Arthur lay dead in the street, due to wounds received from a knife. Glen F., a twenty-two-year-old youth at the party, was arrested for his murder. Another boy was in the local hospital, seriously injured, but expected to survive. . . . That was in June, 1971, and it was one graduation party long remembered in the area.

In the summer of 1972 the house was rented out to a certain Mrs. Gloria Brown. Mrs. Brown and three children were sleeping in the hayloft of the barn, which was located a certain distance from the main house. One of the girls saw a light in the house go on downstairs and the figure of a man which she thought was her father. When she investigated, the man tried to grab her. She screamed and her brothers came to her aid. By that time the "man" had run away. Later that summer, a friend was staying with the Browns one evening. There was a knock at the door of the main house about two o'clock in the morning. The friend got up and answered it, but there was no one outside. She went back to bed, only to be awakened again. This time she opened the door and looked through the screen door to see whether there might be someone outside.

There was a man standing outside all right, and she asked whether he was hurt or needed help. Then she noticed that he had neither face nor hands; he was only a whitish, swirly substance! Horror-stricken, she stared at him when he disappeared just as suddenly as he had come.

The restless young man was still unable to find peace: for him, the unlucky party had never broken up.

Yellow Frame Church was an old country church at Yellow Frame, New Jersey. It stood in one of the most isolated areas of the state and was but little-known to people outside the immediate area. There was only the minister's house and a graveyard across the street, but no other dwellings close by. In the early 1800's a new minister had come to Yellow Frame and, after his very first sermon, dropped dead. He was duly buried in the church yard across from the church. However for unknown reasons, his body was taken some years later from the churchyard and moved to another cemetery at Johnsonburg, two miles down the road.

So much for the background of the old building. I wouldn't be writing about it if it weren't for a report from an alert reader, Mrs. Johanna C., who lived in a nearby town. Apparently there had been an incident involving a woman on her way home early in the morning, while it was still dark, in the 1960's. When the lady passed the church she heard choir music coming from it and saw that both doors were wide open. Curious as to who might be playing the organ that early in the morning, or, rather, that late at night, she stepped up and peered into the church: the inside of the building was quite dark, and when she stepped inside she noticed that there was no one in the church who could have played the organ. Frightened, she left in a hurry.

In the late 1960's, Mr. C. and a group of friends, who had heard the account of the organ music, decided to see for themselves whether there was anything unusual about the church. As so many others who think that Hallowe'en was the time to look for ghosts, Mr. C. and friends picked the night of October 31 to do their ghost hunt. Of course, there was no connection between Hallowe'en, the solemn holiday of witchcraft, the Old Religion, and ghosts; but popular superstition will always link them, since ghosts and witches *seem* to belong to the same level of reference. At any rate, Mr. C. and his friends arrived at Yellow Frame Church at exactly midnight and bravely walked up the steps of the church. At that hour, the church was of course closed. As they confronted the locked doors, the doors suddenly swung open of their own volition, startling the visitors no end. But this did not stop them; they stepped inside the church and, as they did so, each one of the group noticed a strange pressure on his ears as if the air were pushing against them!

One in the group called out, "Reverend, oh Reverend!" but there was no answer. The eerie stillness of the building was too much for them, and they hurried out.

A year later, again on Hallowe'en, Mrs. C. went along with the same group to see whether she could experience anything out of the ordinary. They arrived at the church shortly before midnight, driving by it at first to get a look of it. They noticed that both doors were shut. A few minutes later they returned to see that one of the doors was slightly open. They parked their car and stepped inside the church. At that moment Mrs. C. could also feel the strange pressure on her ears. She also felt as if someone were hiding in the church, watching them. There was a peaceful feeling about it, almost, she explained, as if she were being wrapped in a blanket. Mrs. C. decided to spend some time inside the church to see whether it was truly haunted, but the men would have no part of it and insisted that they all leave again. While they stood around inside, discussing whether or not they should go immediately, they clearly heard what appeared to be footsteps in the leaves. It sounded as if someone were walking around just outside the building. However, they did not stay around long enough to find out whether there was, in fact, someone walking who was not a member of their group.

But the matter did not give Mrs. C. any rest, so she returned to the church once more in the company of a girlfriend, this time during daylight hours. She managed to meet the present minister's wife, telling her of their experiences. To their relief, the minister's wife was not at all shocked: not long ago she had awakened at six in the morning, while it was still quite dark outside, and peering out the window toward the church, she became aware of lights in the church going on and off as if someone were signaling with them. Those were the facts; there was also a tradition in the area that the church was haunted by the restless spirit of the original minister, who doesn't like being buried in the wrong cemetery and comes up the Yellow Frame Road searching for his original resting place.

THE STAY-BEHINDS: AFTER ALL, IT'S THEIR HOUSE, TOO!

The average person thinks that there is just one kind of ghost, and that spirits and ghosts are all one and the same. Nothing could be further from the truth; ghosts are not spirits, and psychic impressions are not the same as ghosts. Basically, there are three phenomena involved when a person dies under traumatic, tragic circumstances and is unable to adjust to the passing from one state of existence to the next. The most common form of passing is of course the transition from physical human being to spirit being, without difficulty and without the need to stay in the denser, physical atmosphere of earth. The majority of tragic passings do not present any problems, because the individual accepts the change and becomes a free spirit, capable of communicating freely with those on the earth plane, and advancing according to his abilities, his likes and dislikes, and the help he or she may receive from others already on the Other Side of life. A small fraction of those who die tragically are unable to recognize the change in their status and become so-called ghosts; that is, parts of human personality hung up in the physical world but no longer part of it or able to function in it. These are the only true ghosts in the literal sense of the term.

However a large number of sightings of so-called ghosts are not of this nature, but represent imprints left behind in the atmosphere by the passing itself. Anyone possessed of psychic ability will sense the event from the past and, in his mind's eye, reconstruct it. The difficulty is that one frequently does not know the difference between a psychic imprint without life of its own and a true ghost. Both seem very real, subjectively speaking. The only way one can differentiate between the two phenomena is when several sightings are compared for minute details. True ghosts move about somewhat, although usually not outside the immediate area of their passing. Imprints are always identical, regardless of observers involved, and do not alter details at any time. Psychic imprints, then, are very much like photographs or films of an actual event while true ghosts are the events themselves, and capable of some measure of reaction to the environment. Whenever there are slight differences in detail concerning an apparition, we are dealing with a true ghost personality; but whenever the description of an apparition or scene from the past is identical from source to source, we are most likely dealing only with a lifeless imprint reflecting the event but in no way suggesting a presence at the time of the observation.

However, there is a subdivision of true ghosts which I have called the Stay-behinds. The need for such a subdivision came to me several years ago when I looked through numerous cases of reported hauntings that did not fall into the category of tragic, traumatic passing, nor cases of death involving neither violence nor great suffering, the earmarks of true ghosts. To the contrary, many of these sightings involved peaceful passings, people who had lived in their respective homes for many years and grown to love them. I realized by comparing these cases one with the other, that they had certain things in common, the most outstanding of which was this: they were greatly attached to their homes, often had lived in them for considerable periods prior to death, and were strong-willed individuals who had managed to develop a routine of life of their own. It appears, therefore, that the Stay-behinds are spirits who are unable to let go of their former homes, are more or less aware of their passing into the next dimension but are unwilling to go on. To them, their earthly home is preferable, and the fact that they no longer possess a physical body is no deterrent to continue to live in it.

Some of these Stay-behinds adjust to their limitations with marvelous ingenuity. They are still capable of causing physical phenomena, especially if they can draw on living people in the house. At times, however, they become annoyed at changes undertaken by successors in their house, and when these changes evoke anger in them they are capable of some mischievous activities, not unlike Poltergeist phenomena, although of a somewhat different nature. Sometimes they are quite satisfied to continue living their former lives, staying out of the way of flesh-and-blood inhabitants of the house and remaining undiscovered until someone with psychic ability notices them by accident. Sometimes, however, they *want* the flesh-and-blood people to know that they are still very much in residence, and in asserting their continuing rights, may come into conflict with the living in the house. Some of these manifestations seem frightening or even threatening to people living in houses of this kind, which should not be, since the Stay-behinds are, after all, human beings like all others who have developed a continuing and very strong attachment to their former homes. Of course, not everyone can come to terms with them.

Take for instance the case of Margaret C. A few years ago, when she lived in New York state, she decided to spend Christmas with her sister and brother-in-law in Pennsylvania. The husband's mother had recently passed away so it would have been a sad Christmas holiday for them. Mrs. C. was given a room on the second floor of the old house, close to a passage which led to the downstairs part of the house. Being tired from her long journey, she went to bed around eleven, but found it difficult to fall asleep. Suddenly she clearly heard the sound of a piano being played in the house. It sounded like a very old piano, and the music on it reminded her of music played in church. At first Mrs. C. thought someone had left a radio on so she checked, but found that this was not the case. Somehow, she managed to fall asleep despite the tinkling sound of the piano downstairs. At breakfast, Mrs. C. mentioned her experience to her sister. Her sister gave her an odd look, then took her by the hand and led her down the stairs where she pointed to an old piano. It had been the property of the dead mother, the one that had recently passed away, but it had not been played in many years since no one else in the house knew how to play the piano. With mounting excitement, the two women pried the rusty lid open. This took some effort, but eventually they succeeded in opening the keyboard.

Picture their surprise when they found that thick dust had settled on the keys—but etched in the dust were the unmistakable imprints of human fingers. They were thin, bony fingers, like the fingers of a very old woman. Prior to her passing, the deceased had been very thin indeed, and church music had been her favorite. Was the lady of the house still around, playing her beloved piano?

The house on South Sixth Street in upstate Hudson, New York, was one of the many fine old town houses dotting this old town on the Hudson River. It was built between 1829 and 1849 and a succession of owners lived in it to the present day. In 1904 it passed into the hands of the Parker family. There was a daughter, first-named Mabel, a very lively, fun person with a zest for life. In her sixties, she contracted a tragic illness and suffered very much, until she finally passed away in a nearby hospital. She had been truly house-proud, and hated to leave for the cold and ominous surroundings of the hospital. After she died, the house passed into the hands of Mr. and Mrs. Jay Dietz, who still owned it when I visited them in 1966. Mrs. Dietz had been employed by Mabel Parker's father at one time.

The psychic did not particularly interest Mrs. Dietz, although she had had one notable experience the night her step-grandfather died, whom she had loved very much. She had been at home taking care of him throughout the daytime and finally returned to her own house to spend the night. Everybody had gone to bed, and as she lay in hers, her face to the wall, she became aware of an unusual glow in the room. She turned over and opened her eyes, and she noticed that on the little nightstand at the head of the bed was a large ball of light, glowing with a soft golden color. As she was still staring at the phenomenon, the telephone rang, and news was brought that her step-grandfather had passed away.

In 1955, the Dietzes moved into the house on South Sixth Street. At first, the house seemed peaceful enough. Previous tenants included a German war bride and her mother. The old lady had refused to sleep upstairs in the room which later became Mrs. Dietz's mother's. There was something uncanny about that room, she explained. So she slept down on the ground floor on a couch instead. The Dietzes paid no attention to these stories until they began to notice some strange things about their house. There were footsteps going up and down the stairs, into the hall and then stopping. The three of them, Mr. and Mrs. Dietz and the mother, all heard them many times.

One year, just before Christmas, Mrs. Dietz was attending to some sewing in the hall downstairs while her husband was in the bathroom. Suddenly she thought he came down the hall and she thought that odd since she hadn't heard the toilet being flushed. But as she turned around, there was no one there. A few nights later she went upstairs and had the distinct impression that she was not alone in the room. Without knowing what she was doing, she called out to the unseen presence, "Mabel?" There was no reply then, but one night, not much later, she was awakened by someone yanking at her blanket from the foot of the bed. She broke out into goose pimples because the pull was very distinct and there was no mistake about it.

She sat up in her upstairs bedroom, very frightened by now, but there was no one to be seen. As she did this, the pull ceased abruptly. She went back to sleep with some relief, but several nights later, the visitor returned. Mrs. Dietz likes to sleep on her left side with her ear covered up by the blanket. Suddenly she felt the covers being pulled off her ear, but being already half-asleep, she simply yanked them back. There was no further movement after that.

The upstairs bedroom occupied by Mrs. Dietz's mother seemed to be the center of activities, however. More than once, after the older lady had turned out the lights to go to sleep, she became aware of someone standing beside her bed, looking down at her.

Sometimes nothing was heard for several weeks or even months, only to resume in full force without prior warning. In February of 1966 Mrs. Dietz happened to wake up at five o'clock in the morning. It so happened that her mother was awake too, for Mrs. Dietz heard her stir. A moment later, the mother went back to bed. At that moment, Mrs. Dietz heard, starting at the foot of the stairs, the sound of heavy footsteps coming up very slowly, going down the hall and stopping, but they were different from the footsteps she had heard many times before.

It sounded as if a very sick person were dragging herself up the stairs, trying not to fall, but determined to get there nevertheless. It sounded as if someone very tired was coming home. Was her friend finding a measure of rest, after all, by returning to the house where she had been so happy? Mrs. Dietz does not believe in ghosts, however. Only in memories left behind.

Thanks to a local group of psychical researchers a bizarre case was once brought to my attention. In the small town of Lafayette, Louisiana, there stands an old bungalow, which had been the property of an elderly couple for many years prior. They were both retired people, and the wife had become an invalid confined to a wheelchair. One day, she suffered a heart attack and died in that chair. Partially because of her demise, or perhaps because of his own fragile state, the husband also died a month later; or, rather, was found dead and declared to have died of a heart attack.

Under the circumstances the house remained vacant for awhile, there being no direct heirs. After about nine months, it was rented to four female students of the university. Strangely, however, they stayed only two months—and again the house was rented out. This time it was taken by two ladies, one a professional microbiologist and the other a medical technician. Both were extremely rational individuals and not the least bit interested in anything supernatural. They moved into the bungalow, using it as it was, including the furniture of the dead couple.

Picture their dismay, however, when they found out that all wasn't as it should be with their house. Shortly after moving in, they were awakened late at night by what appeared to be mumbled conversations and footsteps about the house. At first neither lady wanted to say anything about it to the other, out of fear that they might have dreamt the whole thing or of being ridiculed. Finally, they talked to each other about their experiences and realized that they had shared them, detail for detail. They discovered, for instance, that the phenomena always took place between one a.m. and sunrise. A man and a woman were talking, and the subject of their conversation was the new tenants!

"She has her eyes open—I can see her eyes are open now," the invisible voice said, clearly and distinctly. The voices seemed to emanate from the attic area. The two ladies realized the ghosts were talking about *them;* but what were they to do about it? They didn't see the ghostly couple, but felt themselves being watched at all times by invisible presences. What were they to do with their ghosts, the two ladies wondered?

I advised them to talk to them, plain and simple, for a ghost who can tell whether a living person's eyes were open or not is capable of knowing the difference between living in one's own home, and trespassing on someone else's, even if it *was* their former abode.

When she contacted me, Mrs. Carolyn K. lived in Chicago, Illinois, with her husband, and four children between the ages of eight and thirteen. She had for years been interested in ESP experiences, contrary to her husband who held no beliefs of this kind. The family moved into their home in 1961. She does not recall any unusual experiences for the first six years—but toward the end of April, 1967 something odd happened. She and her husband had just retired and the husband, being very tired, fell asleep almost immediately. Mrs. K., however, felt ill at ease and was unable to fall asleep, since she felt a presence in the bedroom.

Within a few minutes she saw in great detail a female figure standing beside the bed. The woman seemed about thirty years old, had fair skin and hair, a trim figure, and was rather attractive. Her dress indicated good taste and a degree of wealth, and belonged to the 1870's or 1880's. The young woman just stood there and looked at Mrs. K., and vice versa. She seemed animated enough, but no sound was heard from her. Despite this, Mrs. K. had the distinct impression that the ghost wanted her to know something specific. The encounter lasted for about ten or fifteen minutes, then the figure slowly disintegrated.

The experience left Mrs. K. frightened and worried. Immediately she reported it to her husband, but he brushed the incident aside with a good deal of skepticism. In the following two weeks, Mrs. K. felt an unseen presence all about the house without, however, seeing her mysterious visitor again. It seemed that the woman was watching her doing her daily chores. Mrs. K. had no idea who the ghost might be; then, too, she knew that their house was no more than fifty years old and that there had been swamp land on the spot before that. Could the ghost have some connection with the land itself or perhaps some of the antiques Mrs. K. treasured?

About two weeks after the initial experience, Mr. K. was studying in the kitchen located at the far east end of the house, while Mrs. K. was watching television in the living room at the other end of the house. Twice she felt the need to go into the kitchen and warn her husband that she felt the ghost moving about the living room, but he insisted that it was merely her imagination. So she returned to the living room and curled up in an easy chair to continue watching television. Fifteen minutes later she heard a loud noise reverberating throughout the house. It made her freeze with fright in the chair, when her husband ran into the living room to ask what the noise had been.

Upon investigation, he noticed a broken string on an antique zither hanging on the dining room wall. It was unlikely that the string could have broken by itself, and, if it had, how could it have reverberated so strongly. To test such a possibility, they broke several other strings of the same zither, in an effort to duplicate the sound, but without success. A few weeks went by, and the ghost's presence persisted. By then Mrs. K. had the distinct impression that the ghost was annoyed at being ignored. Suddenly, a hurricane lamp which hung from a nail on the wall fell to the floor and shattered to pieces. It could not have moved of its own volition. Again, some time passed, and the ghost was almost forgotten. Mrs. K.'s older daughter, then six years old, asked her mother early one morning who the company was the previous evening. Informed that there had been no guests at the house, she insisted that a lady had entered her bedroom, sat on her bed and looked at her and had then departed. In order to calm the child, Mrs. K. told her she had probably dreamt the whole thing. But the little girl insisted that she had not, and, furthermore, she described the visitor in every detail including the "funny" clothes she had worn. Appalled, Mrs. K. realized that her daughter had seen the same ghostly woman she had. Apparently the ghost felt greater urgency to communicate now, for a few days later, after going to bed, the apparition returned to Mrs. K.'s bedroom. This time she wore a different dress than she had on the first meeting, but it was still of the 1880's. She was wiping her hands on an apron but stayed only for a little while, then slowly disintegrated again. During the following year, her presence was felt only occasionally, but gradually Mrs. K. managed to snatch a few fleeting impressions about her. From this she put together the story of her ghost. She was quite unhappy about a child and one evening the following winter, when Mr. K. felt the ghost wandering about in their basement, she actually heard her cry pitifully for two hours. Obviously, the distraught ghost wanted attention and was determined to get it at all costs.

One day the following summer when Mrs. K. was alone with the children, her husband having left for work, one of the children complained that the door to the bathroom was locked. Since the door could be locked only from the inside of the bathroom and since all four children were accounted for, Mrs. K. assumed that her ghost lady was at it again. When the bathroom door remained locked for half an hour, and the children's needs became more urgent, Mrs. K. went to the door and demanded in a loud tone of voice that the ghost open the door. There was anger in her voice and it brought quick results. Clearly the click of a *lock being turned* was heard inside the bathroom, and, after a moment, Mrs. K. opened the bathroom with great ease. There was no one inside the bathroom, of course. Who, then, had turned the lock—the only way the door could be opened?

For a while things went smoothly. But, a few weeks later, Mrs. K. again felt the ghost near her. One of her daughters was sitting at the kitchen table with her, while she was cutting out a dress pattern on the counter. Mrs. K. stepped back to search for something in the refrigerator a few feet away when all of a sudden the two women saw her box of dressmaking pins rise slightly off the counter and fall to the floor. Neither one of them had been near it. It took them almost an hour to retrieve all the pins scattered on the floor. A little later they clearly heard the door connecting dining room and kitchen fly open and slam shut of its own volition, as if someone in great anger was trying to call attention to their being there. Immediately they closed the door, and made sure there was no draft from any windows.

An instant later it flew open again by itself. Then they attached the chain to the latch—but that didn't seem to stop the ghost from fooling around with the door. With enormous force it flew open again as far as the chain allowed, as if someone were straining at it. Quickly Mrs. K. called a neighbor to come over and watch the strange behavior of the door; but the minute the neighbor arrived, the door behaved normally, just hanging there. The ghost was not about to perform for strangers.

One evening in the summer of 1970, Mr. K. was driving some dinner guests home and Mrs. K. was alone in the house with the children. All of a sudden she felt her ghost following her as she went through her chores of emptying ashtrays and taking empty glasses into the kitchen. Mrs. K. tried bravely to ignore her, at the same being frightened by her, and she knew that her ghost knew it, which made it all the more difficult to carry on.

Shortly later, the K. family had guests again. One of the arriving guests pointed out to Mrs. K. that their basement light was on. Mrs. K. explained that it was unlikely since the basement light bulb had burned out the day before. She even recalled being slightly annoyed with her husband for having neglected to replace the bulb. But the guest insisted, and so the K.'s opened the basement door only to find the light off. A moment later another guest arrived. He wanted to know who was working in the basement at such a late hour since he had seen the basement light on. Moreover, he saw a figure standing at the basement window, looking out. Once more, the entire party went downstairs with a flashlight, only to find the light off and no one about.

That was the last the K.'s saw or heard of their ghost. Why had she so suddenly left them? Perhaps it had to do with a Chicago newspaper woman's call. Having heard of the disturbances, she had telephoned the K.'s to offer her services and that of celebrated psychic Irene Hughes to investigate the house. But the K.'s did not want any attention because of the children. Just the same, Mrs. K. told the reporter what had transpired at the house. To her surprise the reporter informed her that parallel experiences had been reported from another house, not more than seven miles away. In the other case, the mother and one of her children had observed a ghostly figure, and an investigation had taken place with the help of Irene Hughes and various equipment, the result of which was that a presence named Lizzy was ascertained in the other house.

From this Mrs. K. concluded that they were sharing a ghost with a neighbor seven miles away, and began to call the ghostly visitor Lizzy also. Now if Lizzy had two homes and was shuttling back and forth between them, it might account for the long stretches of no activity at the K. home. On the other hand, if the ghost at the K.'s was not named Lizzy, she would naturally not want to be confused with some other, unknown ghost seven miles away. Be this as it may, Mrs. K. wished her well, wherever she may be.

Mrs. J. P. lived in central Illinois, in a three-story house with basement, going back a considerable time. Prior to her acquiring it, it had stood empty for six months. As soon as she had moved in she heard some neighborhood gossip that the house was presumed to be haunted. Although Mrs. P. was not a skeptic, she was level-headed enough not to take rumors at face value. She gave the house a good look. It seemed about eighty years old, and was badly in need of repair. Since they had bought it at a bargain price, they did not mind it. But as time went on they wondered how cheap the house had really been. It became obvious to her and her husband that the price had been low for other reasons. Nevertheless, the house was theirs, and together they set out to repaint and remodel it as best they could. For the first two weeks they were too busy to notice anything out of the ordinary. About three weeks after moving in, however, Mr. and Mrs. P. began hearing things, such as doors shutting by themselves, cupboards opening, and, particularly, a little girl calling for "Mama, Mama" with persistence and a great deal of alarm. As yet, Mr. and Mrs. P. tried to ignore the phenomena.

One evening, however, they were having a family spat over something of little consequence. All of a sudden a frying pan standing on the stove lifted off by itself, hung suspended in mid-air for a moment and then was flung back on the stove with full force. Their twelve-year-old son, who witnessed it, flew into hysterics; Mr. P. turned white, and Mrs. P. was just plain angry. How dared someone invade their privacy? The following week, the ten-year-old daughter was watching television downstairs in what had been turned into Mrs. P.'s office, while Mr. P. and their son were upstairs, also watching television. Suddenly, a glass of milk standing on the desk in the office lifted off by itself and dashed itself to the floor with full force. The child ran screaming from the room and it took a long time for her father to calm her down.

As a result of these happenings, the children implored their mother to move from the house, but Mrs. P. would have none of it. She liked the house fine, and was not about to let some unknown ghost displace her. The more she thought about it, the angrier she got. She decided to go from floor to floor, cursing the unknown ghost and telling her or him to get out of the house, even if it used to be theirs. And, so she stayed.

But that is how it is with Stay-Behinds: they don't care if you paid for the house, and they don't care how much you paid. After all, they can't use the money where they are, and would rather stay on in a place they were familiar with.

Strange places can have Stay-behind ghosts. Take Maryknoll College, of Glen Ellyn, Illinois, a Roman Catholic seminary that closed its doors in June of 1972. In the fall of 1968, a seminarian named Gary M. was working in the photography darkroom of the college. This was part of his regular assignments, and photography had been engaged in for some years by both faculty and students.

On this particular occasion Mr. M. felt as though he was

being watched while in the darkroom. Chalking it up to an active imagination he dismissed the matter from his mind. But in the spring of 1970, Mr. M. was going through some old chemicals belonging to a former priest, when he received the strongest impression of a psychic presence. He was loading some film at the time and, as he did so, he had the uncanny feeling that he was not alone in the room. The chemicals he had just handled once were the property of a priest who had died three years before. The following day, while developing film in an open tank, he suddenly felt as though a cold hand went down his back. He realized also that the chemicals felt colder than before. After he had turned the lights back on, he took the temperature of the developer. At the start it had been 70° F., while at the end it was down to 64° F. Since the room temperature was 68° F., there was a truly unaccountable decrease in temperature.

The phenomena made him wonder, and he discussed his experiences with other seminarians. It was then learned that a colleague of his had also had experiences in the same area. Someone, a man, had appeared to him and he felt the warm touch of a hand at his cheek. Since he was not alone at the time but in a group of five students, he immediately reported the incident to them. The description of the apparition was detailed and definite. Quickly, Mr. M. went into past files, and came up with several pictures, so that his fellow student could pick out that of the ghostly apparition he had seen. Without the slightest hesitation, he identified the dead priest as the man he had seen. This was not too surprising; the students were using what was once the priest's own equipment and chemicals, and perhaps he still felt obliged to make sure they used them properly.

Mr. and Mrs. E. lived in an average home in Florida, which was built about thirteen years before. They moved into this house in August of 1971. Neither of them had any particular interest in the occult, and Mr. E., if anything, could be classified as a complete skeptic. For the first few months of their residence they were much too busy to notice anything out of the ordinary, even if there were such occurrences.

It was just before Christmas when they got their first inkling that something was not as it should be with their house. Mrs. E. was sitting up late one night, busy with last-minute preparations for the holiday. All of a sudden the front door, which was secured and locked, flew open with a violent force, and immediately shut itself again, with the handle turning by itself and the latch falling into place. Since Mrs. E. hadn't expected any visitors, she was naturally very surprised. Quickly walking over to the door to find out what had happened, she discovered that the door was locked. This was the kind of lock that could only be unlocked by turning a knob. Shaking her head in disbelief, she returned to her chair, but before she could sit down again and resume her chores, the door to the utility room began to rattle as though a wind were blowing. There were no open windows there that could have caused it. Suddenly, as she was staring at it, the knob turned and it opened. Somehow nonplussed, Mrs. E. thought, rather sarcastically, "While you're at it, why don't you shake the Christmas tree too?" Just as she had completed the thought, the tree began to shake. For a moment, Mrs. E. stood still and thought all of this over in her mind. Then she decided that she was just overtired and had contracted a case of the holiday jitters. It was probably all due to imagination. She went to bed and didn't say anything about the incident.

Two weeks later, her fourteen-year-old daughter and Mrs. E. were up late talking when all of a sudden every cupboard in the kitchen opened by itself, one by one. Mrs. E.'s daughter's eyes stared at the phenomena in disbelief. But Mrs. E. simply said, "Now close them." Sure enough, one by one, the doors shut with a hard slam, by themselves, almost like a little child whose prank had not succeeded. At this point Mrs. E. thought it best to tell her daughter of her first encounter with the unseen, and implored her not to be scared of it, nor to tell the younger children or anyone else outside the house. She didn't want to be known as a weird individual in this neighborhood into which they had just moved. However, she decided she had to inform her husband of what had happened. He didn't say much, but it was clear he was not convinced. However, as with so many cases of this kind where the man in the house took a lot longer to be convinced than the women, Mr. E.'s time came about two weeks later.

He was watching television when one of the stereo speakers began to tilt back all of a sudden, tilting back and forth without falling over, of its own volition, as if held by unseen hands. Being of a practical bent, Mr. E. got up to find an explanation, but there was no wind that would have been strong enough to tilt a twenty-pound speaker box. At this point Mr. E. agreed that there was something peculiar about the house. This was the more likely as their dog, an otherwise calm and peaceful animal, went absolutely wild at the moment the speakers tilted, and ran about the house for half an hour afterwards, barking, sniffing, and generally raising Cain.

However, the ghost was out of the bag, so to speak. The two younger children, then nine and ten years old, noticed him—it was assumed to be a man all along. A house guest remarked how strange it was that the door was opening seemingly by itself. This, Mrs. E. explained with a remark that the latch was not working properly. "But how did the knob turn, then?" the house guest wanted to know. Evidently, she had also seen the knob turn by itself.

Under the circumstances, Mrs. E. owned up to their ghost. The ghost didn't scare Mrs. E., but he made it somewhat unpleasant for her at times, such as when she was taking a shower and the doors fly open. After all, one doesn't want to be watched by a man while showering, even if he *is* a ghost. The Stay-behind wasn't noticeable all the time, to be sure, but frequently enough to count as an extra inhabitant of the house. Whenever she felt him near, there was a chill in the hall, and an echo. This happened at various times of day or night, early or late. To the children, he was a source of some concern and they would not stay home alone.

But to Mrs. E. he was merely an unfortunate human being, caught up in the entanglement of his own emotions from the past, desperately trying to break through the time barrier to communicate with her, but unable to do so because conditions weren't just right. Sometimes she wished she were more psychic than she was, but in the meantime she had settled down to share the appointments with someone she could not see, but who, it appears, considered himself part of the family.

One of the most amazing stories I heard concerns a family of farmers in central Connecticut. Some people have a ghost in the house, a Stay-behind who likes the place so much he or she doesn't want to leave. But this family had entire *groups* of ghosts staying on simply because they liked the sprawling farmhouse, and simply because it happened to be their home too. The fact that they had passed across the threshold of death did not deter them in the least. To the contrary, it seemed a natural thing to stay behind and watch what the young ones were doing with the house, possibly help them here and there, and, at the very least, have some fun with them by causing so-called "inexplicable" phenomena to happen.

After all, life could be pretty dull in central Connecticut, especially in the winter. It wasn't any more fun being a ghost in central Connecticut, so one cannot really hold it against these Stay-behinds if they amuse themselves as best they could in the afterlife. At this time, the house was showing its age; it wasn't in good condition, and needed lots of repairs. The family wasn't as large as it was before some of the younger generation moved out to start lives of their own, but it was still a busy house and a friendly one, ghosts or not ghosts. It stood on a quiet country road, off the main route, and on a clear day you could see the Massachusetts border in the distance; that is, if you were looking for it. It was hardly noticeable, for, in this part of the country, all New England looks the same.

Because of the incredible nature of the many incidents, the family wanted no publicity, no curious tourists, and no reporters. To defer to their wishes, I have changed the family name to help them retain that anonymity and the peace and quiet of their country house. The house in question was already old when a map of the town, drawn in 1761, showed it. The-then owners, the Harveys, had lived in it all their lives, with interruption. Mrs. Harvey's great-great-grandparents bought it from the original builder, and when her great-great-grandfather died in 1858, it happened at the old homestead. Likewise, her great-great-grandmother passed on in 1871, aged eighty, and again it happened at home. One of their children died at age ninety-one in 1921, also at home.

This was important, you see, because it accounts for the events which transpired later in the lives of their descendants. A daughter named Julia married an outsider and moved to another state, but considered herself part of the family just the same, so much so that her second home was still the old homestead in central Connecticut. Another daughter, Martha, was Mrs. Harvey's great-grandmother. Great-grandmother Martha died at age ninety-one, also in the house. Then there was an aunt, a sister of her great-great-grandfather's, by the name of Nancy, who came to live with them, being a widow;

she lived to be ninety and died in the house. They still had some of her furniture there. Mrs. Harvey's grandparents had only one child, Viola, who became her mother, but they took in boarders, mostly men working in the nearby sawmills. One of these boarders died in the house too, but his name was unknown. Possibly, several others died there too.

Of course the house didn't look the way it originally did; additions were built onto the main part, stairs were moved, a well in the cellar was filled in because members of the family going down for more cider used to fall into it, and many of the rooms which later became bedrooms originally had other purposes. For instance, daughter Marjorie's bedroom was once called the harness room because horses' harnesses were made in it, and the room of one of the sons used to be called the cheese room for obvious reasons. What became a sewing room was originally used as a pantry with shelves running across the south wall.

The fact that stairs were changed throughout the house was important, because in the mind of those who lived in the past, the original stairs would naturally take precedence over later additions or changes. Thus phantoms may appear out of the wall, seemingly without reason, except that they would be walking up staircases which no longer existed. Mrs. Harvey was born in the house, but at age four her parents moved away from it, and did not return until much later. But even then, Mrs. Harvey recalls an incident which she was never to forget. When she was only four years old, she remembers very clearly an old lady she had never seen before appear at her crib. She cried, but when she told her parents about it, they assured her it was just a dream. But Mrs. Harvey knew she had not dreamt the incident; she remembered every detail of the old lady's dress.

When she was twelve years old, at a time when her family had returned to live in the house, she was in one of the upstairs bedrooms and again the old lady appeared to her. But when she talked about it to her parents, the matter was immediately dropped. As Frances Harvey grew up in the house, she couldn't help but notice some strange goings-on. A lamp moved by itself, without anyone being near it. Many times she could feel a presence walking close behind her in the upstairs part of the house, but when she turned around, she was alone. Nor was she the only one to notice the strange goings-on. Her brothers heard footsteps around their beds, and complained about someone bending over them, yet no one was to be seen. The doors to the bedrooms would open by themselves at night, so much so that the boys tied the door latches together so that the doors could not in fact open by themselves. Just the same, when morning came, the doors were wide open with the knot still in place.

It was at that time that her father got into the habit of taking an after-dinner walk around the house before retiring. Many times he told the family of seeing a strange light going through the upstairs rooms, a glowing luminosity for which there was no rational explanation. Whenever Frances Harvey had to be alone upstairs she felt uncomfortable, but when she mentioned this to her parents she was told that all old houses made one feel like that and to never mind. One evening Frances was playing a game with her grandfather when both of them clearly heard footsteps coming up the back stairs. But her grandfather didn't budge. When Frances asked him who this could possibly be, he merely shrugged and said there was plenty of room for *everyone.*

As the years passed the Harveys would come back to the house from time to time to visit. On these occasions Frances would wake up in the night because someone was bending over her. At other times there was a heavy depression on the bed as if someone were sitting there! Too terrified to tell anyone about it, she kept her experiences to herself for the time being. Then, in the early 1940's, Frances married and with her husband and two children eventually returned to the house to live there permanently with her grandparents. No sooner had they moved in when the awful feeling came back in the night. Finally she told her husband, who of course scoffed at the idea of ghosts. The most active area in the house seemed to be upstairs, roughly from her son Don's closet, through Lolita the daughter's room, and especially the front hall and stairs. It felt as if someone were standing on the landing of the front stairs, just watching. This goes back a long time. Mrs. Harvey's mother frequently complained, when working in the attic, that all of a sudden she would feel someone standing next to her, someone she could not see.

One day Mrs. Harvey and her youngest daughter went grocery shopping. After putting the groceries away, Mrs. Harvey reclined on the living room couch while the girl sat in the dining room, reading. Suddenly they heard a noise like thunder even though the sky outside was clear. It came again, only this time it sounded closer as if it were upstairs! When it happened the third time, it was accompanied by a sound as if someone were making up the bed in Mrs. Harvey's son's room upstairs.

Now, they had left the bed in disorder, because they had been in a hurry to go shopping. No one else could have gone upstairs, and yet when they entered the son's room, the bed was made up as smoothly as possible. As yet, part of the family scoffed at the idea of having ghosts in the house and considered the mother's ideas as dreams or hallucinations. They were soon to change their minds, however—when it happened to them as well.

The oldest daughter felt very brave and called up the stairs, "Little ghosties, where are you?" Her mother told her she had better not challenge them, but the others found it amusing. That night she came downstairs a short time after she had gone to bed, complaining that she felt funny in her room but thought it was just her imagination. The following night, she awoke to the feeling that someone was bending over her. One side of her pillow was pulled away from her head as though a hand had pushed it down. She called out and heard footsteps receding from her room, followed by heavy rumbling in the attic above. Quickly she ran into her sister's room where both of them lay awake the rest of the night listening to the rumbling and footsteps walking around overhead. The next day she noticed a dusty, black footprint on the light-colored scatter rug next to her bed. It was in the exact location where she had felt someone standing and bending over her. Nobody's footprint in the house matched the black footprint, for it was long and very narrow. At this point the girls purchased special night lights and left them on all night in the hope of sleeping peacefully.

One day Mrs. Harvey felt real brave and started up the stairs in response to footsteps coming from her mother's bedroom. She stopped—and as the footsteps approached along the top of the stairs, a loud, ticking noise came with them, like a huge pocket watch. Quickly she ran down the stairs and outside to get her son to be a witness to it. Sure enough, he too could hear the ticking noise. This was followed by doors opening and closing by themselves. Finally, they dared go upstairs, and when they entered the front bedroom they noticed a very strong, sweet smell of perfume. When two of the daughters came home from work that evening the family compared notes and it developed that they, too, had smelled the strange perfume and heard the ticking noise upstairs. They concluded that one of their ghosts, at least, was a man.

About that time, the youngest daughter reported seeing an old woman in her room, standing at a bureau with something shiny in her hand. The ghost handed it to her but she was too frightened to receive it. Since her description of the woman had been very detailed, Mrs. Harvey took out the family album and asked her daughter to look through it in the hope that she might identify the ghostly visitor. When they came to one particular picture, the girl let out a small cry: that was the woman she had seen! It turned out to be Julia, a great-great aunt of Mrs. Harvey's, the same woman whom Mrs. Harvey herself had seen when she was twelve years old. Evidently the lady was still staying around.

Mrs. Harvey's attention had been deflected from the phenomena in the house by her mother's illness. Like a dutiful daughter, she attended her to the very last, but in March of 1966 her mother passed away. Whether there was any connection with her mother's death or not, the phenomena started to increase greatly, both in volume and intensity in July of that same year—to be exact, on July 20, 1966. Mrs. Harvey was hurrying one morning to take her daughter Lolita to the center of town so she could get a ride to work. Her mind was preoccupied with domestic chores, when a car came down the road, brakes squealing. Out of habit, she hurried to the living room window to make sure that none of their cats had been hit by the car. This had been a habit of her mother's and hers whenever there was the sound of sudden brakes outside.

As she did so, for just a fleeting glance, she saw her late mother looking out of the window that had been her favorite one. It didn't register at first, then Mrs. Harvey realized her mother couldn't possibly have been there. However, since time was of the essence, Mrs. Harvey and her daughter Lolita left for town without saying anything to any of the others in the house. When they returned, her daughter Marjorie was standing outside waiting for them. She complained of hearing someone moving around in the living room just after they had left, and it sounded just like Grandma when she straightened out the couch and chair covers.

It frightened her, so she decided to wait in the dining room for her mother's return. But while there, she heard footsteps coming from the living room and then go into the den, then the sound of clothes being folded. This was something Mrs. Harvey's mother was also in the habit of doing there. It was enough for Marjorie to run outside the house and wait there. Together with her sister and mother she returned to the living room, only to find the chair cover straightened. The sight of the straightened chair cover made the blood freeze in Mrs. Harvey's veins; she recalled vividly how she had asked her late mother not to bother straightening the chair covers during her illness, because it hurt her back. In reply, her mother had said, 'Too bad I can't come back and do it after I die.'

Daughter Jane was married to a Navy man, who used to spend his leaves from the service at the old house. Even during his courtship days, he and Mrs. Harvey's mother got along real fine, and they even used to do crossword puzzles together. He was sleeping at the house some time after the old lady's death when he awoke to see her standing by his bed, with her puzzle book and pencil in hand. It was clear to Mrs. Harvey by then that her late mother had joined the circle of dead relatives to keep a watch on her and the family. Even while she was ill, Mrs. Harvey's mother wanted to help in the house. One day after her death, Mrs. Harvey was baking a custard pie and lay down on the couch for a few minutes while it was baking.

She must have fallen asleep, for she awoke to the voice of her mother saying, 'Your pie won't burn, will it?' Mrs. Harvey hurriedly got up and checked, the pie was just right and would have burned if it had been left in any longer. That very evening something else happened. Mrs. Harvey wanted to watch a certain program on TV which came on at seven-thirty p.m. But she was tired and fell asleep on the couch in the late afternoon. Suddenly she heard her mother's voice say to her, 'It's time for your program, dear.' Mrs. Harvey looked at the clock, it was exactly seven-thirty p.m. Of course, her mother did exactly the same type of thing when she was living, so it wasn't too surprising that she should continue with her concerned habits after she passed on into the next dimension.

But if Mrs. Harvey's mother had joined the ghostly crew in the house, she was by no means furnishing the bulk of the phenomena, not by a long shot. Lolita's room upstairs seemed to be the center of many activities, with her brother Don's room next to hers also very much involved. Someone was walking from her bureau to her closet, and her brother heard the footsteps, too. Lolita looked up and saw a man in a uniform with gold buttons standing in the back of her closet. At other times she smelled perfume and heard the sound of someone dressing near her bureau. All the time she heard people going up the front stairs, mumbling, go into her closet, where the sound stopped abruptly. Yet, they could not see anyone on such occasions.

Daughter Jane wasn't left out of any of this either. Many nights she would feel someone standing next to her bed, between the bed and the wall. She saw three different people and felt hands trying to lift her out of bed. To be sure, she could not see their faces; their shapes were like dark shadows. Marjorie, sleeping in the room next to Jane's, also experienced an attempt by some unseen forces to get her out of bed. She grabbed the headboard to stop herself from falling old woman whom Mrs. Harvey had seen when she heard several people leave her room for the front hall.

One night she awoke to catch a glimpse of someone in a long black coat hurrying through the hall. Mumbling was heard in that direction, so she put her ear against the door to see if she could hear any words, but she couldn't make out any. Marjorie, too, saw the old woman standing at the foot of her bed—the same old woman whom Mrs. Harvey had seen when she was twelve years old. Of course, that isn't too surprising; the room Marjorie slept in used to be Julia's a long time ago. Lolita also had her share of experiences: sounds coming up from the cellar bothering her, footsteps, voices, even the sound of chains. It seemed to her that they came right out of the wall by her head, where there used to be stairs but were no more. Finally, it go so bad that Lolita asked her mother to sleep with her. When Mrs. Harvey complied the two women clearly saw a glow come in from the living room and go to where the shelves used to be. Then there was the sound of dishes, even the smell of food.

Obviously, the ghostly presences were still keeping house in their own fashion, reliving some happy or at least busy moments from their own past. By then Mr. Harvey was firmly convinced that he shared the house with a number of dead relatives, if not friends. Several times he woke to the sound of bottles being placed on the bureau. One night he awoke because the bottom of their bed was shaking hard; as soon as he was fully awake, it stopped. This was followed by a night in which Mrs. Harvey could see a glow pass through the room, at the bottom of the bed. When "they" got to the hall door, which was shut, she could hear it open, but it actually did not move. Yet the sound was that of opening a door. Next she heard several individuals walk up the stairs, mumbling as they went.

The following night a light stopped by their fireplace and as she looked closely it resembled a figure bending down. It got so that they compared notes almost every morning to see what had happened next in their very busy home. One moonlit night Mrs. Harvey woke to see the covers of her bed folded in half, the entire length of the bed. Her husband was fully covered, she was totally uncovered. At the same time she saw some dark shadows by the side of the bed. She felt someone's hand holding her own, pulling her gently. Terrified, she couldn't move, just lay there wondering what would happen next. Then the blankets were replaced as before, she felt something cold touch her forehead and the ghosts left. But the Stay-behinds were benign, and meant no harm. Some nights Mrs. Harvey would wake up because of the cold air, and notice that the blankets were standing up straight from the bed as if held by someone—even after she pushed them back hard, they would not stay in place.

On the other hand, there were times when she accidentally uncovered herself at night and felt someone putting the covers back on her, as if to protect her from the night chills. This was the more important as the house had no central heating. Of course it wasn't always clear what the ghosts wanted with her; on the one hand, they clearly were concerned with her well-being and that of the family; on the other they seemed to crave attention for themselves also.

Twice they tried to lift Mrs. Harvey out of her bed. She felt herself on unseen hands several inches above it, and tried to call out to her husband but somehow couldn't utter a single word. This was followed by a strange, dreamlike state in which she remembered being taken to the attic and shown something. Unfortunately she could not remember it afterwards except that she had been to the attic and how the floorboards looked there; she also recalled that the attic was covered with black dust. When morning came, she took a look at her feet: they were dusty, and the bottom of her bed was grayish as if from dust. She was just contemplating these undeniable facts, when her husband asked her what had been the matter with her during the night. Evidently he had awakened to find her gone from the bed.

One night daughter Marjorie was out on a date. Mrs. Harvey awoke to the sound of a car pulling into the driveway, returning Marjorie home. From her bed she could clearly see four steps of the back stairs. As she lay there, she saw the shape of a woman coming down without any sound, sort of floating down the stairs. She was dressed in a white chiffon dress. At the same moment her daughter Marjorie entered the living room. She too saw the girl in the chiffon dress come down the stairs into the living room and disappear through a door to the other bedroom. Even though the door was open wide and there was plenty of room to go through the opening, evidently the ghostly lady preferred to walk through the door.

The miscellaneous Stay-behinds tried hard to take part in the daily lives of the flesh-and-blood people in the house. Many times the plants in the living room would be rearranged and attended to by unseen hands. The Harveys could clearly see the plants move, yet no one was near them; no one, that is, visible to the human eye. There was a lot of mumbling about now, and eventually they could make out some words. One day daughter Marjorie heard her late grandmother say to her that "they" would be back in three weeks. Sure enough, not a single incident of a ghostly nature occurred for three weeks. To the day, after the three weeks were up, the phenomena continued. Where had the ghosts gone in the meantime? On another occasion, Marjorie heard someone say, "That is Jane on that side of the bed, but who is that on the other side? The bed looks so smooth." The remark made sense to Mrs. Harvey. Her late mother sometimes slept with Jane, when she was still in good health. On the other hand, daughter Marjorie likes to sleep perfectly flat, so her bed did look rather smooth.

Many people believe ghosts only walk at night. Nothing could be further from the truth, as Mrs. Harvey could testify. Frequently, when she was alone in the house during the daytime, she would hear doors upstairs bang shut and open again. One particular day she heard the sound of someone putting things on Jane's bureau, so she tried to go up and see what it was. Carefully tiptoeing up the stairs to peek into her door to see if she could actually trap a ghost, she found herself halfway along the hall when she heard footsteps coming along the foot of son Don's bed, coming in her direction. Quickly, she hurried back down the stairs and stopped halfway down. The footsteps sounded like a woman's, and suddenly there was the rustle of a taffeta gown. With a *whooshing* sound she passed Mrs. Harvey and went into Jane's room. Mrs. Harvey waited, rooted to the spot on the stairs.

A moment later the woman's footsteps came back, only this time someone walked with her, someone heavier. They went back through Don's room, and ended up in Lolita's closet—the place where Lolita had seen the man in the uniform with the shining gold buttons. Mrs. Harvey did not follow immediately but that night she decided to go up to Lolita's room and have another look at the closet. As she approached the door to the room, it opened, which wasn't unusual, since it was in the habit of opening at the slightest vibration. But before Mrs. Harvey could close it, it shut itself tight and the latch moved into place of its own volition. Mrs. Harvey didn't wait around for anything further that night.

For a while, there was peace. Then, in October, the phenomena resumed. One night Mrs. Harvey woke up when she saw a shadow blocking the light coming from the dining room. She looked towards the door and noticed a lady dressed all in black come into her bedroom and stand close to her side of the bed. This time she clearly heard her speak.

"Are you ready? It is almost time to go."

With that, the apparition turned and started up the stairs. The stairs looked unusually light, as if moonlight were illuminating them. When the woman in black got to the top step, all was quiet and the stairs were dark again, as before. Mrs. Harvey could see her clothes plainly enough, but not her face. She noticed that the apparition had carried a pouch-style pocket-book, which she had put over her arm, so that her hands would be free to lift up her skirt as she went up the stairs. The next morning, Mrs. Harvey told her husband of the visitation. He assured her she must have dreamt it all. But before she could answer, her daughter Marjorie came in and said that she had heard someone talking in the night, something about coming, and it being almost time. She saw a figure at the foot of her bed, which she described as similar to what Mrs. Harvey had seen.

The night before Thanksgiving, 1967, Marjorie heard footsteps come down the stairs. She was in bed, and tried to get up to see who it was, but somehow couldn't move at all, except to open her eyes to see five people standing at the foot of her bed! Two of them were women, the others seemed just outlines or shadows. One of the two women wore a hat shaped like an old-fashioned one, and she looked very stern. As Marjorie was watching the group, she managed to roll over a little in her bed and felt someone next to her. She felt relieved at the thought that it was her mother, but then whoever it was got up and left with the others in the group. All the time they kept talking among themselves, but Marjorie could not make out what was being said. Still talking, the ghostly visitors went back up the stairs.

Nothing much happened until Christmastime. Again the footsteps running up and down the stairs resumed, yet no one was seen. Christmas night Jane and her mother heard walking in the room above the living room where Mrs. Harvey's mother used to sleep. At that time Mr. Harvey was quite ill and was sleeping in what used to be the sewing room, so as not to awake when his wife got up early.

On two different occasions Mrs. Harvey had "visitors." The first time someone lifted her a few inches off the bed. Evidently someone else was next to her in bed, for when she extended her hand that person got up and left. Next she heard footsteps going up the stairs and someone laugh, and then all was quiet again. About a week later she woke one night to feel someone pulling hard on her elbow and ankle. She hung onto the top of her bed with her other hand. But the unseen entities pushed, forcing her to brace herself against the wall.

Suddenly it all stopped. Yet there were no sounds of anyone leaving. Mrs. Harvey jumped out of bed and tried to turn the light on. It wouldn't go on. She went back to bed when she heard a voice telling her not to worry, that her husband would be all right. She felt relieved at the thought, when the voice added, "But you won't be." Then the unseen voice calmly informed her that she would die in an accident caused by a piece of bark of some sort of tree. That was all the voice chose to tell her, but it was enough to start her worrying. Under the circumstances, and in order not to upset her family, she kept quiet about it, eventually thinking that she had dreamed the whole incident. After all, if it were just a dream there was no point in telling anyone, and if it were true, there was nothing she could do anyway, so there was no point in worrying her family. She had almost forgotten the incident, when she did have an accident about a week later. She hurt her head rather badly in the woodshed, requiring medical attention. While she was still wondering whether that was the incident referred to by the ghostly voice, she had a second accident: a heavy fork fell on her and knocked her unconscious.

But the voice had said that she would die in an accident, so Mrs. Harvey wasn't at all sure that the two incidents, painful though they had been, were what the voice had referred to. Evidently ghosts get a vicarious thrill out of making people worry, because Mrs. Harvey was alive and well—many years after the unseen voice had told her she would die in an accident.

But if it were not enough to cope with ghost people, Mrs. Harvey also had the company of a ghost dog. Their favorite pet, Lucy, passed into eternal dogdom in March, 1967. Having been treated as a member of the family, she had been permitted to sleep in the master bedroom, but as she became older she started wetting the rug, so eventually she had to be kept out.

After the dog's death, Marjorie offered to get her mother another dog, but Mrs. Harvey didn't want a replacement for Lucy; no other dog could take her place. Shortly after the offer, and its refusal, Lolita heard a familiar scratch at the bathroom door. It sounded exactly as Lucy had always sounded when Lolita came home late at night. At first, Mrs. Harvey thought her daughter had just imagined it, but then the familiar wet spot reappeared on the bedroom rug again. They tried to look for a possible leak in the ceiling but could find no rational cause for the rug to be wet. The wet spot remained for about a month. During that time several of the girls heard a noise which reminded them of Lucy walking about. Finally the rug dried out and Lucy's ghost stopped walking.

Then, suddenly, the house was quiet. Years passed by. Had the ghosts gone on to their just rewards, been reincarnated, or simply tired of living with their flesh-and-blood relatives? Stay-behinds generally stay indefinitely; unless, of course, they feel they were really not wanted. Or perhaps they just got bored with it all.

Years ago, a tragic event took place at a major university campus in Kansas. A member of one of the smaller fraternities, TKE, was killed in a head-on automobile accident on September 21, 1971. His sudden death at so young an age—he was an undergraduate—brought home a sense of tragedy to the other members of the fraternity, and it was decided to attend his funeral in New York *enmasse*.

Not quite a year after the tragic accident, several members of the fraternity were at their headquarters. Eventually, one of the brothers and his date were left behind alone, studying in the basement of the house. Upon completion of their schoolwork they left. When they had reached the outside, the girl remembered she had left her purse in the basement and returned to get it. When she entered the basement, she noticed a man sitting at the poker table, playing with chips. She said something to him, explaining herself, then grabbed her purse and returned upstairs. There she asked her date who the man in the basement was, since she hadn't noticed him before. He laughed and said that no one had been down there but the two of them. At that point one of the other brothers went into the basement, and was surprised to see a man get up from his chair and walk away. That man was none other than the young man who had been killed in the automobile crash a year before.

One of the other members of the fraternity had also been in the same accident, but had been only injured, and survived. Several days after the incident in the fraternity house basement, this young man saw the dead boy walking up the steps to the second floor of the house. By then the fraternity realized that their dead brother was still very much with them, drawn back to what to him was his true home—and so they accepted him as one of the crowd, even if he was invisible at times.

On January 7, 1971, Mr. and Mrs. S. moved into an older house on South Fourth Street, a rented two-bedroom house, fully furnished, in a medium-sized city in Oklahoma. Mrs. S.'s husband was a career service man in the Army, stationed at a nearby Army camp. They had a small boy and looked forward to a pleasant stay where the boy could play with neighbor kids, while Mrs. S. tried to make friends in what to her was a new environment.

She was a determined lady, not easily frightened off by anything she cannot explain, and the occult was the last thing on her mind. They had lived in the house for about two weeks when she noticed light footsteps walking in the hall at night.

But, when she checked on them, there was no one there. Her ten-year-old son was sleeping across the hall and she wondered if perhaps he was walking in his sleep. But each time she heard the footsteps, and would check on her son, she found him sound asleep. The footsteps continued on and off for a period of four months.

Then, one Sunday afternoon about two o'clock, when her husband was at his post and her son in the back yard playing, she found herself in the kitchen. Suddenly she heard a child crying, very softly and muted as if the child were afraid to cry aloud. At once she ran into the back yard to see if her son was hurt. There was nothing wrong with him, and she found him playing happily with a neighbor boy. It then dawned on her that she could not hear the child crying outside the house, but immediately upon re-entering the house the faint sobs were clearly audible again.

She traced the sound to her bedroom, and, when she entered the room, it ceased to be noticeable. This puzzled her no end, since she had no idea what could cause the sounds. Added to this were strange sounds of a thumping nature, which frequently awakened her in the middle of the night. It sounded as if someone had fallen out of bed. On these occasions she would get out of bed quickly and rush into her son's room, only to find him fast asleep. A thorough check of the entire house revealed no source for the strange noises. But Mrs. S. noticed that their Siamese cat, who slept at the foot of her bed when these things happened, also reacted to them: his hair would bristle, his ears would fly back, he would hiss and stare into space at something or someone she could not see.

About that time her mother decided to visit them. Since her mother was an invalid, Mrs. S. decided not to tell her about the strange phenomena in order to avoid upsetting her. She stayed at the house for three days, when one morning she wanted to know why Mrs. S. was up at two o'clock in the morning making coffee? Since the house had only two bedrooms, they had put a half-bed into the kitchen for her mother, especially as the kitchen was very large and she could see the television from where she was sleeping. Her mother insisted she had heard footsteps coming down the hall into the kitchen. She called out to what she assumed was her daughter, and when there was no answer she assumed that her daughter and her son-in-law had had some sort of disagreement and she had gotten up to make some coffee.

From her bed she could not reach the light switch, but she could see the time by the illuminated clock and realized it was two o'clock in the morning. Someone came down the hall, entered the kitchen, put water into the coffee pot, plugged it in, and then walked out of the kitchen and down the hall. She could hear the sound of coffee perking and actually smell it. However, when she didn't hear anyone coming back, she assumed that her daughter and son-in-law had made up and gone back to sleep.

She did likewise and decided to question her daughter about it in the morning. Mrs. S. immediately checked the kitchen, but there was no trace of the coffee to be found, which did not contribute to her state of mind. A little later she heard some commotion outside the house and on stepping outside noticed that the dogcatcher was trying to take a neighbor's dog with him. She decided to try and talk him out of it, and the conversation led to her husband being in the service, a statement which seemed to provoke a negative reaction on the part of the dogcatcher. He informed Mrs. S. that the last GI to live in the house was a murderer. When she wanted to know more about it he clammed up immediately. But Mrs. S. became highly agitated. She called the local newspaper and asked for any and all information concerning her house. It was then that she learned the bitter truth.

In October, 1969, a soldier stationed at the same base as her husband, had beaten his two-year-old baby girl to death. The murder took place in what had then become Mrs. S.'s bedroom. Mrs. S., shocked by the news, sent up a silent prayer, hoping that the restless soul of the child might find peace and not have to haunt a house where she had suffered nothing but unhappiness in her short life. . . .

A HAUNTED HOUSE IS NOT A HOME: HOW TO LIVE WITH A GHOST

A lot of people are particular about the privacy of their home. They like it fine when nobody bothers them, except of course their own kinfolk. Some do not even mind if a relative or friend stays over, or comes to visit them, because, after all, they will leave again in time. But when a guest overstays his welcome, and stays on and on and on, the matter can become upsetting, to say the least. This becomes even more of a problem when the guest was not aware of the passage of time, or when he thinks that your home was actually his home. When that happens, the owner of the house or apartment is faced with a difficult choice: fight the intruder and do everything at one's command to get rid of him, or accept the invasion of privacy and consider it a natural component of daily living.

When the ghost comes with the house—that is, if he or she lived there before you did—there is a certain sentimentality involved; after all, the previous owner had earlier rights to the place, even if he is dead and you paid for the house, and an attempt to chase him away may create a sense of guilt in some sensitive souls. However, as often as not, the spectral personality had nothing to do with the house itself. The ghost may have lived in a previous dwelling standing on the spot prior to the building of the present one, or he may have come with the land and go back even further. This was entirely possible, because a ghost lives in his own environment, meaning that the past was the only world he knows. In some of these cases, telling the ghost to pack up and leave and join the regular spirits on the Other Side of life, will meet resistance: after all, to the ghost, you are the invader, the usurper. He was there first. But whatever the status of the phantom in the house or place, panic will not help much.

The more the current tenant of a house or apartment becomes frightened, the more the ghost derives benefit from it, because the negative nervous energy generated by the present-day inhabitants of a house could be utilized by the ghost to create physical phenomena—the so-called Poltergeist disturbances, where objects move seemingly of their own volition. The best thing to do is to consider the ghost a fellow human being, albeit in trouble, and perhaps not quite in his right mind. Ghosts have to be dealt with compassion and understanding; they have to be *persuaded* to leave, not forcefully ejected.

Ms. Sally S. lived in what was then a nice section of Brooklyn, half an hour from Manhattan, and at the time of the happenings I am about to report, was semi-retired, working two days a week at her old trade, which was that of a secretary. A year after the first phenomena occurred, she moved away to Long Island, not because of her ghostly experiences, but because the neighborhood had become too noisy for her: ghosts she could stand, human disturbances were too much.

Ms. S. moved into her Brooklyn apartment in May of 1964. At first, it seemed nice and quiet. Then, on August 3, she had an unusual experience. It must have been around 3:15 in the morning when she awoke with an uncanny feeling that she was not alone. In the semi-darkness of her apartment, she looked around and had the distinct impression that there was an intruder in her place. She looked out into the room and in the semi-darkness saw what appeared to be a dark figure. It was a man, and though she could not make out any features, he seemed tall and as lifelike as any human intruder might be.

Thinking that it was best for her to play possum, she lay still and waited for the intruder to leave. But, he came by her bed and started to touch her quilt cover. About fifteen minutes prior to this experience, she had herself awakened because she was cold, and had pulled the cover over herself. Thus she was very much awake when the "intruder" appeared to her. She lay still, trembling, watching his every move. Suddenly, he vanished into thin air and it was only then that Ms. S. realized she wasn't dealing with any flesh and blood person, but a ghost.

A month later, again around 3:00 A.M., Ms. S. awoke to see a white figure gliding back and forth in her room. This time, however, she was somewhat sleepy, so she did not feel like doing much about it. However, when the figure came close to her bed, she stuck out her arm to touch it and at that moment it dissolved into thin air again. Wondering who the ghost might be, Ms. S. had another opportunity to observe it in November, when around 6:00 in the morning she went into her kitchen to see the dark outline of a six-foot-tall man standing in the archway between kitchen and dinette. She looked away for a moment, and then returned her gaze to the spot. The apparition was still there. Once more Ms. S. closed her eyes and looked away, and when she returned her eyes to the spot, he was gone.

She decided to speak to her landlady about the incidents.

No one had died in the house, nor had there been any tragedy to the best of her knowledge, the owner of the house assured her. As for a previous owner, she wouldn't know. Ms. S. realized that it was her peculiar psychic talent that made the phenomena possible. For some time then she had been able to predict the results of horse races with uncanny accuracy, getting somewhat of a reputation in this area. Even during her school days, she came up with answers she had not been taught. In April of 1965, Ms. S. visited her sister and her husband in New Jersey. They had bought a house a year prior and knew nothing of its history. Sally was assigned a finished room in the attic. Shortly after 2:00 A.M., a ghost appeared to her in that room. But before she could make out any details, the figure vanished. By then Ms. S. knew that she had a talent for such things, and preferred not to talk about them with her sister, a somewhat nervous individual. But she kept wondering who the ghost at her house was.

In 1951, a close friend named John had passed away. A year before he had given her two nice fountain pens as gifts, and Ms. S. had kept one at home, while the other one was used by her at her office. A year after her friend's death, she was using one of the pens in the office, when the point broke. As she couldn't use it anymore, she put the pen into her desk drawer. Then she left the office for a few minutes. When she returned, she found a lovely, streamlined black pen on top of her desk. Immediately she inquired whether any of the other workers had left it there, but no one had, nor had anyone been seen near her desk. The pen was a rather expensive Mont Blanc, and just the thing she needed. It made her wonder whether her late friend John had not presented her with it even from the Beyond.

This belief was reinforced by an experience she had on the exact anniversary of his passing, in April, 1952, when she heard his voice loud and clear calling her 'sweetheart'—the name he had always used to address her by, rather than her given name Sally.

All this ran through her head in April, 1965, when she tried to come to terms with her ghostly experiences. Was the ghost someone who came with the house, someone who had been there before, or was it someone who somehow linked up with her? Then Sally began to put two and two together. She was in the habit of leaving her feet outside her quilt cover, because the room was rather warm with the steam heat on. However, in the course of the night, the temperature in the room fell, and frequently her feet became almost frostbitten as a result. One Saturday night in March, 1965, she was still awake, lying in bed around 11:00 P.M. Her feet were sticking out of the quilt, as the temperature was still tolerable. Suddenly she felt a terrific tug on her quilt; it was first raised from above her ankles and then pulled down to cover her feet. Yet, she saw no one actually doing it.

Suddenly she remembered how her late friend John had been in the habit of covering her feet, when she had fallen asleep after one of his visits with her. Evidently he was still concerned that Sally should not get cold feet or worse, and had decided to watch over her in this manner.

Mrs. I.B. was a recently married young wife, expecting a baby some months later. She and her husband were looking for a furnished apartment—the year was 1945. They had picked their favorite neighborhood, and decided to just look around until they saw a sign saying 'Apartment for Rent.' In 1945 this was still possible. They stopped into a candy store in the area and asked the owner if he knew of a vacant apartment. As they were speaking to the owner of the store, a young soldier, who had been standing in the rear of the store and had overheard the conversation, came over to them. He informed them that he had an apartment across the street from the store. When the inquired why he offered them the apartment, the soldier, very quietly, explained that he had come home to bury his wife. In his absence abroad, she had gone on a diet and, because of a weakened condition, had suddenly passed away. It had been the serviceman's intention to live with her in the apartment after the War. Under the circumstances, Mr. and Mrs. B. could have it until he returned, for he still wanted to live in it at War's end.

This was agreeable to the young couple, especially as the apartment was handsomely furnished. A deal was quickly made, and, that very night, Mr. and Mrs. B. went to sleep in the bedroom of the apartment, with nothing special on their minds.

At four-thirty A.M., Mr. B. got up to go to work, while his wife was still fast asleep. It was around five, when she heard someone running around in the room, in what seemed to her bare feet. The noise awoke her, and as she looked up, Mrs. B. saw at the foot of her bed the figure of a young woman, very pretty, wearing a nightgown.

Mrs. B. had no idea who the stranger might be, but thought that the young woman had somehow wandered into the apartment and asked her what she wanted. Instead of answering her, however, the young woman simply disappeared into thin air.

Mrs. B. flew into panic. Dressing in haste, she left the apartment while it was still dark outside and took refuge in her mother's home. Nobody would believe her story, not her mother, not her husband. And, because Mrs. B. was pregnant at the time, her condition was blamed for the "hallucination." Reluctantly, Mrs. B. went back to the apartment and to sleep the following evening. Shortly after her husband left for work again early in the morning, Mrs. B. was awakened by the same apparition. This time Mrs. B. did not run out of the house, but closed her eyes, and eventually the figure faded.

As soon as she was fully awake the next day, Mrs. B. determined to try and find out who the ghost might have been. Going through the various drawers in the apartment, she came across some photo albums belonging to the soldier. Leafing through them, she gave out a startled cry when her eyes fell on a photograph of the soldier, wearing plain clothes, with the very woman she had seen early in the morning next to him! Then Mrs. B. knew that she hadn't imagined the experiences. She showed the album to her husband, feeling that she had been visited by the soldier's dead wife. This time her husband was somewhat more impressed, and it was decided to obtain the "services" of a dog Mrs. B. had grown up with.

That night the dog slept on her bed, at the foot of it, as she had done many times before Mrs. B. was married. This made her feel a lot safer. But early in the morning she was awakened by her dog. The animal was standing on the foot of her bed, growling at the same spot where Mrs. B. had seen the apparition. The dog's fur was bristling on her back, and it was obvious that the animal was thoroughly scared.

But Mrs. B. did not see the ghost this time. It occurred to her that the ghost might resent her sleeping in what was once the bride's bed, so she and her husband exchanged beds the following night. From that moment on, the apparition did not return in the early mornings. Gradually, Mrs. B. got over her fear. A few weeks passed; then she noticed that some cups would fall off the shelf in the kitchen of their own volition, whenever she tried to cook a meal in it. Then the clock fell off the wall by itself, and it became apparent to her that objects were moved about by unseen hands. Some of this happened in the presence of her husband, who was no longer skeptical about it.

He decided it was time for them to move on. He wrote to the soldier, informing him that he was turning the apartment back to the landlord, so that he could have it for himself again upon his return. Undoubtedly, that was exactly what the ghostly woman had wanted in the first place. . . .

Not all ghostly visitors are necessarily frightening, or negative influences. Take the case of Mrs. M. N. In October of 1939 she signed a lease for a lovely old house on Commerce Street in New York's Greenwich Village. Legend had it that the house had been built by Washington Irving, although nothing was offered to substantiate this claim. It was a charming white house, small, with three stories and basement—and with five steps leading up from the street and guarded by wrought iron rails. On the first floor, there was a narrow hallway, stairs to the right, then the living room running the full depth of the house to the left. The second story contained the master bedroom with bath and a small room, possibly used as a dressing room originally. On the third floor were three small bedrooms with dormer windows and a bathroom.

Mrs. N. loved the house like a friend; and as she was then going through a personal crisis in her life, a group of human friends had gathered around her and moved into the house with her. These were people much younger than herself, and who decided to share the old house with her. Before actually moving into the house, Mrs. N. made the acquaintance of a neighbor, who was astonished at her having taken this particular house.

"For goodness' sake," the neighbor said, "why are you moving in *there?* Don't you know that place is haunted?"

Mrs. N. and her friends laughed at the thought, having not the slightest belief in the supernatural. Several days before the furniture was to be moved into the house, the little group gathered in the bare living room, lit their first fire in the fireplace and dedicated the house with prayers. It so happened they were all followers of the Baha'i faith, and they felt that that was the best way to create a harmonious atmosphere in what was to be their home.

They had been in the empty living room for perhaps an hour, praying and discussing the future, when suddenly there was a knock on the door. Dick, one of the young people who was nearest the door, went to answer the knock. There was no one there. It was a brilliant, moonlit night and the whole of little Commerce Street was empty. Shaking his head, Dick went back into the room, but fifteen minutes later somebody knocked again. Again, there was no one outside, and the knocking sounded once more that night. Just the same, they moved in, and almost immediately heard the footsteps of an unseen person. There were six in the house at the time: Kay sleeping on the couch in the basement dining room, Dick on a huge divan in the living room, Mrs. N. in the master bedroom on the second floor, and her fifteen-year-old daughter Barbara in one of the dormer bedrooms; Evie in another room and Bruce in the third. The first time they heard the steps they were all at dinner in the basement dining room. The front door, which was locked, opened and closed by itself, and footsteps went into the living room where they seemed to circle the room, pausing then and then, and then continuing.

Immediately Dick went upstairs to investigate and found there was no one about. Despite this, they felt no sense of alarm. Somehow they knew that their ghost was benign. From that moment on the footsteps of an unseen person became part of their lives. They were heard going upstairs and downstairs, prowling the living room, but somehow they never entered one of the bedrooms. Once in awhile, they heard the opening and then a loud slamming of the front door. They checked, but there was nobody to be seen, and eventually they realized that whoever it was who was sharing the house with them, preferred to remain unseen.

Since there were no other uncanny phenomena, the group accepted the presence of a ghost in their midst without undue alarm. One night however they had invited a group of Baha'i

65

Youth to stay with them and as a result Mrs N. had to sleep on the couch in the basement dining room. It turned into a night of sheer terror for her; she didn't see anything, but somehow the terror was all about her like thick fog. She didn't sleep a moment that night. The following morning, Mrs. N. queried Kay, who had ordinarily slept on the basement couch, as to whether she had had a similar experience. She had not. However, a few days later Kay reported a strange dream she had had while occupying the same couch.

She had been awakened by the opening of the areaway door. Startled, she had sat up in bed and watched fascinated as a file of Native Americans came through the door, along the end of the dining room, went through the kitchen and out the back door again, where she could hear their feet softly scuffing the dead leaves! They paid no attention to her at all, but she was able to observe that they were in full war paint.

Since Kay had a lively sense of imagination, Mrs. N. was inclined to dismiss the story. As there were no further disturbances, the matter of the ghost receded into the back of their minds. About a year after they had moved into the house, some of the little group were leaving town, and the household was being broken up. It was a week before they were to part, when Mrs. N. had an early morning train to catch, and not having an alarm clock herself had asked Dick to set up his alarm clock and wake her.

Promptly at six A.M., there was a knock at her door, to which Mrs. N. responded with thanks, and just as promptly went back to sleep. A few minutes later, there was a second knock on the door and this time Mrs. N. replied that she was already getting up. Later she thanked her friend for waking her and he looked at her somewhat sheepishly, asking her not to rub it in, for he hadn't heard the alarm at all. It appears that he had slept through the appointed hour and not awakened Mrs. N. as promised.

However, the friendly ghost had seen to it that she didn't miss her morning train. Was it the same benign specter which had shielded them from the Indians during their occupancy? That is, if the "dream" of Indians in war paint belonged to the past of the house, and was not merely an expression of a young girl's fancy.

Adriana Victoria was a spunky, adventurous lady of Mexican ancestry, of whom I have written before in one of my books. At one time, she worked as a housekeeper in a Hollywood mansion that was once the property of noted actress Carole Lombard. One night, Adriana awoke to see the blood-stained body of the actress standing by her bed, as if begging for attention. . . . By then Adriana knew that she was psychic, she knew that her mother was psychic also and that this particular talent ran in the family. She accepted it as something perfectly natural and learned to live with it, although at times she underwent frightening experiences not easily forgotten.

In 1966 Ms. Victoria lived in an apartment in New York City, which consisted of two-and-a-half rooms. In view of the small size of the apartment, it was something of a problem to put up her mother and her two children, who were living with her then; but Adriana managed somehow, when they came for a visit to New York in the summer of that year. They were on their way from Florida to Europe, and were staying for only a few days.

Since there was little room for everybody, they put a mattress on the living room floor. One night Ms. Victoria, sleeping on the mattress, was awakened by two invisible hands which she saw only in her mind's eye. At the same time she was shaken strongly by the ankles and opened her eyes wide. She couldn't see any intruder, and didn't dare to wake the others in the apartment. But nothing further happened until the end of summer, when her mother left with her daughter, leaving her nine-year-old son with her.

About two months later, Ms. Victoria was doing the dishes after dinner, and a girl friend from an apartment in the same building was watching television, waiting for her to finish with the dishes. Suddenly her son came running in and locked himself into the bathroom next to the kitchen, as if he were frightened by something. Before she could figure out what was happening, Ms. Victoria heard heavy footsteps coming from the living room in the direction of the kitchen and stopping right behind her. Quickly, she turned around, but her friend was still sitting on the living room couch, watching TV. Obviously, she hadn't heard the footsteps.

With her friend in the living room on the couch and her nine-year-old son in the bathroom, there was no one present who could have caused the footsteps. Besides, they were heavy, like those of a man. That same night, Adriana entered her bedroom. Her bed stood against the wall with a night table on either side of it. Suddenly she saw the figure of a woman standing next to her bed, moving her hands as if she were trying to get some papers or letters in a hurry.

As Adriana watched in fascinated horror, the apparition was putting imaginary things down from the night table onto the bed. There were some real books on the night table, but they did not move. Standing at the entrance to the room, Adriana looked at the apparition: she could see right through her, but was able to make out that the woman had brown hair down to her shoulders, stood about five foot two or three, and seemed to be about thirty years old. When Adriana made a move towards the bed, the figure looked up and straight at her—and then vanished before her very eyes. A little later, her little boy came to sleep with her and, of course, she did not tell him about the apparition. Evidently the child had heard the footsteps, too, and there was no need to frighten him further.

The following evening around nine o'clock the boy complained about being frightened by footsteps again. It was difficult for Adriana to explain them to her son, but she tried to calm his fears. The ghost reappeared from time to time, always in the same spot, always looking for some papers or seeming to be, and not necessarily at night: there were times when Adriana saw her standing by her bed in plain daylight.

In July of 1967 Adriana had to go into the hospital for a minor operation. A Spanish-speaking lady, a neighbor, was asked to stay with her son for the four days Adriana was to be in the hospital. The baby sitter left the bed to the young man and slept on the couch herself.

When Adriana returned from the hospital on the fifth day, the baby sitter grabbed her by the hand and rushed her into the bedroom, for she didn't want to talk in front of the boy. She was absolutely terrified. It seems that the previous night she was awakened toward three in the morning by heavy footsteps right next to her. She was sure that it was a man and heard him bump into a chair! Frightened, she screamed and called out, "Who's there?" But there was no answer. Through all this the boy had slept soundly.

She turned on the lights and noticed that the chair had been moved a little from where it had stood before. That was enough for her! She crawled into bed with the little boy—and decided never to stay in the apartment overnight again unless Adriana was there also.

Adriana decided to make some inquiries about the past of her apartment, but all she could ascertain was that two nurses had lived there for about eight years. The building was very old and had a long history, so it may well be that one or more tragedies have taken place in what was then Adriana's apartment.

Adriana found herself invited to a Christmas party and somehow the conversation drifted to ghosts. Her host did not believe in such things, and doubted Adriana's experiences. When they brought her back to her apartment, Adriana invited them in. She was just bending down trying to open a bottle of soda, when she suddenly heard those heavy footsteps again, coming from the bedroom and stopping right at the entrance to the living room. At the same time, the thought crossed her mind that it was like a husband, waking from sleep to greet his wife returning from a party. Somehow this terrified her and she let out a loud scream. That night, she stayed with friends.

After her son left in July of the following year, things seemed to quiet down a little. Shortly afterward, around six P.M., Adriana returned home from work. As soon as she opened the door she could smell burned papers. Immediately she checked the kitchen. Everything seemed in order. Suddenly she realized that she could smell the strange smell better in her mind than with her nose. At the same time, a thought crossed her mind, "My lady ghost finally found the papers and burned them." Adriana knew that they were love letters, and that all was right then with her ghost. There were no further disturbances after that.

Some ghostly invasions have a way of snowballing from seemingly quiet beginnings into veritable torrents of terror. Mrs. C. of North Dakota was a housewife with an eight-year-old daughter, a husband who did not believe in ghosts or anything of that nature, and an old house which would be a comfortable, roomy house if it weren't for—*them*. Mrs. C. and her family moved into the house in 1970. Whether it was because both she and her husband worked and at different times, thus being absent from the house a great deal of the time, or whether the unseen forces had not yet gathered enough strength to manifest, nothing of an uncanny nature occurred until January, 1973.

One day during January Mrs. C. was working in the basement, doing some clothes. All of a sudden she heard someone whistle; no definite tune, just one long whistle repeated several times. Immediately her dog, Pud, ran around the basement to see where the noise came from, but neither Mrs. C. nor her dog could find the origin of the whistle.

The whistling continued on several occasions during the month, and, while it seemed puzzling, it did not upset her greatly. At the time, she was working nights, returning home between midnight and one A.M. One night during February she returned home and as soon as she had entered the house, had a very strange feeling of being watched by someone. At the same time it became freezing cold and the hair on her arms stood up. She looked all over the house, but found no intruder, nothing human that could account for the strange feeling.

Mrs. C. decided to prepare for bed, and changed clothes in the kitchen, as was her custom, in order not to wake her husband who was already asleep. She then went toward the bedroom, in semi-darkness, with the lights off, but sufficient illumination to make out details of the room. All of a sudden, about a foot and a half in front of her face and a little above her head, she noticed a smoky, whitish-gray haze. To her horror she saw that in the middle of it there was a human face without either body or neck. It was the head of a bald man, very white, with distinctive black eyes, and a very ugly face. All through it and around it was this strange white fog. Mrs. C. had never seen anything like it and became very frightened. She dashed into the bedroom, not sure whether the whole thing had been her imagination, and eventually she fell asleep. The next day, the whistling returned and in fact continued all month long. This was followed by a mumbling human voice, at first one person, later two people speaking. Both she and her seven-year-old girl heard it. At first the mumbling was heard only in the daytime; later it switched to nighttime as well.

At the time, Mrs. C.'s husband left for work at four o'clock in the morning, and she was in the habit of sleeping on till about eight. But then she could not; as soon as her husband had left for work, the mumbling would start, always in the bedroom and seemingly coming from the foot of the bed, moving to the side of the bed opposite where she slept, then back to the foot of the bed again, and directly in front of her feet. She tried hard not to pay any attention to it and after listening to it for awhile, managed to fall asleep. Soon it sounded as if several women and one man were speaking, perhaps as many as four individuals. This continued every morning until April of that year. Then something new was added to the torment: what sounded like a faint growling noise.

The growling was the last straw. Mrs. C. became very frightened and decided to do something to protect herself. She recalled a small cross which her husband had given her the previous Christmas. She put the cross and chain around her neck, never taking it off again.

Mrs. C. loved animals. At the time of the haunting, the family owned two parakeets, six guinea pigs, two dogs and two cats. Since the uncanny events had started in her house, she had kept a day-to-day diary of strange happenings, not because she hoped to convince her husband of the reality of the phenomena, but to keep her own sanity and counsel. On May 5, 1973, Mrs. C. awoke and found her blue parakeet dead, horribly disfigured in its cage; the green parakeet next to it acted as if it were insane, running back and forth all day and screaming. The following day, May 6, Mrs. C. awoke to find the green bird dead, destroyed in exactly the same way as the first parakeet had been.

Four days later, as she was washing her hair, Mrs. C. felt the chain with the cross being lifted up from the back of her neck by an unseen hand and unclasped and then dropped to the floor. When she turned around, there was no one in back of her. Still shaken, she left her house at 9:30 to do some errands. When she returned at eleven o'clock, she found one of her guinea pigs lying on the living room floor, flopping its head in a most pitiful fashion. A short time later the animal died. Its neck had been broken by an unseen force. No one had been in the house at the time, as her daughter and a friend, who had slept over, had accompanied Mrs. C. on her errands. What made the incident even more grisly was the fact that the guinea pig had been kept in a cage, that the cage was locked and that the key rested safely in Mrs. C.'s cigarette case, on her person when she went out of the house.

Two weeks passed. On May 25, while taking a bath, Mrs. C. felt the necklace with the cross being lifted up into the air from the back of the neck and pulled so hard it snapped and fell into the tub. This was the beginning of a day of terror. During the night the two children heard frightening noises down in the basement, which kept them from sleeping. Mrs. C., exhausted from the earlier encounters, had slept so deeply she had not heard them. The children reported that the dogs had growled all night and that they had heard the meowing of the cats as well.

Mrs. C. went downstairs to check on things. The dogs lay asleep as if exhausted; the cats were not there, but upstairs by now; and on the floor, scattered all over the basement, lay the remaining guinea pigs except for one. That one was alive and well in its cage, but two others lay dead inside their cage, which was still locked and intact. Their bodies were bloody and presented a horrible sight—fur all torn off, eyes gone and bodies torn apart. At first, Mrs. C. thought that the dogs might have attacked them, but soon realized that they could not have done so inside the animals' cages.

For a few days, things quieted down somewhat. Then, one morning the ominous growling started again while Mrs. C. was still in bed. Gradually, the growling noise became louder and louder, as if it were getting closer. This particular morning the growling had started quietly but when it reached a deafening crescendo, Mrs. C. heard over it a girl's voice speak quite plainly, "No, don't hurt her! Don't hurt her!" The growling continued, nevertheless. Then, as Mrs. C. looked on in horror, someone unseen sat down in front of her feet on the bed, for the bed sank down appreciably from the weight of the unseen person.

Then the spectral visitor moved up closer and closer in the bed towards her, while the growling became louder. Accompanying it was the girl's voice, "No, no! Don't do it!" That was enough for Mrs. C. Like lightning she jumped out of bed and ran into the kitchen and sat down trembling. But the growling followed her from the bedroom, started into the living room across from the kitchen, then went back to the bedroom—and suddenly stopped.

That was the last time Mrs. C. slept on in the morning after her husband left for work. From that moment on she got up with him, got dressed and sat in the kitchen until the children got up, between 7:30 and 9:00 A.M.

About that time, they heard the sound of water running, at night and in the morning upon arising. Even her husband heard it then and asked her to find out where it was coming from. On checking the bathroom, kitchen, upstairs sink, basement bathroom and laundry room, Mr. and Mrs. C. concluded that the source of the running water was invisible.

From time to time they heard the sound of dishes being broken and crashing and furniture being moved with accompanying loud noise. Yet, when they looked for the damage, nothing had been touched, nothing broken.

At the beginning of summer, 1973, Mrs. C. had a sudden cold feeling and all of a sudden she felt a hand on her neck, coming around from behind her, and she could actually feel fingers around her throat! She tried to swallow and felt as if she were being choked. The sensation lasted just long enough to cause her great anxiety and then it went away as quickly as it had come.

Some of the phenomena were then accompanied by rapping on the walls, with the knocks taking on an intelligent pattern, as if someone were trying to communicate with them. Doorknobs would rattle by themselves or turn themselves, even though there was no one on the other side of them. All over the house, footsteps were being heard. One particular day, when Mrs. C. was sitting in the kitchen with her daughter, all the doors in the house began to rattle. This was followed by doors all over the house opening and slamming shut by themselves, and the drapes in the living room opening wide and closing quickly, as if someone were pulling them back and forth. Then the window shades in the kitchen went up and then down again, windows would open by themselves, going up, down, up, down, in all the rooms, crashing as they fell down without breaking.

It sounded as if all hell had broken loose in the house. At the height of this nightmare, the growling started up again in the bedroom. Mrs. C. and her little daughter sat on the bed and stared towards where they thought the growling came from. Suddenly Mrs. C. could no longer talk, no matter how she tried; not a word came from her mouth. It was clear to her that something extraordinary was taking place. Just as the phenomena reached the height of fury, everything stopped dead silent, and the house was quiet again.

Thus far only Mrs. C. and her little daughter shared the experiences, for her husband was not only a skeptic but prided himself on being an atheist. No matter how pressing the problem was, Mrs. C. could not unburden herself to him.

One night, when the couple was returning from a local stock car race, and had gone to bed, the mumbling voices started up again. Mrs. C. said nothing, in order not to upset her husband, but the voices became louder. All of a sudden Mr.

C. asked, "What is that?" and when she informed him that those were the ghostly voices she had been hearing all along, he chided her for being so silly. But *he* had heard them *also*. A few days later Mr. C. told his wife he wanted a cross necklace similar to the one she was wearing. Since his birthday was about to occur, she bought one for him as a gift. From that moment on, Mr. C. also wore a necklace with a cross on it all the time.

In despair, Mrs. C. turned to her brother, who had an interest in occult matters. Together with him and her young brother-in-law, Mrs. C. went downstairs one night in August, to try and lay the ghosts. In a halting voice, her brother spoke to the unseen entities, asking them to speak up or forever hold their peace. There was no immediate response. The request to make their presence felt was repeated several times.

All of a sudden, all hell broke loose. Rattling and banging in the walls started up around them, and the sound of walking on the basement steps was clearly heard by the three of them. Mrs. C.'s brother started up the stairs and, as he did so, he had the chilly impression of a man standing there.

Perhaps the formula of calling out the ghosts worked, because the house went quiet after that experience. Sometimes Mrs. C. looks back on those terrible days and nights, and wishes it had happened to someone else, not her. But the empty cages where her pet animals had been kept were a grim reminder that it had all been only too true.

Mrs. J.H. was a housewife living in Maryland. At the time of the incidents I am about to report, her son Richard, was seven and her daughter Cheryl, six. Hers was a conventional marriage, until the tragic death of her husband, Frank. On September 3, 1969, he was locking up a restaurant where he was employed near Washington, D.C. Suddenly, two men entered the rear door and shot him, while attempting a robbery. For more than a year after the murder, no clue as to the murderers was found by the police.

Mrs. H. was still grieving over the sudden loss of her husband when something extraordinary took place in her home. Exactly one month to the day from his death, she happened to be in her living room, when she saw a "wall of light" and something floated across the living room towards her. From it stepped the person of her late husband Frank. He seemed quite real to her, but somewhat transparent. Frightened, the widow turned on the lights and the apparition faded.

From that moment on, the house seemed to be alive with strange phenomena: knocks at the door, which disclosed no one who could have caused them, and the dog barking for no good reason in the middle of the night, or the cats staring as if they were looking at a definite person in the room. Then one day the two children went into the bathroom, and saw their dead father taking a shower! Needless to say, Mrs. H. was at a loss to explain that to them. The widow had placed all of her late husband's clothes into an unused closet which was kept locked. She was the last one to go to bed at night and the first one to arise in the morning. One morning she awoke to find Frank's shoes in the hallway; nobody could have placed them there.

One day Mrs. H.'s mother, Mrs. D., who lived nearby, was washing clothes in her daughter's basement. When she approached the washer, she noticed that it was spotted with what appeared to be fresh blood. Immediately she and the widow searched the basement, looking for a possible leak in the ceiling, to account for the blood, but they found nothing. Shortly afterwards, a sister of the widow arrived, to have lunch at the house. A fresh tablecloth was placed on the table. When the women started to clear the table after lunch, they noticed that under each dish there were blood spots the size of a fifty-cent piece. Nothing they had eaten at lunch could possibly have accounted for such a stain.

But the widow's home was not the only place where manifestations took place. Her mother's home was close by, and one night a clock radio alarm went off by itself in a room which had not been entered by anyone for months. It was the room belonging to Mrs. H.'s grandmother, who had been in the hospital for some time before.

It became clear to Mrs. H. that her husband was trying to get in touch with her, since the phenomena continued at an unabated pace. Early in 1972, two alarm clocks in the house went off at the same time, although they had not been set, and all the kitchen cabinets flew open by themselves. The late Frank H. appeared to his widow punctually on the third of each month, the day he was murdered, but the widow could not bring herself to address him and ask him what he wanted. Frightened, she turned on the light and caused him to fade away. In the middle of the night Mrs. H. would feel someone shake her shoulder, as if to wake her up. She recognized this touch as that of her late husband, for it was his habit to wake her in just that manner.

Meanwhile, the murderers were caught. Unfortunately, by one of those strange quirks of justice, they got off very lightly, one of the murderers with three years in prison, the other with ten. It seemed like a very light sentence for having taken a man's life so deliberately.

Time went on, and the children became ten and eleven years of age respectively. Mrs. H. could no longer take the phenomena in the house, and moved out. The house was rented to strangers, who lived in it for years. They had no experiences of an uncanny nature, since, after all, Frank wants nothing from *them*.

As for the new house where Mrs. H. and her children moved, Frank did not put in an appearance. But there were occasional tappings on the wall, as if he still wanted to communicate with his wife.

*   *   *

At the time of this story, Alice H. was sixty-nine years old, and lived in a five-room bungalow flat in the Middle West. She still worked part-time as a salesperson, but lived alone. Throughout her long life she never had any real interest in psychic phenomena. She even went to a spiritualist meeting with a friend and was not much impressed one way or another. She was sixty-two years old when she had her first personal encounter with the unknown.

One night she went to bed and awoke because something was pressing against her back. Since she knew herself to be alone in the apartment, it frightened her. Nevertheless, she turned around to look—and to her horror she saw the upper part of her late husband's body. As she stared at him, he glided over the bed, turned to look at her once more with a mischievous look in his eye and disappeared on the other side of the bed. Mrs. H. could not figure out why he had appeared to her, because she had not been thinking of him at that time. But evidently he was to instigate her further psychic experiences.

Not much later, she had another manifestation which shook her up a great deal. She had been sound asleep when she was awakened by the whimpering of her dog. The dog, a puppy, was sleeping on top of the covers on the outside of the bed. Mrs. H. was fully awake then and looked over her shoulder, and there stood a young girl of about ten years, in the most beautiful shade of blue tailored pajamas, with a T pattern. She was looking at the dog. As Mrs. H. looked closer, she noticed that the child had neither face, hands nor feet showing. Shaken, she jumped out of bed and went toward the spirit. The little girl moved back toward the wall, and Mrs. H. followed her. As the little girl in the blue pajamas neared the wall, it somehow changed into a beautiful flower garden with a wide path!

She walked down the path in a mechanical sort of way, with the wide cuffs of her pajamas showing, but still with no feet. Nevertheless, it was a happy walk. Then it all disappeared.

The experience bothered Mrs. H., so she moved into another room. But her little dog stayed on in the room where the experience had taken place, sleeping on the floor under the bed. That first experience took place on a Sunday in October, at four A.M. The following Sunday, again at four o'clock, Mrs. H. heard the dog whimper, as if he were conscious of a presence. By the time she reached the other room, however, she could not see anything. These experiences continued for some time, always on Sunday at four in the morning. It became clear to Mrs. H. then that the little girl hadn't come for her in particular—but only to visit her little dog.

Mrs. S.F. worked in an assembly plant, assembling electronic parts. She was a middle-aged woman of average educational background, divorced, and living in a house in central Pennsylvania. A native of Pittsburgh, she went to public school in that city, her father worked for a steel company, and she had several brothers and sisters.

When she was fourteen years of age, she had her first remembered psychic experience. In the old house her parents then lived in, she saw a column of white smoke in front of her, but, as she didn't understand it, it didn't bother her, and she went off to sleep anyway.

Many times she would get impressions of future events and foretell things long before they happened, but she paid little attention to her special gift. It was only when she moved into her house that the matter took on new dimensions.

The house Mrs. F. moved into was a small attached house, two stories high, and connected to two similar houses by what was locally called a party wall: two houses sharing the same wall. Two rooms were downstairs, two rooms upstairs. Her house had its bathroom down in the cellar, and when you first entered it you were in the living room, then the kitchen. Upstairs, there were two bedrooms, with the stairs going up from the kitchen. There was no attic; the house was small and compact, and it was just the thing Mrs. F. needed, since she was going to live in it alone. The house next door was similar to hers, and it belonged to a woman whose husband had passed away some time previously. Next to that was another, similar house in which some of this widowed woman's family lived at the time Mrs. F. moved into her house. There were four houses in all, identical and connected by "party walls." The four houses share a common ground, and seemed rather old to her, when she first saw them.

When Mrs. F. moved into the house she decided to sleep in the bedroom in back of the upper story, and she put her double bed into it. But after she had moved into the house, she discovered that the back room was too cold in the winter and too hot in the summer, so she decided to sleep in the front room, which had twin beds in it. Depending upon the temperature, she would switch from one bedroom to the other. Nothing much out of the ordinary happened to her at first, or perhaps she was too busy to notice.

Then, one spring night, when she was asleep in the back bedroom, she woke from her sound sleep around four o'clock in the morning. Her eyes were open and, as she looked up, she saw a man bending over her, close to her face. She could see that he had a ruddy complexion, a high forehead, and was partly bald with white hair around his ears.

When he noticed that she was looking at him, he gave her a cold stare and then slowly drifted back away from her until he disappeared. She could not see the rest of his body, but had the vague impression of some sort of robe. Immediately Mrs F. thought she had had a hallucination or dreamt the whole thing, so she went back to sleep.

Not much later, Mrs. F. was in bed, reading. It was around two-thirty in the morning. The reading lamp was on and the light in the hall as well—when she suddenly heard a swish-like sound followed by a thump. At the same time something punched her bed and then hit her in the head. She clearly felt a human hand in the area of her eye, but could not see anything. Immediately, she wondered, what could have hit her? There was no one in the room but her. After a while, she dismissed the matter from her mind and went back to reading.

A few days later, when she was reading again in the late hours of the night, she noticed that the bed would go down as if someone had sat on it. It clearly showed the indentation of a human body, yet she could not see anything. This disturbed her, but she decided to pay it no attention—until one night she also heard a man's voice coming to her as if from an echo chamber. It sounded as if someone were trying to talk to her but couldn't get the words out properly: like a muffled 'hello.'

Mrs. F. never felt comfortable in the back bedroom, and so she decided to move into the front room. One night she was in bed in that room, when her eyes apparently opened by themselves and rested on a cupboard door across from the bed. This time she clearly saw the figure of a man, but she couldn't make out legs or feet. It was a dark silhouette of a man, but she could clearly make out his rather pointed ears. His most outstanding features were his burning eyes and those strange pointed ears. When he saw her looking at him, he moved back into the door and disappeared.

Again, Mrs. F. refused to acknowledge that she had a ghost but thought it was all a hallucination, seeing that she had been awakened from a deep sleep. Not much later she happened to be watching television, a little after midnight, because her work ended at twelve. She felt like getting some potato chips from a cupboard in the corner. As she got up to get the potato chips, and rounded the bend of the hall, she happened to glance at the wall in the hallway—and there was the same man again. She could clearly make out his face and the pointed ears, but again he had neither legs nor feet. As soon as the ghost realized that she had discovered him, he quickly moved back into the wall and disappeared. Then Mrs. F.'s composure was gone; clearly, the apparition was not a hallucination, since she was fully awake then and could not blame her dreams for it.

While she was still debating within herself what this all meant, she had another experience. She happened to be in bed reading when she thought she heard something move in the kitchen. It sounded like indistinct movements, and so she tried to listen but after awhile she didn't hear anything further and went back to reading. A little later she decided to go down to get a fruit drink out of the refrigerator. The hall lights were on, so the kitchen wasn't too dark. Just the same, when she reached the kitchen, Mrs. F. turned on the fluorescent lights in the kitchen, two long tubes. As soon as the lights came on she saw the same ghostly apparition standing there in the kitchen, only this time there was a whole view of him, with feet and legs and even shoes with rounded toes. He wore pants and a shirt, and she could see his color; she could see that he had curly hair, a straight nose and full lips. She particularly noted the full lips and, of course, the pointed ears.

At first, the apparition must have been startled by her, perhaps because he had thought that it was the cat coming down the stairs into the kitchen. He turned towards her and Mrs. F. could see his profile. As soon as he noticed her, he ran into the wall and disappeared. But she noticed that his legs started to shake when the lights went on, as if he were trying to get going and didn't quite know how. Then he hunched over a little, and shot into the wall.

Mrs. F. was shocked. She shut off the light and went back to bed. For a long time she just lay there, with the eeriest, chilliest feeling. Eventually she drifted off to sleep again. The entire incident puzzled her, for she had no idea who the ghost might be. One day she was leaving her house and, as she passed her neighbor's house, there was a young man sitting on the steps, looking out into the street. She saw his profile, and like a flash it went through her mind that it was the same profile as that of the man she had seen in her kitchen! She looked again, and noticed the same full lips, the same pointed ears she had seen in the face of the ghost!

Immediately, she decided to discuss the matter with a neighbor, a Mrs. J.M. Mrs. M. lived at the end of the street, and she was a good person to talk to, because she understood about such matters. In fact, Mrs. F. had spent a night at her house at one time when she was particularly upset by the goings-on in her own house. The neighbor assured her that the widow's son, the one she had seen sitting on the steps, was the spit and image of his father. The reason Mrs. F. had not seen him before was that he was married and lived somewhere else, and had just been visiting here that particular day.

Well, Mrs. F. put two and two together, and realized that the ghost she had seen was her late neighbor. On making further inquiries, she discovered that the man had suffered from rheumatic fever, and had been in the habit of lying on a couch to watch television. One day his family had awakened him so he wouldn't miss his favorite program. At that moment he had a heart attack, and died, right there on the couch. He was only middle-aged.

With this information in her hands, Mrs. F. wondered what she could do about ridding herself of the unwelcome visitor from next door. In August, 1972, a niece was visiting her with some friends and other relatives. One of the people in the group was an amateur medium, and suggested that they try their hand at a seance. There were about seven in the group, and they sat down and tried to make contact with the late neighbor. The seance was held in the upstairs bedroom, and they used a card table borrowed from Mrs. M. from the other end of the street.

Everybody put his hands on the table, and immediately felt that the table was rising up. Nothing much happened, however, beyond that, and eventually the amateur medium had to leave. But Mrs. F. wanted an answer to her problem, so she continued with those who were still visiting with her. They moved the table down into the kitchen, turned out all the lights but one, and waited. Mrs. F. asked the ghost questions: who he was, what he wanted, etc. Sure enough, her questions were answered by knocks. Everybody could hear them, and after awhile, they managed to get a conversation going. From this communication Mrs. F. learned that her neighbor had been forty-three years old when he died, that his name was Bill, and that he wasn't very happy being dead! But apparently he appreciated the fact that they had tried to get through to him. He never appeared to Mrs. F. again after that.

Only a small fraction of ghosts are "fortunate" enough to be relieved of their status by an investigation in which they are freed from their surroundings and allowed to go out into the greater reaches of the world beyond. The majority has no choice but to cling to the environment in which their tragedy had occurred. But what about those who are in an environment which suddenly ceases to exist? As far as houses are concerned, tearing down one house and building another on the spot doesn't alter the situation much. Frequently, ghosts continue to exist in the new house, even more confused then they were in the old one. But if the environment is radically changed, and no new dwelling erected on the spot, what is there to occupy the ghost in his search for identity?

Mrs. Roberta B. was a housewife, mother of four children,

leading a busy life in Pittsburgh. Because of her interest in parapsychology she was able to assist her parents in a most unusual case. In a small town north of Pittsburgh, on the Ohio River, her parents occupied a house built approximately seventy-five years before. They were the second owners, the house having been planned and partially built by the original owner, a certain Daniel W.

Mr. W. had lived in the house with his brother and sister for many years, and had died a bachelor at the age of ninety-four. His last illness was a long one, and his funeral was held in what later became the living room of Mrs. B.'s parents. Thus, Mr. W. not only "gave birth" to the little house, but he lived in it for such a long period that he must have become very attached to it, and formed one of those rare bonds which frequently lead to what I have called "Stay-behinds," people who live and die in their houses and just don't feel like leaving them.

In the late spring of 1965, Mrs. B.'s parents decided to remodel the house somewhat. In particular, they tore through the wall connecting her bedroom with that of her husband, next to it. Each room had a cupboard in it, but instead they decided to build a new closet with sliding doors. Although they had occupied the house for fourteen years, this was the first change they had made in it.

One week after the alteration had been completed, Mrs. B.'s mother found it difficult to fall asleep. It was toward one o'clock in the morning and she had been tossing for hours. Suddenly from the direction of the cupboard in the left-hand corner of the room came the sound of heavy breathing. This startled her, as she could also hear her husband's breathing from the room next to hers. The mysterious breathing was husky, labored, and sounded as though it came from an echo chamber. Frightened, she lay still and listened. To her horror, the breathing sound moved across the room and stopped in front of the bureau against the far wall. Then, as she concentrated on that spot, she saw a mist starting to form above the chest. At this point, she managed to switch on the light and call out, "Who was there?" Immediately the breathing stopped.

Mrs. B's mother then called her daughter, knowing of her interest in the occult, and reported the incident to her. Her daughter advised her not to be alarmed, but to watch out for further occurrences, which were bound to happen. Sure enough, a few days later a curtain was pulled back in full view of her mother, as if by an unseen hand, yet no window was open which would have accounted for it. Shortly thereafter a chair in the living room sagged as if someone were sitting in it, yet no one was visible. That was enough for one day! A few days later a window was lowered in the hall while Mrs. B.'s mother was talking to her on the telephone and while there was no one else in the house. Shadow-like streaks began to appear on the dining room and living room floors. A Japanese print hanging in the living room, two-by-four feet in size and very heavy, moved of its own volition on the wall. Mrs. B.'s father began to hear the heavy breathing on his side of the dividing wall, but as soon as he had taken notice of it, it moved to the foot of his bed.

By then it was clear to both parents that they had a ghost in the house; they suspected the original owner. Evidently he was displeased with the alterations in the house and this was his way of letting them know. Mr. W.'s continued presence in the house also shook up their dog. Frequently she would stand in the hall downstairs and bark in the direction of the stairs, with the hair on her back bristled, and unable to move up those stairs. At times she would run through the house as if someone were chasing her—someone unseen, that is.

It looked as if Mrs. B.'s parents would have to get used to the continued presence of the original owner of the house when the authorities decided to run a six-lane state highway smack through the area, eliminating about half of the little town in which they lived, including their house. This has since been done, and the house exists no more. But what about Mr. W.? If he couldn't stand the idea of minor alterations in his house, what about the six-lane highway eliminating it altogether?

Ghosts, as a rule, do not move around much. They may be seen in one part of the house or another, not necessarily in the room in which they died as people, but there are few cases on record where ghosts have traveled any kind of distance to manifest.

YANKEE PHANTOMS AND DIXIE GHOSTS— TWO DIFFERENT WORLDS

*T*here are two areas of the United States that are frequently connected with hauntings in the imaginations of the average person: New England and the South. Perhaps it is because these two regions are more likely to inspire romantic notions; perhaps it's because their physical appearance is more conducive to unusual phenomena than, let us say, the plains states, or the Rocky Mountains.

But it is not only the unusual and varied geographical appearance of New England and the South that is seemingly conducive to the occurrence of hauntings, but the people who live there as well. Both regions have one thing in common: they were settled at an early stage in American history, mainly from western European roots, and they share a fierce loyalty to basic nationalistic values. With New England, it was one of continuing the traditions of the mother country, England, and of extending the cultural backgrounds of the old country into the new. In the South, the traditions of Great Britain have been largely overshadowed by native-grown values, inherent in the background of the region, such as the country appeal of the wide-open spaces, the gentility of a closely-knit society going back several hundred years.

The ghosts of an area are likely to reflect the people of that region; frequently, they *are* people who once lived in the region. Thus the appearances of specters may differ greatly in New England and the South; but the degree of their involvement with the land, with traditions and with strongly parochial points of view was very similar. It was for that reason that I have grouped the following cases together, not so much to reconcile the erstwhile Civil War foes.

Mrs. Geraldine W. was a graduate of Boston City Hospital, and worked as a registered nurse; her husband was a teacher, and they had four children. Neither Mr. nor Mrs. W. ever had the slightest interest in the occult; in fact, Mrs. W. remembers as a child hearing some chilling stories about ghosts and considering them just so many fairy tales.

In July, 1968, the W.'s decided to acquire a house about twenty miles from Boston, as the conditions in the city seemed inappropriate to bring up their four children. Their choice fell upon a Victorian home sitting on a large rock overlooking a golf course in this little town. Actually, there were two houses, built next door one to the other by two brothers. The one to the left had originally been used as a winter residence and the one upon which their choice fell, as a summer home. It presented a remarkable sight, high above the other houses in the area. The house so impressed the W.'s that they made immediate inquiry toward acquiring it. They were told that it had once formed part of the H. estate, and had remained in the same family until nine years prior to their visit. Originally built by a certain Ephraim Hamblin, it had been sold to the H. family and remained a family property until it passed into the hands of a family initialed P. It remained in their possession until the W.'s acquired it in the spring of 1968.

Prior to obtaining possession of the house, Mrs. W. had a strange dream in which she saw herself standing in the driveway, looking up at the house. In the dream she had a terrible feeling of foreboding, as if something dreadful had happened in the house. On awakening the next morning, however, she thought no more about it and later put it out of her mind.

Shortly after they moved in, which was July 15, 1968, Mrs. W. awoke in the middle of the night. Her eyes fell upon the ceiling and she saw what looked to her like a sparkler-type of light. It swirled about in a circular movement and then disappeared. On checking, Mrs. W. found that all the shades were drawn in the room, so it perplexed her how such a light could have occurred on her ceiling. But the matter slipped from her mind soon after.

Several days later she happened to be sitting in the living room one evening, with the television sound on very low, since her husband was asleep on the couch. Everything was very quiet. On the arm of a wide-armed couch there were three packages of cigarettes, side by side. As she looked at them, the middle package suddenly flipped over by itself and fell to the floor. Since Mrs. W. had no interest in psychic phenomena, she dismissed this as probably due to some natural cause. A short time thereafter she happened to be sleeping in her daughter's room, facing directly alongside the front hall staircase. The large hall light was left on, since the lamp near the children's rooms had burned out. As she lay in the room, she became aware of heavy, slow, plodding footsteps coming across the hallway.

Terrified, she kept her eyes closed tight because she thought there was a prowler in the house. Since everyone was accounted for, only a stranger could have made the noises. She started to pray over and over in order to calm herself. But the footsteps continued on the stairs, progressing down the staircase and around into the living room, where they faded away.

Mrs. W. was thankful that her prayers had been answered and that the prowler had left again.

Just as she started to doze off again the footsteps returned. Although she was still scared, she decided to brave the intruder, whoever he might be. As she got up and approached the area where she heard the steps, they resounded directly in front of her—yet she could see absolutely no one. The next morning she checked all doors and windows and found them securely locked, as she had left them the night before. She mentioned the matter to her husband, who ascribed it to nerves. A few nights later Mrs. W. was awakened again in the middle of the night, this time in her own bedroom. As she came to and sat up in bed, she heard a woman's voice from somewhere in the room. It tried to form words, but Mrs. W. could not make them out. The voice was of a hollow nature and resembled something from an echo chamber. It seemed to her that the voice had come from an area near the ceiling, over her husband's bureau, but the matter did not prevent her from going back to sleep, perplexing though it was.

By then Mrs. W. was convinced that they had a ghost in the house. She was standing in her kitchen, contemplating where she could find a priest to have the house exorcised, when all of a sudden a trash bag, which had been resting quietly on the floor, burst and crashed with its contents spilling all over the floor. The disturbances had become so frequent that Mrs. W. took every opportunity she could to leave the house as early as possible in the morning with her children, and not arrive home until she had to. She did not bring in a priest to exorcise the house, but managed to obtain a bottle of blessed water from Lourdes, and went through each room sprinkling it with a prayer for the soul of whoever was causing the haunting in the house.

About that time her husband came home from work one evening around six o'clock, and went upstairs to change his clothes while Mrs. W. was busy setting the table for dinner.

Suddenly, Mr. W. called his wife and asked her to open and close the door to the back hall stairs. Puzzled by his request, she did so, five times, each time increasing the operation in strength. Finally she asked her husband what was the purpose of this exercise. He admitted that he wanted to test the effect of the door being opened and closed in this manner, because he had just observed the back gate to the stairs opening and closing by itself!

This was as good a time as any to have a discussion of what was going on in the house, so Mrs. W. went up the stairs to join Mr. W. in the bedroom, where he was standing. As she did so, her eye caught a dim, circular light that seemed to skip across the ceiling in two strokes; at the same time the shade at the other end of the room suddenly snapped up, flipping over vigorously a number of times. Both Mr. and Mrs. W. started to run from the room; then, catching themselves, returned to the bedroom.

On looking over these strange incidents, Mr. W. admitted that there had been some occurrences that could not be explained by natural means. Shortly after they had moved to the house, he had started to paint the interior of the house, at the same time thinking about making some structural changes in the house, because there were certain things in it he did not like. As he did so, two cans of paint were knocked out of his hands, flipping over and covering a good portion of the living room and hall floors.

Then there was that Saturday afternoon when Mr. W. had helped his wife vacuum the hall stairs. Again he started to talk about the bad shape the house was in, in his opinion, and as he condemned the house, the vacuum cleaner suddenly left the upper landing and traveled over the staircase all by itself, to hit him on the head with a solid thud!

But their discussion did not solve the matter; they had to brace themselves against further incidents, even though they did not know why and who caused them. One evening Mrs. W. was feeding her baby in the living room near the fireplace when she heard footsteps overhead and a dragging movement of something very heavy across the floor. This was followed by a crashing sound on the staircase, as if something very heavy had fallen against the railing. Her husband was asleep, but Mrs. W. woke him up and together they investigated, only to find the children asleep and no stranger in the house.

It was then virtually impossible to spend a quiet evening in the living room without hearing some uncanny noises. There was scratching along the tops of the doors inside the house, a rubbing sound along the door tops, and once in awhile the front doorknob would wiggle by itself, as if an unseen hand were twisting it. No one could have done this physically, because the enclosed porch leading to the door was locked and the locks were intact when Mrs. W. examined them.

The ghost, whoever he or she was, roamed the entire house. One night Mrs. W. was reading in her bedroom, at around midnight, when she heard a knocking sound halfway up the wall of her room. It seemed to move along the wall and then stop dead beside her night table. Needless to say, it did not contribute to a peaceful night. By then the older children were also aware of the disturbances. They, too, heard knocking on doors with no one outside, and twice Mrs. W.'s little girl, then seven years old, was awakened in the middle of the night because she heard someone walking about the house. At the time both her parents were fast asleep.

Coming home Christmas night, 1968, to an empty house, or what they *presumed* to be an empty house, the W.'s noticed that a Christmas light was on in the bedroom window. Under the circumstances the family stayed outside while Mr. W. went upstairs to check the house. He found everything locked and no one inside. The rest of the family therefore moved into the lower hall, waiting for Mr. W. to come down from upstairs. As he reached the bottom of the stairs, coming from what he assured his family was an empty upper story, they all heard footsteps overhead from the area he had just examined.

It was the eve of St. Valentine's Day, and Mrs. W. was readying the house for a party the next evening. She had waxed the floors and spruced up the entire house and it had gotten late. Just before going to bed, she decided to sit down for awhile in her rocking chair. Suddenly she perceived a moaning and groaning sound coming across the living room from left to right. It lasted perhaps ten to fifteen seconds then ended as abruptly as it had begun.

During the party the next evening, the conversation drifted to ghosts, and somehow Mrs. W. confided in her sister-in-law what they had been through since moving to the house. It was only then that Mrs. W. found out from her sister-in-law that her husband's mother had had an experience in the house while staying over one night during the summer. She, too, had heard loud footsteps coming up the hall stairs, she had heard voices, and a crackling sound as if there had been a fire someplace. On investigating these strange noises she had found nothing that could have caused them. However, she had decided not to tell Mrs. W. about it in order not to frighten her.

Because of her background and position and her husband's respected position as a teacher, the W.'s were reluctant to discuss their experiences with anyone who might construe them as imaginary, or think them silly. Eventually, however, a sympathetic neighbor gave her one of my books, and Mrs. W. contacted me for advice. She realized, of course, that her letter would not be read immediately and that in any event I might not be able to do anything about it for some time. Frightening though the experiences had been, she was reconciled to living with them, hoping only that her children would not be hurt or frightened.

On March 3, 1969, she had put her three young boys to bed for a nap, and decided to check if they were properly covered. As she went up over the stairway she thought she saw a movement out of the corner of her eye. Her first thought was that her little boy, then four years old, had gotten up instead of taking his nap, but, on checking, she found him fast asleep. Exactly one week later, Mrs. W. was in bed trying to go to sleep, when she heard a progressively louder tapping on the wooden mantle at the foot of the bed. She turned over to see where the noise was coming from or what was causing it and immediately it stopped. She turned back to the side, trying to go back to sleep, when suddenly she felt something or some-one shake her foot as though trying to get her attention. She looked down at her foot and saw absolutely nothing.

Finally, on March 26, she received my letter, explaining some of the phenomena to her and advising her what to do. As she was reading my letter, she heard the sound of someone moving about upstairs, directly over her head. Since she knew that the children were sleeping soundly, Mrs. W. realized that her unseen visitor was not in the least bit put off by the advice dispensed to her by the Ghost Hunter. Even a dog the W.'s had acquired around Christmas had its difficulty with the unseen forces loose in the house.

At first, he had slept upstairs on the rug beside Mrs. W.'s bed. But a short time after, he began to growl and bark at night, in the direction of the stairs. Eventually he took to sleeping on the enclosed porch and refused to enter the house, no matter how one would try to entice him. Mrs. W. decided to make some inquiries in the neighborhood, in order to find out who the ghost might be or what he might want.

She discovered that a paper-hanger who had come to do some work in the house just before they had purchased it, had encountered considerable difficulties. He had been hired to do some paper-hanging in the house, changing the decor from what it had been. He had papered a room in the house as he had been told to, but on returning the next day found that some of his papers were on upside down, as if moved around by unseen hands. He, too, heard strange noises and would have nothing further to do with the house. Mrs. W. then called upon the people who had preceded them in the house, the P. family, but the daughter of the late owner said that during their stay in the house they had not experienced anything unusual. Perhaps she did not care to discuss such matters; at any rate, Mrs. W. discovered that the former owner, Mr. P., had actually died in the house three years prior to their acquisition of it. Apparently, he had been working on the house, which he loved very much, and had sustained a fracture. He recovered from it, but sustained another fracture in the same area of his leg. During the recovery, he died of a heart attack in the living room.

It was conceivable that Mr. P. did not like the rearrangements made by the new owners, and resented the need for repapering or repainting, having done so much of that himself while in the flesh; but if it was he who was walking up and down the stairs at night, turning doorknobs, and appearing as luminous balls of light—who, then, was the woman whose voice had also been heard?

So it appears that the house overlooking the golf course for the past hundred and fifty years had more than one spectral inhabitant in it. Perhaps Mr. P. was only a Johnny-come-lately, joining the earlier shades staying on in what used to be their home. As far as the W.'s were concerned, the house was big enough for all of them; so long as they knew their place!

Peter Q. came from a devout Catholic family, part Scottish, part Irish. In June, 1968, Peter Q. was married, and his brother Tom, with whom he had always maintained a close and cordial relationship, came to the wedding. That was the last time the two brothers were happy together. Two weeks later Tom and a friend spent a weekend on Cape Cod. During that weekend, Tom lost his prize possession—his collection of record albums worth several hundred dollars had been stolen. Being somewhat superstitious, he feared that his luck had turned against him, and, sure enough, a hit-and-run driver hit his car shortly afterwards.

Then, in August of the same year, Tom and his father caught a very big fish on a fishing trip and won a prize consisting of a free trip during the season. As he was cleaning the fish to present it to the jury, the line broke and Tom lost the prize fish. But his streak of bad luck was to take on ominous proportions soon after: two weeks later, Tom Q. and the same friend who had been with him when his record collection had been stolen, were planning another trip together. Tom was very happy the night before, because he was looking forward to the trip. He was joyful, and in the course of conversation said, "When I die, I want a good send-off," meaning, a good traditional Irish wake. His friend, first-named David, on the other hand, was quiet and withdrawn, not quite himself that evening. The following morning, the two young men set out for their trip. Before the day was out, they were involved in an automobile accident. Tom Q. died instantly. David died the next day.

Even before the bad news was brought home to Peter Q. and the family, an extraordinary thing happened at their house. The clock in the bedroom stopped suddenly. When Peter checked it, and wound it again, he found that there was nothing wrong with it. By then, word of Tom's death had come, and, on checking out the time, Peter found that the clock had stopped at the very instant of his brother's death.

During the following days, drawers in their bedroom would open by themselves, when there was no one about. This continued for about four weeks, then it stopped again. On the anniversary of Tom's death, Peter, who was then a junior at the university, was doing some studying and using a fountain pen to highlight certain parts in the books. Just then his mother called him and asked him to help his father with his car. Peter placed the pen inside the book to mark the page and went to help his father. On returning an hour later, he discovered that a picture of his late brother with his family had been placed where he had left the pen, and the pen was lying outside the book, next to it. No one had been in the house at the time, since Peter's wife was out working.

Under the influence of Tom's untimely death, and the phenomena taking place at his house, Peter Q. became very interested in life after death and read almost everything he could, talking with many of his friends about the subject, becoming all the time more and more convinced that man does in some mysterious way survive death. But his wife disagreed with him and did not wish to discuss the matter. One night, while her husband was away from the house, she received a telepathic impression concerning continuance of life, and, as she did so, a glowing object about the size of a softball appeared next to her in her bed. It was not a dream, for she could see the headlights from passing cars shine on the wall of the room, yet the shining object was still there next to her pillow, stationary and glowing. Eventually, it disappeared.

Many times Peter Q. had felt the presence of his brother after his untimely death—a warm, wonderful feeling; yet it gives him goose bumps all over. As for the real big send-off Tom had wanted from this life, he truly received it. The morning after his accident, a number of friends called the house without realizing that anything had happened to the boy. They had felt a strong urge to call as if someone had communicated with them telepathically to do so.

Tom Q. was a collector of phonograph records and owned many, even though a large part of his collection had been stolen. The night before his fatal accident, he had played some of these records. When Peter checked the record player later he discovered that the song his brother had played last was entitled, "Just One More Day." Of the many recordings by Otis Redding that his brother owned, why had he chosen that one?

Mr. Harold B. was a professional horse trainer who traveled a good deal of the time. When he did stay at home, he lived in an old home in W., a small town in Massachusetts. Prior to moving to New England, he and his wife lived in Ohio, but he was attracted by the old world atmosphere of New England and decided to settle down in the East. They found a house which was more than two hundred years old but unfortunately it was in dire need of repair. There was neither electricity nor central heating, all the rooms were dirty, neglected and badly in need of renovating. Nevertheless, they liked the general feeling of the house and decided to take it.

Much of the sad state the house was in was due to the fact that it had been lived in for fifty-five years prior to their arrival by a somewhat eccentric couple who had shut themselves off from the world. They would hardly admit anyone to their home, and it was known in town that three of their dogs had died of starvation. Mr. and Mrs. B. moved into the house on Walnut Road in October, 1967. Shortly after their arrival, Mrs. B. fractured a leg, which kept her housebound for a considerable amount of time. This was unfortunate, since the house needed so much work. Nevertheless, they managed. With professional help, they did the house over from top to bottom, putting in a considerable amount of work and money to make it livable until it became a truly beautiful, neat house.

Although Mrs. B. was not particularly interested in the occult, she had a number of psychic experiences in the past, especially of a precognitive nature, and had accepted her psychic powers as a matter of course. Shortly after the couple had moved into the house on Walnut Road, they noticed that there *was* something peculiar about their home.

One night Mrs. B. was sleeping alone in a downstairs front room off the center entrance hall. Suddenly she was awakened by a sense of presence and as she looked up she saw the figure of a small woman before her bed, looking at her. She could make out all details of the woman's face and stature, and noticed that she was wearing a veil, as widows sometimes do. When the apparition became aware of Mrs. B.'s attention, she lifted the veil and spoke to her, assuring her that she was not there to harm her, but came as a friend. Mrs. B. was too overcome by it all to reply, and before she could gather her wits, the apparition drifted away.

Immediately, Mrs. B made inquiries in town, and since she was able to give a detailed description of the apparition, it was not long until she knew who the ghost was: the description fit the former owner of the house, Mrs. C., to a tee. Mrs. C. died at age eighty-six a short time before the B.'s moved into what was her former home. Armed with this information, Mrs. B. braced herself for the presence of an unwanted inhabitant in the house. A short time afterwards, she saw the shadowy outline of what appeared to be a heavy-set person move along the hall from her bedroom. At first she thought it was her husband, so she called out to him, but soon discovered that her husband was actually upstairs. She then examined her room and discovered that the shades were drawn, so there was no possibility that light from traffic on the road outside could have cast a shadow into the adjoining hall. The shadowy figure which she had seen did not however look like the outline of the ghost she had earlier encountered in the front bedroom.

While she was still wondering about this, she heard the sound of a dog running across the floor. There was no dog to be seen. Evidently her own dog also heard or sensed the ghostly dog's doings, because he reacted with visible terror.

Mrs. B. was still wondering about the second apparition, when her small grandson came and stayed overnight. He had never been to the house before and had not been told of the stories connected with it. As he was preparing to go to sleep, but still fully conscious, he saw a heavy-set man wearing a red shirt standing before him in his bedroom. This upset him greatly, especially as the man suddenly disappeared without benefit of door. He described the apparition to his grandparents, who reassured him by telling him a white lie: namely, that he had been dreaming. To this the boy indignantly replied that he had not, but in fact had been fully awake. The description given by the boy not only fitted the shadowy outline of the figure Mrs. B. had seen along the corridor, but was a faithful description of the late Mr. C., former owner of the house.

Although the ghost of Mrs. C. had originally assured the B.'s that they meant no harm and that she had, in fact, come as a friend, Mrs. B. had her doubts. A number of small items of no particular value disappeared from time to time and were never found again. This was at times when intruders were completely out of the question.

Then Mrs. B. heard the pages of a wallpaper sampler lying on the dining room table being turned one day. Thinking that it was her husband that was doing it, she called out to him, only to find that the room was empty. When she located him in another part of the house he reported having heard the pages being turned also, and this reassured Mrs. B. since she then had her husband's support in the matter of ghosts. It was clear to her that the late former owners did not appreciate the many changes they had made in the house. But Mrs. B. also decided that she was not about to be put out of her home by a ghost. The changes had been made for the better, she decided, and the C.'s, even in their present ghostly state, should be grateful for what they had done for the house and not resent them. Perhaps these thoughts somehow reached the two ghosts telepathically; at any rate, the house settled down to a quiet atmosphere after that.

Not all ghosts have selfish motives, so to speak, in reasserting their previous ownership of a home: some even help later occupants, although the limits of a ghost's rationality are very narrow. For one thing, if a ghost personality was aware of later inhabitants of a house, and wants to communicate with them not in order to get them out but to warn them—such a ghost was still unable to realize the warning may be entirely unnecessary because time had passed, and the present reality no longer corresponds to the reality he or she knew when his or her own tragedy occurred.

Still, there was the strange case of Rose S., at one time living in Fort Worth, Texas. Ms. S. was a secretary by profession, and during the middle 1960's worked for a well-known social leader. In the summer of 1968, Ms. S. moved into an old house in Fort Worth, renting one room at one end of the house. At the time she wanted to be near her fiance, an army pilot, who was stationed not far away.

The old house she chanced upon was located on Bryce Avenue, in one of the older sections of Fort Worth. The owner was renting out a furnished room because the house had become too large for her. Her husband, who had been an attorney, had passed away and their children were all grown and living away from home.

The house seemed pleasant enough, the room large and suitable, so Ms. S. was indeed happy to have found it. Moreover, her landlady did not restrict her to the rented room, but allowed her to use the kitchen and in fact have the freedom of the house, especially as there were no other tenants, and the landlady and Ms. S. were the only people living at that address. The landlady seemed pleasant enough, a woman in her middle or late sixties at the time, and except for an occasional habit of talking to herself, there was nothing particularly unusual about her. Ms. S. looked forward to a pleasant, if uneventful stay at the house on Bryce Avenue.

Not long after moving in, it happened that the landlady went off to visit a daughter in Houston, leaving the house entirely to Ms. S. That night Rose S. decided to read and then retire early. As soon as she switched off the lights to go to sleep, she began to hear footsteps walking around the house. At the same time the light in the bathroom, which she had intended leaving on all night, started to grow dimmer and brighter alternately, which puzzled her. Frightened, because she thought she had to face an intruder, Ms. S. got up to investigate but found not a living soul anywhere in the house. She then decided that the whole thing was simply her imagination, on being left alone in the house for the first time, and went to bed. The days passed, and the incident was forgotten. A few weeks later the landlady was off again for Houston, but this time Ms. S.'s fiance was visiting her. It was evening, and the couple was spending the time after dinner, relaxing.

Ms. S.'s fiance, the pilot, had fallen asleep. Suddenly, in the quiet of night, Ms. S. heard someone whistle loudly and clearly from the next room. It was a marching song which vaguely reminded her of the well-known melody, the Colonel Bogey March. Neither TV nor radio were playing at the time, and there was no one about. When she realized that the source of the whistling was of an uncanny nature, she decided not to tell her fiance, not wishing to upset him.

Time went on, and another periodical trip by her landlady left Ms. S. alone in the house. This time she was in the TV den, trying to read and write. It was a warm night, and the air conditioner was on.

As she was sitting there, Ms. S. gradually got the feeling that she was not alone. She had the distinct impression that someone was watching her, and then there came the faint whining voice of a woman above the sound of the air conditioner. The voice kept talking, and though Ms. S. tried to ignore it, she had to listen. Whether by voice or telepathy, she received the impression that she was not to stay in the house, and that the voice was warning her to move out immediately. After another restless night with very little sleep, Ms. S. decided she could take the phenomena no longer.

As soon as the landlady returned, she informed her that she was leaving, and moved in with friends temporarily. Eventually, her experiences at the house on Bryce Avenue left her no peace and she made some quiet inquiries. It was then that she discovered the reasons for the haunting. On the very corner where the house stood, a woman and a girl had been murdered by a man, while waiting for a bus.

As if that were not enough to upset her, something happened to her fiance from that moment on. Following the incident with the whistling ghost, of which her fiance knew nothing, his behavior towards her changed drastically. It was as if he was not quite himself any more, but under the influence of another personality. Their relationship changed drastically; shortly afterwards Ms. S. and her pilot broke off the engagement.

Mike L. lived in Tennessee, in an area where his family had been in residence for several generations. Ever since he could remember he had had psychic ability. At the time when a favorite uncle was in the hospital, he was awakened in the middle of the night to see his uncle stand by his bed. "Goodbye, Michael," the uncle said, and then the image faded away. That instant Mike knew that his uncle had passed away, so he went back to sleep. The following morning his mother awoke him to tell him that his uncle had passed away during the night. In April, 1964, he and his wife moved to a residential section in one of the large cities of Tennessee. They bought a house from a lady well up in her seventies. She had the reputation of being somewhat cranky and was not too well-liked in the neighborhood.

Shortly after they had settled down in the house, they noticed footsteps in the rafters over their bedroom. Regardless of the hour, these footsteps would come across the ceiling from one side of the room to the other. Whenever they checked, there was nothing there that could have caused the footsteps. While they were still puzzled about the matter, though not shocked, and since they had had psychic presences in other houses, something still more remarkable occurred. There were two floor lamps in the living room, on opposite sides of the room. In order to make them work, a switch had to be turned on physically. One night Mr. L. awoke and noticed one of the floor lamps lit. Since he clearly remembered having turned it off on going to bed, he was puzzled by this, but got out of bed and switched it off again. As if to complement this incident, the other floor lamp came on by itself a few nights later, even though it had been turned off by hand a short time before.

This was the beginning of an entire series of lights being turned on in various parts of the house, seemingly by unseen hands. Since it was their practice not to leave any lights on, except for a small night light in their daughter's room, there was no way in which this could be explained by negligence or on rational grounds. The house had a basement, including a small space below the wooden front porch. As a result of this hollow space, if anyone were walking on the porch, the steps would reverberate that much more audibly. Frequently the L.'s heard someone coming up the porch, approaching the door and stopping there. Whenever they looked out, they saw no one about. Not much later they were awakened by the noise of a large number of dishes crashing to the floor of the kitchen, at least so they thought. When they checked, everything was in order, no dish had been disturbed.

They were still wondering about this when they caught the movement of something—or someone—out of the corner of their eye in the living room. When they looked closer, there was no one there. Then the dresser in the bedroom *seemed* as if it were moving across the floor, or so it sounded. By the time they got to the room, nothing had been changed.

One night, just after retiring, Mr. L. was shocked by a great deal of noise going on in the basement. It sounded as if someone were wrecking his shop. He jumped out of bed, grabbed a gun, opened the basement door and turned on the light. There was an audible scurrying sound, as if someone were moving about, followed by silence.

Immediately Mr. L. thought he had a burglar but realized he would be unable to go downstairs without exposing himself. Under the circumstances he called for his wife to telephone the police while he was staying at the head of the stairs guarding the basement exit. As soon as he heard the police arrive, he locked the only door to the basement and joined them on the outside of the house. Together they investigated—only to find no one about, and no evidence of foul play. Even more inexplicable, nothing in the shop had been touched. About that time Mr. L. noticed a tendency of the basement door to unlock itself seemingly of its own volition, even though it was Mr. L.'s custom to lock it both at night and when leaving the house. During the daytime Mrs. L. frequently heard footsteps overhead when she was in the basement, even though she was fully aware of the fact that there was no one in the house but her.

By then Mr. and Mrs. L. realized that someone was trying to get their attention. They became aware of an unseen presence staring at them in the dining room, or bothering Mrs. L. in one of the others rooms of the house. Finally, Mike L. remembered that a Rosicrucian friend had given them a so-called Hermetic Cross, when they had encountered ghostly troubles in another house. He brought the cross to the dining room and nailed it to the wall. This seemed to relieve the pressure somewhat, until they found a calendar hung in front of the cross, as if to downgrade its power.

Mr. L. made some further inquiries in the neighborhood, in order to find out who the unseen intruder might be. Eventually, he managed to piece the story together. The woman from whom they had bought the house had been a widow of about nine years, when they had met her. The husband had been extremely unhappy in the house; he was not permitted to smoke, for

instance, and had to hide his cigarettes in a neighbor's basement. Nothing he did in his own house met with his wife's
approval, it appeared, and he died a very unhappy man. Could it
not be that his restless spirit, once freed from the shackles of the
body, finally enjoyed his unobstructed powers, to roam the
house and do whatever he pleased? Or perhaps even enjoy the
vicarious thrill of frightening the later owners, and, for the first
time in his long life, becoming the ruler of the house.

There was the strange case of Dorothy B., a young woman
then in her early thirties, a native of Pennsylvania, who spent
several years living with a maternal uncle and aunt in North
Carolina. The house was a two-hundred-year-old farmhouse,
surrounded by a medium-sized farm. Her uncle and aunt were
people in their late fifties who continued farming on a reduced
scale, since they lived alone; and their two children had long
left and gone to the city. Dorothy was assigned a pleasant corner room in the upper story of the house, and when she moved
into it in April of 1961, she thought she had at last found a
place where she could have peace and quiet.

This was very necessary, you see, because she had just been
through a nervous breakdown due to an unhappy love affair,
and had decided to withdraw from life in the city. Fortunately
she had saved up some money, so she could afford to live quietly by herself for at least a year. When her uncle had heard of
her predicament, he had offered the hospitality of the house, in
return for some light chores which she could easily perform for
them. The first night after her arrival at the farmhouse,
Dorothy slept soundly, due probably to the long journey and
the emotional release of entering a new phase of her life. But
the following night, and she remembers this clearly, because
there was a full moon that night, Dorothy went to bed around
ten P.M., feeling very relaxed and hopeful of the future. The
conversation at the dinner table had been about art and poetry,

two subjects very dear to Dorothy's heart. Nothing about the house or its background had been mentioned by her uncle and aunt, nor had there been any discussion of psychic phenomena. The latter subject was not exactly alien to Dorothy for she had had a number of ESP experiences over the years, mainly pre-cognitive in nature and not particularly startling.

She extinguished the lights and started to drift off to sleep. Suddenly her attention was focused on a low level noise, seemingly emanating from below the ceiling. It sounded as if someone were tapping on the wall. At first, Dorothy assumed that the pipes were acting up, but then she remembered that it was the middle of spring and the heat was not on.

She decided not to pay any attention, assuming it was just one of those noises you hear in old houses, due to their settling. Again she tried to drift off to sleep. She was almost asleep when she had the feeling of a presence close to her bed. There was an intense chill accompanying that feeling, and she sat bolt upright in bed, suddenly terrified. As she opened her eyes and looked toward the corner of her room, she saw that she was not alone. Due to the strong moonlight streaming in from the window she could make out everything in the room. Perhaps a yard or a yard and a half away from her stood the figure of a young girl, motionless, staring at her with very large, sad eyes!

Despite her terror, Dorothy could make out that the girl was dressed in very old-fashioned clothes, of the kind that are not worn today. She seemed liked a farm girl; the clothes were simple but clean, and her long brown hair cascaded down over her shoulders. There was a terrible feeling of guilt in her eyes, as if she were desperately seeking help. "What do you want?" Dorothy said, trembling with fear as she spoke. The apparition did not reply, but continued to stare at her. At this moment Dorothy had the clear impression that the girl wanted her to know how sorry she was. At this point Dorothy's fear got the better of her and she turned on the light. As she did so, the apparition vanished immediately.

Still shaken, she went back to sleep and managed a some-what restless night. The following morning she asked her aunt whether there had ever been any psychic experience in the fam-ily, in particular whether anyone had ever seen or heard any-thing unusual in the house. Her aunt gave her a strange look, and shook her head. Either there hadn't been anything, or she didn't care to discuss it. Dorothy, as the newcomer, did not feel like pressing her point, so she changed the subject.

That night she went to bed with anticipatory fears, but nothing happened. Relieved that it might all have been her imagination due to the long trip the day before, Dorothy began to forget the incident. Three days later, however, she was again awakened by the feeling of a presence in her room. The cold was as intense as it had been the first time, and when she opened her eyes, there was the same apparition she had seen before. This time she was even more pleading for help, and since Dorothy did not feel the same gripping fear she had experienced the first time, she was able to communicate with the apparition.

"I want to help you; tell me who you are," she said to the specter, waiting for some sort of reply. After what seemed to her an eternity but could have been no more than a few sec-onds, Dorothy received the impression that the girl was in trouble because of a man she had become involved with. To be sure, the ghost did not speak to her; the thoughts came to Dorothy on a telepathic level, haltingly, in bits, picturing the apparition with a tall, good-looking man, also wearing old-fashioned farm clothes. In her mind's eye, Dorothy saw the two lovers, and then she heard the sound of what seemed a tiny infant. At that point, the apparition vanished, leaving Dorothy very much shaken.

The following morning she broached the subject of ghosts to her aunt. But the reaction she got from her relative was so cold, she hesitated to go on, and, again, she did not relate her experiences. Several weeks passed, without any incident of any kind. That is, except for some strange noises which Dorothy ascribed to a settling of the house, or perhaps a squirrel or two in the rafters above her room. It sounded like furtive, light foot-steps if one were so inclined to interpret the sounds. Again, there was a full moon, and Dorothy was aware that she had been at the house for a full month. That night, Dorothy went to bed earlier than usual, hoping to get a good start toward a night's sleep, since she had been particularly active during the day, help-ing her aunt clear out a woodshed in back of the farmhouse.

It had not been an easy chore: somehow the atmosphere in the woodshed was very depressing, and Dorothy wanted to leave more than once, but hesitated to do so lest her aunt accuse her of being lazy. But the feeling inside the woodshed was heavy with tragedy and unhappiness, even though Dorothy could not pinpoint the reasons for it.

Now she lay in bed, waiting for sleep to come. She had drawn the blinds, but the moonlight kept streaming in through them, bathing the room in a sort of semi-darkness, which allowed Dorothy to see everything in the room in good detail. After a few minutes she became aware of an intense chill to the left side of her bed. She realized she was not about to drift into peaceful sleep after all, and prepared herself for what she knew would be her nocturnal visitor. In a moment, there was the pale-looking girl again, this time standing by the window as if she did not dare come near Dorothy.

Very well, Dorothy thought, let's get to the bottom of this. I've had about enough of it, and if this ghost is going to make my life miserable here, I might as well know why. Somehow the ghost seemed to have read her mind, because she came closer to the bed, looking at Dorothy again with her tearful, large eyes. As if someone had told her to, Dorothy then closed her own eyes, and allowed the apparition to impress her with further details of her story. Again she saw the husky young man and the ghost girl together, and this time there was an infant with them. Next she saw an old woman entering what appeared to be a very run-down shack or room, and something in Dorothy recognized the shack as the woodshed she had been in during the day!

Then something horrible happened: although she could not see it with her mind's eye, Dorothy knew that the child was being *butchered,* and that the old woman was the instigator of it! Quickly, Dorothy opened her eyes and looked at the apparition. For a moment the girl looked at Dorothy again as if to say *now you understand why I am still here*—but then the ghost faded into the woodwork. Somehow Dorothy was able to sleep peacefully that night, as if a burden had been lifted from her.

The following morning, she told her aunt everything that had happened from the very first day on. This time her aunt did not interrupt her, but listened in stony silence, as Dorothy recounted her ghostly experiences. Finally, she said, "I wish you had been left in peace; that is why I did not want to tell you anything about this ghost." She explained that a young girl named Anne, who had been working for them for a number of years prior to Dorothy's arrival, had also slept in the same room. She, too, had seen the apparition, although she was unable to understand the reasons for the ghostly encounter. A few years after taking over the farm, Dorothy's uncle had stumbled across an unmarked grave in back of the woodshed. It was clear to him that it was a grave, even though the headstone had been partially destroyed by time and weather. He had assumed that it belonged to a slave, for there were slaves in the area at the time when the farm was first built.

But the grave seemed unusually small, and Dorothy's aunt wondered whether perhaps it might not be that of a child. As she said this, Dorothy felt a distinct chill and received the distinct impression that her aunt had hit on something connected with her ghost. On the spur of the moment, the two women went to the spot where the grave had been discovered. It was barely discernible amid the surrounding rocks and earth, but eventually they located it. Dorothy fetched some flowers from the house and placed them upon what must have been the headstone at one time. Then she fashioned a crude cross from two wooden sticks and placed them in the center. This done, she said a simple prayer, hoping that the soul of whoever was underneath the stones would find an easy passage into the world beyond.

When Dorothy went to bed the following night, she had a sense of relief at having done something constructive about her ghost. She half-expected the ghostly girl to appear again, but nothing happened that night, nor the following night, nor any night thereafter until Dorothy left the farmhouse to go back to the city years later.

MR. HULSE'S PSYCHIC EXPERIENCES

*G*eorge Hulse was a quiet, soft-spoken gentleman who lived in Baltimore, Maryland, and dealt in real estate. Now, if there is any profession with its feet more firmly on the ground than real estate, I wouldn't know it. Mr. Hulse was a typical member of his profession, not given to guesswork or fantasy, but who had, nevertheless, learned to cope with some extraordinary facets of his personality, abilities which do not seem as substantial as his ability to appraise the value of a house or a piece of land, but which, nevertheless, partake of a higher reality, and he had learned to live with it.

Originally from Liverpool, England, he had arrived in the United States in June 1962. Hulse worked at a variety of professions; he worked on ships, he worked on the docks, in offices, as a salesman, and even as a truck driver. During World War II, he was a tail-gunner in the Royal Air Force and was wounded in August, 1941. Although he had some ESP experiences in his younger years, he had not accepted them as valid. The first experience he remembered clearly happened when he was only a child.

He had been in bed asleep when he awoke and saw the figure of his grandmother standing at the side of the bed. The six-year-old George was his grandmother's favorite. He had given her a nickname, Pepper, because his grandmother used to take snuff and he thought she was taking pepper. From that evolved her peculiar nickname. Since George knew that his grandmother was dead, and yet he saw her standing next to his bed, he let out a yell and his mother came running into the bedroom. But she didn't persuade the little boy that he had dreamt it, but merely told him that if grandmother had come to see him, it was just to make sure that he was all right. As a matter of fact, she might have been telling the truth: shortly afterward, George contracted scarlet fever and had to go to a hospital.

Even when he was in his teens, George scoffed at the idea that there was anything to psychic phenomena. When his sister invited a medium to come to their house, George scoffed at the idea of a seance, and warned his sister not to meddle in such nonsense. However, in 1937, he awakened one night from deep sleep, and, still in a state bordering on sleep, but half-awake, he saw a vision of marching soldiers, with guns and other equipment. He was lying flat on his bed at the time, and as he looked up toward the ceiling, he saw this vision which reminded him of a television image. The soldiers wore British uniforms, of pre-World War II days, khaki, and puttees, which were still worn on the legs of British soldiers in those days. The men seemed to be advancing over rough ground, and, George thought, when he saw this vision, whether his mind was playing him tricks. But he had not been to any movies, not seen any war pictures, nor discussed the subject of war with anyone prior to having this vision.

During the year he had the same vision again; three times more, in fact, and always in total silence. The second time he had the vision, the word *war* seemed to be flashed across his mental horizon, like a newspaper headline. When it happened for the fourth time that year, it seemed more urgent. Yet, the vision was almost identical with the three previous ones.

Two years later George's vision became reality, when World War II broke out. But he was not one of the marching soldiers of his vision, since he joined the Royal Navy in September, 1939. He considered the visions a warning and at the time discussed them freely with his parents. During the War, when he was married, his wife was sharing a house with one of her sisters whose husband was also away in the Forces. But George wanted a house of his own, for the time when he would be done with war, and so he decided to look for one in the Boodle section of Liverpool. He found just what he had in mind in a little row of houses right in the center of the district.

No sooner found than rented, he and his wife moved in on a Friday, and as soon as the movers had left, he and his wife worked like beavers to set up the beds and the rest of the furniture. But Saturday morning he had a terrible feeling that he had to get out of the house immediately. Giving in to his impulse, he jumped on his motorcycle, raced back to the people who had moved them in, and asked them to come back and take the furniture back where they had brought it from. The movers shook their heads, but did what he requested. That night there was a tremendous air raid on Liverpool; and, after it was over, Hulse jumped back on his motorcycle and went down to where the house stood. There was only rubble there now: the house had taken a direct hit.

Although Mr. Hulse's wife thought him crazy when he decided to move before even settling down in the house, she was no longer as skeptical after she learned that his psychic awareness had saved their lived. His psychic ability had been helpful to him many times in his life. One year, in October, he had a vision that his mother would die the following February; he saw the roads which the funeral procession would be taking, and the cemetery, and the kind of weather it would be on that day.

Consequently, he was prepared for it and when it came to pass, exactly as he had foreseen it in his vision, he was able to withstand the emotional shock better. At the time, Mr. Hulse was living in Australia while his mother made her home in England: nevertheless, the impression of her impending passing was so strong it crossed both time and space without difficulty.

But not all of Mr. Hulse's psychic experiences were on the grim side. After he had become a widower in Australia, he returned to England, married again, this time to an American. His wife's family wanted them to come to the United States, and since he had made a fair amount of money as a salesman in Australia, he decided to do so. But after he figured out the fare for the family, he realized that there wouldn't be much left. Now, in those days, he was in the habit of going to Bingo games in Liverpool every Thursday evening. One particular Thursday evening, he left his sister after the Bingo games, and he went to his late mother's home. There he sat in what used to be her chair and suddenly had a vision, in which he saw himself win the following week's Bingo.

It was a very strange feeling, a picture suspended in front of the wall, lasting perhaps forty-five seconds, but clearly visible to his eyes. This gave him enough of a chance to study the vision in detail: he saw a man in a brown suit, with his face turned away from him, and he knew that this was the man in charge of handing out the prizes. He knew this was the Jackpot Night, next Friday, and as he looked closer, he saw the man in the brown suit put the amount of the winnings on a blackboard. Unfortunately, he was unable to make out whether the amount was three hundred forty or three hundred and four pounds, but he was sure it was beyond three hundred pounds.

The next morning Mr. Hulse telephoned his sister and told her that he was going to win the Bingo the following week. She laughed at this preposterous idea, but he assured her that he meant it. The following Friday the entire family went to the Bingo, instead of the usual Thursday night, since they wanted to be present when Mr. Hulse won the big prize. When they got on line for tickets, Mr. Hulse turned to one of the ushers and assured him that he was going to win the jackpot that evening. The man laughed, of course, but again Mr. Hulse assured him that he would.

When he got to the ticket window, and picked up the tickets to play Bingo, they felt very hot in his hand. Quickly he looked at the girl selling tickets and said, "Now look at me very close, miss, because I'm going to win the jackpot this evening." It never occurred to him that he might be accused of fixing the game, but then there was no possibility of that, since an ordinary player like himself had no access to the machinery where the game was decided.

When he returned to his seat, he realized that he had forgotten to buy some tickets for his sister, and he was about to hand her two of those he had bought for himself. At that moment he had the feeling of a tremendous roaring in his ears, and he heard a voice saying to him, "No! Do not do this." He recognized the voice as that of his late wife. Even though the ticket line was by now several blocks long, he went back on line to get two new tickets for his sister. Then they settled down to play the game. The last game of the evening was to be the jackpot, and when the man came out to put the figures on the board, there he was, the man of his vision: brown suit and all. The actual amount of the jackpot was 347.17 pounds.

Sure enough, Mr. Hulse had the winning ticket. When he walked out into the aisle to claim his prize, the usher looked at him in complete surprise, and said, "This is the man who said he was going to win," and when he passed the girl who had sold him the tickets, she, too, recognized him and shook her head. Fate had been kind to him: now he had all the money he needed to go to America.

After Mr. Hulse had settled down in Baltimore, it happened that he had to work half a day on a warm Saturday. In the morning, his wife had gone to the beach with a sister and another friend and their children, and she had left a note informing him that they would be home by four o'clock in the afternoon. George likes punctuality, so promptly at four o'clock he telephoned his home, but received no answer. When he called back ten minutes later and again at half-past four, there still was no answer, so he became somewhat annoyed, if not worried. He slammed down the phone and became angry, and as he was sitting in his office, he had a vision of his living room as big as a picture. It seemed as if he were looking at a giant TV screen. He saw the beach and his wife sitting on it, and to her left was the friend, and the children were playing around them; but lying on the sand in front of them were two men with their chins resting on their hands, and talking to the ladies. He even observed that his wife was wearing a black bathing suit and that one of the men had on a red speckled pair of shorts.

At ten minutes to five, he telephoned his home again, and this time his wife answered. When he informed her as to what she had been doing the previous hour, she accused him of spying on her. But all the details of his vision checked out correctly. At the time, Mr. Hulse's wife found it difficult to accept the psychic explanation, and continued to suspect that her husband was spying on her.

However, she changed her mind about this some time shortly thereafter, when they were sitting in the kitchen one evening, having a cup of tea before going to bed.

Suddenly the kitchen turned into an icebox, for no apparent reason, and as they noticed the sudden chill, Hulse saw a vision appearing in the doorway, out of nowhere, and pointed it out to his wife. There, in their doorway, stood a woman, and he went on to describe her face and apparel in great detail. As he did so, his wife turned white with emotion, the apparition he had described was that of her late mother, who had passed away several years before. George had never met her.

Mr. Hulse used his psychic gift whenever it could be useful; for instance, he knew way ahead of time whether he was going to make a sale or not. In each instance, his hunches had been correct. When he found that a certain transaction was not going to jell, he didn't try to push it through, but walked away from it, letting another salesman handle it.

In July of 1971 he heard a warning voice in his ear, telling him not to let his wife use the car. He tried to confirm the inner voice by using the Ouija board, and a communicator identifying himself as Mr. Hulse's late father, confirmed the fact that the car should not be used.

So, because of Hulse's insistence, Mrs. Hulse used her sister's car that afternoon. But, they had an accident just the same. When the spirit advisor had said, don't use the car that afternoon, he meant don't go at all, but the Hulses thought it merely meant their particular car. Fortunately, no one was seriously hurt.

THE GHOSTLY USHER
OF MINNEAPOLIS

I am indebted for this account to then-very-young creative production assistant in a Minneapolis advertising agency by the name of Deborah Turner. Ms. Turner got hooked on some of my books, and started to look around in the Twin Cities for cases that might whet my appetite for ghost hunting. Being also musically inclined, with an interest in theater, it was natural that she should gravitate toward the famed Guthrie Theater, named after the famous director, which was justly known as the pride of Minneapolis. At the theater she met other young people, also in their early twenties, and shared her interest in psychic phenomena with them. Imagine her surprise when she discovered that she had stumbled upon a most interesting case.

Richard Miller was born in Manhattan, Kansas in 1951. Until age ten, he lived there with his father, a chemist in government service. Then his father was transferred to England, and Richard spent several years going to school in that country. After that, he and his family returned to the United States, and moved to Edina, Minnesota, just outside Minneapolis. This left Richard not only with a vivid recollection of England, but also somewhat of an accent, which, together with his childhood in Kansas gave him a somewhat unusual personality.

His strange accent became the subject of ridicule by other students at Edina Morningside High School, where he went to school, and it did not go down well with the shy, introspective young man. In the tenth grade at this school he made friends with another young man, Fred Koivumaki, and a good and close relationship sprang up between the two boys. It gave Fred a chance to get to know Richard better than most of the other fellows in school.

As if the strange accent were not enough to be standing out from the other boys in the area, Richard was given to sudden, jerky movements which made him a good target for sly remarks and jokes on the part of his fellow students. The Millers did not have much of a social life, since they also did not quite fit into the pattern of life in the small town of Edina.

During the years spent in an English school, Richard had known corporal punishment, since it was still part of the system in some English schools. This terrified him and perhaps contributed towards his inability to express himself fully and freely. He couldn't for the world understand why people didn't like him more, and often talked about it to his friend, Fred.

When both young men reached the age of sixteen, they went to the Guthrie Theater where they got jobs as ushers. They worked at it for two years. Richard Miller got along well with the other ushers, but developed a close friendship only with Fred Koivumaki and another fellow, Barry Peterson. It was perhaps a strange quirk of fate that both Richard Miller and Barry Peterson never reached manhood, but died violently long before their time.

However, Richard's parents decided he should go to the university, and therefore he quit his job as usher at the theater. In order to oblige his parents, Richard Miller gave up the job as usher, and moved into Territorial Hall, in his first year at the university.

However, the change did not increase his ability to express himself or to have a good social life. Also, he seemed to have felt that he was catering to his parents' wishes, and became more antagonistic toward them. Then, too, it appears that the other students also made him the butt of their jokes. Coincidentally, he developed a vision problem, with cells breaking off his retinas and floating in the inner humor of the eye, thus causing him to see spots before his eyes, a condition for which there was no cure. However, he did enjoy skiing because he knew how to do it well, and joined the university ski club.

But Richard's bad luck, somehow, was still with him. On a trip to Colorado, he ran into a tree, luckily only breaking his skis. When summer came to the area, Richard rode his bike down a large dirt hill into rough ground and tall weeds at the bottom, seriously injuring himself in the process. Fortunately, a motorcyclist came by just then and got Richard to the emergency ward of a nearby hospital. All this may have contributed towards an ultimate breakdown, or, as the students would call it, Richard just "flipped out."

He was hospitalized at the university hospital and allowed home only on weekends. During that time he was on strong medication, but when the medication did not improve his condition, the doctor took him off it and sent him home.

On February 4, 1964 he decided to try skiing again and asked his father to take him out to Buck Hill, one of the skiing areas not far from town. But to his dismay Richard discovered that he couldn't ski anymore, and this really depressed him. When he got home, there was a form letter waiting for him from the university advising him that because he had skipped all the final exams, due to having had his emotional problems at the time, he had received F's in all his classes and was on probation.

All this seemed to be too much for him. He asked his mother for forty dollars, ostensibly to buy himself new ski boots. Then he drove down to Sears on Lake Street, where he bought a high-powered pistol and shells. That was Saturday, and he killed himself in his car. He wasn't found until Monday morning when the lot cleaning crew found him with most of his head shot off.

Richard Miller was given a quiet burial in Fort Snelling National Cemetery. His parents, Dr. and Mrs. Byron S. Miller, requested that memorials to the Minnesota Association for Mental Health be sent instead of flowers. Richard's mother had always felt that her son's best years had been spent as an usher at the Guthrie Theater; consequently he was cremated wearing his Guthrie Theater blazer. The date was February 7, 1967, and soon enough the shock of the young man's untimely death wore off, and only his immediate family and the few friends he had made remembered Richard Miller beyond that.

A few weeks after the death of the young usher, a woman seated in the theater in an aisle seat came up to the usher in charge of this aisle and asked him to stop the other usher from walking up and down during the play. The usher in charge was shocked, since he had been at the top of the aisle and had seen no one walk up and down. All the other ushers were busy in their respective aisles. However, the lady insisted that she had seen this young man walk up and down the aisle during the play. The usher in charge asked her to describe what she had seen. She described Richard Miller, even to the mole on his cheek. The incident is on record with the Guthrie Theater. Minneapolis Tribune columnist Robert T. Smith interviewed Craig Scherfenberg, director of audience development at the theater, concerning it. "There was no one in our employ at the time who fit the description," the director said, "but it fit the dead young man perfectly."

In the summer of 1971, two ushers were asked to spend the night in the theater to make sure some troublesome air conditioning equipment was fully repaired. The Guthrie

Theater had a thrust stage with openings onto the stage on all three sides; these openings lead to an actors' waiting area, which, in turn, had a door opening onto an area used as a lounge during intermissions.

The two young men were sitting in this waiting area, with both doors open, and they were the only people in the building. At one o'clock in the morning, they suddenly heard the piano onstage beginning to play. Stunned by this, they watched in silence when they saw a cloud-like form floating through the lounge door and hovering in the center of the room. One of the ushers thought the form was staring at him. As quickly as they could gather their wits, they left the room.

One of Deborah Turner's friends had worked late one evening, shortly after this incident, repairing costumes needed for the next day's performance. She and a friend were relaxing in the stage area, while waiting for a ride home. As she glanced into the house, she noticed that the lights on the aisle which had been the dead usher's were going on and off, as if someone were walking slowly up and down. She went to the Ladies' Room a little later, and suddenly she heard pounding on one wall, eventually circling the room and causing her great anxiety, since she knew that the two of them were the only people in the house.

When the Guthrie Theater put on a performance of *Julius Caesar*, one of the extras was an older woman by the name of Mary Parez. She freely admitted that she was psychic and had been able to communicate with her dead sister, and she told her fellow actors that she could sense Richard Miller's presence in the auditorium. Somehow she thought that the ghost would make himself known during Mark Antony's famous speech to the Romans after Caesar's death.

The scene was lit primarily by torches, as the body of Julius Caesar was brought upon the stage. Jason Harlen, a young usher, and one of his colleagues, were watching the performance from different vantage points in the theater. One was in one of the tunnels leading to the stage, the other in the audience. Both had been told of Mary Parez's prediction, but were disappointed when nothing happened at that time. In boredom, they began to look around the theater. Independently of each other, they saw smoke rising to the ceiling and shape itself into human form. Both young men said that the form had human eyes.

The aisle which the late Richard Miller worked was number eighteen. Two actresses in the company during the performance of Julius Caesar, first-named Terry and Gigi, complained that they had much trouble with the door at the top of aisle eighteen, for no apparent reason. Bruce Benson, who then worked aisle eighteen, told of people complaining of an usher walking up and down the aisle during performances. Bruce Margolis, whose duty was the stage door, and who leaves the building after everyone else had left, was there one night all alone, when the elevator began running on its own.

All this talk about a ghost induced some of the young ushers to try and make contact with him via the Ouija board. Dan Burg, head usher, took a board with him to the stage, and, along with colleagues Bruce Benson and Scott Hurner, tried to communicate with the ghost. For awhile, nothing happened. Then, all of a sudden, the board spelled, "Tiptoe to the tech room." When they asked why, the board spelled the word ghost. They wanted to know which tech room the ghost was referring to, downstairs? No, the communicator informed them, upstairs. Then the board signed off with the initials MIL. At that, one of the men tipped over the board and wanted nothing further to do with it.

In November, 1972, an usher working at the theater told columnist Robert Smith, "It was after a night performance. Everyone had left the theater but me. I had forgotten my gloves and had returned to retrieve them. I glanced into the theater and saw an usher standing in one of the aisles. It was him. He saw me and left. I went around to that aisle and couldn't find anything."

There was also an opera company connected with the Guthrie Theater. One night years ago, one of the ladies working for the opera company was driving home from the Guthrie Theater. Suddenly she felt a presence beside her in the car. Terrified, she looked around and became aware of a young man with dark, curly hair, glasses, and a mole on his face. He wore a blue coat with something red on the pocket—the Guthrie Theater blazer. With a sinking feeling she realized she was looking at the ghost of Richard Miller.

The years have passed, however, and no new reports have come in concerning the unfortunate young man. Could it be that he had finally realized that there await him greater opportunities in the next dimension, and that though his life on earth was not very successful, his passing into the spiritual life might give him most of the opportunities life on earth had denied him? At any rate, things have quieted down then in aisle eighteen at the Guthrie Theater, Minneapolis, Minnesota.

THE GHOSTLY
ADVENTURES OF A
NORTH CAROLINA FAMILY

*T*oni S. was a young woman of good educational background, a psychologist by profession, working for a large business concern, and not given to daydreaming or fantasizing. She was the daughter of Mrs. Elizabeth K., or rather the daughter of Mrs. K.'s second marriage. The thrice-married Mrs. K. was a North Carolina lady, a socially prominent woman who had traveled extensively. Both ladies were taken aback by what transpired. Neither was the kind of person who pulls out a Ouija board to while away the time, or to imagine that every shadow cast upon the wall was necessarily a ghost. Far from it; but both ladies were taken aback by what transpired in their old house at the town of East La Porte, built on very old ground.

Originally built about one hundred years ago, it was to be a home for Mrs. K.'s father who then owned a large lumber company, and the tract of timber surrounding the house extended all the way across the Blue Ridge Parkway. Undoubtedly, an older dwelling stood on the same spot, for Mrs. K. had unearthed what appears to be the remains of a much older structure. The house was renovated and a second story built on, about sixty years ago. At that time her father had lost one leg as the result of an automobile accident, and retired from his lumber mill activities to East La Porte, where he intended to spend his remaining years in peace and quiet. He had liked the climate to begin with, and then there was a sawmill nearby, which he could oversee at the same time. The house was a double-boxed frame house, perhaps fifty-by-fifty square, containing around fifteen rooms.

Mrs. K.'s family refered to it as the summer cottage, even though it was a full-sized house; but they had other houses that they visited from time to time, and the house in East La Porte was merely one of their lesser properties. Downstairs there was a thirty-by-fifteen foot reception room, richly carpeted with chestnut from Furnace Creek, one of the sawmills owned by the family. It was in this room that Mrs. K.'s father eventually passed on.

The house itself was built entirely from lumber originating in one of the family's sawmills. There was a center hall downstairs and two thirty-foot rooms, then three smaller rooms, a bath, a card room and what the family referred to as a sleeping porch. On the other side of the center hall was a lounge, a kitchen and a laundry porch. Running alongside the south and east walls of the house was a veranda. Upstairs was reached by a very gentle climb, with the stairs in the middle, and as one climbs the steps there was a bedroom at the head of the stairs, and in back of the stairs two more bedrooms, then a bathroom, and finally a storage room; to the left of the stairs were three bedrooms.

The attic was merely a structure to hold up the roof, but did not contain any rooms. There was a cellar, but it contained only a furnace. Although the acreage surrounding the house ran to about sixty acres, only three acres belong to the house proper. All around the house, there was nothing but wilderness and to get to the nearest town, East La Porte, one needs a car.

Mrs. K. enjoyed traveling, and didn't mind living in so many residences; in fact, she considered the house at East La Porte merely a way station in her life. In fact, she was born in Alaska, where the family also had a sawmill. Her early years were spent traveling from one sawmill to another, accompanying her parents on business trips.

Under the circumstances, they were never very long in residence at the house in East La Porte. Any attempt to find out about the background of the land on which the house stood proved fruitless. This was Cherokee territory, but there was little written history concerning the time before the Cherokees. Anything remotely connected with psychic phenomena was simply not discussed in the circles in which Mr. K. grew up.

The first time Mrs. K. noticed anything peculiar about the house was after her father had passed away. She and her father had been particularly close, since her mother had died when she was still a small child. That particular day she was sitting at her late father's desk in the part of the house where her father had died. The furniture had been rearranged in the room, and the desk stood where her father's bed had previously stood. Her father was on her mind, and so she thought it was all her imagination when she became aware of a distinctive sound as if someone were walking on crutches, coming down the hall.

Since Mrs. K. knew for a fact that she was the only person in the house at the time, she realized that something out of the ordinary was happening. As the footsteps came closer she recognized her father's tread. And then she heard her father's familiar voice say, "Baby" coming from the direction of the door. It gave her a feeling of great peace, for she had been troubled by emotional turmoil in her life. She felt that her late father was trying to console her, and give her spiritual strength.

Nothing else happened until about a year later. It was August, and she had been in New York for awhile. As she was coming down the stairs of the house, she found herself completely enveloped with the fragrance of lilacs. She had not put any perfume on, and there were no lilacs blooming in August. No one was seen, and yet Mrs. K. felt a presence, although she was sure it was benign, and loving.

A short time later she was sitting at a desk in what used to be her father's study upstairs, thinking about nothing in particular. Again she was startled by the sound of footsteps, but this time they were light steps, certainly not her father's. Without thinking, she called out to her daughter, "Oh, Toni, is that you?" telling her daughter that she was upstairs.

But then the steps stopped, and no one came. Puzzled, Mrs. K. went to the head of the stairs, called out again, but when she saw no one she realized that it was not a person of flesh and blood that had walked upon the stairs.

During the same month, Mrs. K.'s daughter Toni was at the house also. Her first experience with the unseen happened that month, in an upstairs bedroom.

She was asleep one night when someone shook her hard and said, "Hey, you!" Frightened, she did not open her eyes, yet with her inner eyes, she "saw" a man of about fifty years of age, but she was much too frightened to actually look. Instead she dived underneath the covers and lay there with her eyes shut. There was nothing further that night.

In the fall of the same year, 1962, Toni decided to have a pajama party and spent the night with a group of friends. Her mother had gone to bed because of a cold. Toni and her friends returned to the house from bowling around eleven-thirty. They were downstairs, talking about various things, when all of a sudden one of Toni's girl friends said,

"Your mother is calling you."

Toni went out into the hallway, turning on the lights as she approached the stairs. Footsteps were coming down the stairs, audible not only to her but also to her two girl friends, who had followed her into the house. And then they heard a voice out of the clear blue sky, calling out, "Toni, it is time to go to bed." It was a voice Toni had never heard before. She went up the stairs and into her mother's room. But her mother was fast asleep, and had not been out of bed. The voice had been a woman's voice, but it had sounded strangely empty, as if someone were speaking to her from far away.

The following year, Toni was married and left the house. Under the circumstances, Mrs. K. decided to sublease part of the house to tenants. This turned out to be a pleasant woman by the name of Alice H. and her husband The lady had been injured and was unable to go far up the mountain where she and her husband were building a summer home at the time. Although Mrs. K. and her new tenants were not associated in any way except that they were sharing the same house, she and Alice H. became friendly after a while. One afternoon Alice H. came to Mrs. K.'s apartment in order to invite her to have supper with her and her husband that night. She knew that Mrs. K. was in her apartment at the time because she heard her light footsteps inside the apartment. When there was no reply from inside the apartment, Alice was puzzled so she descended to the ground floor, thinking that perhaps Mrs. K. was downstairs.

Sure enough, as she arrived downstairs, she saw a shadow of what she assumed to be Mrs. K.'s figure walking along the hallway. She followed this shadowy woman all the way from the ground floor guest room through the bath into Mrs. K.'s bedroom and then through another hallway and back to the bedroom. All the time she saw the shadowy figure, she also heard light footsteps. But when she came to the bedroom again, it suddenly got very cold and she felt all the blood rush to her head. She ran back to her husband in their own apartment and informed him that there was a stranger in Mrs. K.'s rooms.

But there was no one in the house at the time, except themselves, for Mrs. K. had gone off to Asheville for the day. The experience shook Alice H. to the point where she could no longer stand the house, and shortly afterward she and her husband left for another cottage.

In August of the same year, Toni S. returned to her mother's house. By then she was a married lady, and she was coming for a visit only. Her husband was a car dealer, in business with his father. At the time of the incident he was not in the house. It was raining outside, and Toni was cleaning the woodwork in the house.

Then, suddenly her Pekinese dog came running down the stairs, nearly out of her mind with terror, barking at the top of her lungs. Toni thought a mouse had frightened the dog, so she picked her up and proceeded up the stairs. But the dog broke away from her and ran behind the door. All of a sudden, Toni felt very cold. She kept walking down the hall and into the room where there was a desk standing near the window. Someone was going through papers on her desk, as if looking for a certain piece of paper, putting papers aside and continuing to move them! But there was no one there. No one, that is, to be seen. Yet the papers were moving as if someone were actually shuffling them. It was two o'clock in the afternoon; the light was fairly good.

Suddenly, one letter was pulled out of the piles of papers on the desk, as if to catch her attention. Toni picked it up and read it. It was a letter her father had sent her in February, at the time she got married, warning her that the marriage would not work out, after all, and to make sure and call him if anything went wrong. Things *had* gone wrong since, and Toni understood the significance of what she had just witnessed. At that very moment, the room got warm again, and everything returned to normal. But who was it standing at her desk, pulling out her father's letter for her? The one person who had been close to her while he was in the flesh, was her grandfather.

During Toni's visit at the house, her husband, later her ex-husband, also had some uncanny experiences. Somebody would wake him in the middle of the night by calling out, "Wake up!" or

"Hey you!" This went on night after night until both Toni and her husband awoke around two in the morning because of the sound of loud laughing, as if a big party were going on downstairs.

Toni thought that the neighbors were having a party, and decided to go down and tell them to shut up. She looked out the window, and realized that the neighbors were also fast asleep. So she picked up her dog and went downstairs, and as she arrived at the bottom of the stairs she saw a strange light, while the laughing kept going on and on. There were voices, as if many people were talking all at once, having a social. In anger, Toni called out to them to shut up, she wanted to sleep, and all of a sudden the house was quiet, quiet as the grave. Evidently, Southern ghosts have good manners!

After her daughter left, Mrs. K. decided to sublease part of the house to a group of young men from a national fraternity, students at a nearby university. On one occasion, Mitchell, one of the students, was sleeping in a double bed, and he was all alone in the house. Because the heat wasn't turned up, it being rather costly, he decided to sleep in a sleeping bag, keeping warm in this manner. He went to sleep with his head at the head of the bed, which meant due east, and his feet going due west. When he awoke, he found himself facing in the opposite direction, with his head where his feet should have been, and vice versa. It didn't surprise the young man, though, because from the very first his fraternity brothers had moved into the house, they had heard the sounds of an unseen person walking up and down the stairs.

One of their teachers, a pilot who had been a colonel in the Korean War, also had an experience at the house. One day while he was staying there, he was walking up the stairs and when he reached about the halfway mark, someone picked him up by the scruff of his neck and pushed him up the rest of the way to the landing.

But the night to remember was Halloween Eve, 1963. Mrs.

K. was in the house, and the night was living up to its reputation: it sounded as if someone with manacles on were moving about. Mrs. K. was downstairs, sleeping in one of the bunk beds, and a noise came from an upstairs hall. This went on for about two hours straight. It sounded as if someone with a limp were pulling himself along, dragging a heavy chain. Mrs. K. was puzzled about this, since the noise did not sound anything like her father. She looked into the background of the area and discovered that in the pre-colonial period there had been some Spanish settlers in the area, most of whom kept slaves.

Toni S. took her involvement with hauntings in stride. She had had psychic experiences ever since she could remember; nothing frightening, you understand, only such things as events before they actually happen—if someone was going to be sick in the family, for instance, or who might be calling. Entering old houses was always a risky business for her: She picks up vibrations from the past and sometimes she simply can't stand what she feels and must leave at once.

But she thought she had left the more uncanny aspects of the hauntings behind when she came to New York to work. Somehow she wound up residing in a house which was 110 years old. After a while, she became aware of an old man who liked sitting down on her bed. She couldn't actually see him, and he appeared to her more like a shadow. So she asked some questions, but nobody ever died in the apartment, but it was difficult for Toni to accept the reality of the phenomena under the circumstances. As a trained psychologist, she had to approach all this on a skeptical level and yet there did not seem to be any logical answers.

Soon afterward she became aware of footsteps where no one was walking, and of doors closing by themselves, which were accompanied by the definite feeling of another personality present in the rooms. On checking with former upstairs neighbors who had lived in the house for seventeen years, Toni discovered that they, too had heard the steps and doors closing by themselves but had put no faith in ghosts and dismissed the matter as simply an old structure settling. Toni tried her innate psychic powers and hoped that the resident ghost would communicate with her. She began to sense that it was a woman with a very strong personality. By a process of elimination Toni came to the conclusion that the last of the original owners of the house, a Mrs. A., who had been a student of the occult, was the only person who could be the presence she was feeling in the rooms.

Toni didn't mind sharing her rooms with a ghost, except for the fact that appliances in the house had a way of breaking down without reason. Then, too, she had a problem with some of her visiting friends; they complained of feeling extremely uncomfortable and cold, and of being watched by someone they cannot see. What was she to do? But then Toni recalled how she had lived through the frightening experiences at East La Porte, North Carolina, and had somehow come to terms with the haunts there. No ordinary ghost was going to dispossess her! With that resolve, Toni decided to ignore the presence as much as she could and go about her business—the business of the living. And, her life went on.

REBA'S GHOSTS

*R*eba B. was a sensitive, fragile-looking lady with two grown children, born in Kentucky, and from an old family in which the name Reba had occurred several times before. She worked as a medical secretary and doctor's assistant, and shared her home with three cats, her children having moved away. Reba. B., who was divorced, wondered whether perhaps she had a particular affinity for ghosts, seeing that she had encountered denizens of the Other World so many times in so many houses. It wasn't that it bothered her to any extent but she had gotten use to living by herself except for her cats, and the idea of having to share her home with individuals who could pop in and out at will, and who might hang around her at times when she could not see them, did not contribute to her comfort.

Her psychic ability went back to age three, when she was living with her grandparents in Kentucky. Even then she had a vivid feeling of presences all around her, not that she actually saw them with her physical eyes. It was more a sensitivity to unseen forces surrounding her—an awareness that she was never quite alone. As soon as she would go to bed, as a child, she would see the figure of a man bending over her, a man she did not know. After a long period of this she wondered whether she was dreaming but in her heart she knew she was

137

not. However, she was much too young to worry about such things and as she grew up, her ability became part of her character, and she began to accept it as "normal."

In 1961 she was living in Cincinnati, already divorced. Her mother shared an old house with her, a house that was built around 1900; it had all the earmarks of the post-Victorian era: brass door knobs, little door bells which were to be turned by hand, and the various trimmings of that age. The house consisted of three floors; the ground floor contained an apartment, and the two ladies took the second and third floors of the house. Reba had her bedroom on the third floor; it was the only bedroom up there and was situated in the middle of the floor.

One day she was coming up those stairs and was approaching the window, when she saw a man standing by the window. He vanished as she came closer. She gave this no more thought until a few days later. At that time she happened to be lying in bed, propped up and reading a book.

She happened to look up and saw a man who had apparently come up the stairs. She noticed his features fully, his eyes were brown, and he also had brown hair. Immediately she could sense that he was very unhappy, even angry. It wasn't that she heard his voice but somehow his thoughts communicated themselves to her, mind to mind. From her bed she could see him approach, walking out onto a small landing and standing in front of her door. Next to her room was a storage room. He looked straight at Reba and at that moment she received the impression that he was very angry because she and her mother were in the house—that they had moved into *his* house.

Although Reba B. was fully conscious and aware of what was going on, she rejected the notion that she was hearing the thoughts of a ghost. But it did her no good; over and over she heard him say, or think, "Out, out. I want you out, I don't want you here." At that moment, he raised his arm and pointed outward, as if to emphasize his point. The next moment he was gone. Reba thought about it for a moment, whether she should tell her mother whose bedroom was downstairs. She decided against it, since her mother had a heart condition and because she herself wasn't too sure the incident had been quite real. Also, she was a little frightened and did not want to recall the incident any more than she had to. After a while, she went off to sleep.

Not too long after that her daughter, who was then fourteen, and her eleven-year-old son were home with her from school. It was a weekend, and she wanted the children to enjoy it. Consequently she did not tell them anything about her ghostly experience. She had gone into the front storage room when she thought she saw someone sitting on the boxes stacked in the storage area.

At first, she refused to acknowledge it, and tried to look away, but when her gaze returned to the area, the man was still sitting there, quietly staring at her. Again she turned her head, and when she looked back, he was gone. The following weekend her children were with her again. They had hardly arrived when her daughter returned from the same storage room and asked her, "Mother, is there someone sitting in there?" and all Reba could do was nod, and acknowledge that there was. Her daughter then described the stranger and the description matched what her mother had seen. Under the circumstances, Reba B. freely discussed the matter with her children. But nothing further was done concerning the matter, no inquiries made as to the background of the house.

Summer came, and another spring and another summer and they got into the habit of using the entrance at the side of the house. There were some shrubs in that area, and in order to enter the apartment in which they lived, they had to come up the stairs where they would have a choice of either walking into the living room on the second floor or continuing on to the third floor where Reba's bedroom was. The tenant who had the ground floor apartment also had his own entrance to it.

One warm summer evening she suddenly felt the stranger come into the downstairs door and walk up the stairs. When she went to check, she saw nothing. Still, she *knew* he was in the house. A few days passed, and again she sensed the ghost nearby. She looked, and as her eyes peered down into the hall, she saw him walking down the hall towards her. While she was thinking, "I am imagining this, there is no such thing as a ghost," she slowly walked toward him. As he kept approaching her, she walked right through him! It was an eerie sensation: for a moment she could not see, and then he was gone. The encounter did not help Reba to regain her composure, but there was little she could do about it.

Many times she sensed his presence in the house without seeing the man, but early one evening, it was a Sunday, just as it got dark, she found herself in the living room on the second floor of the house. She had turned on the television set which was facing her, and she kept the volume down so as not to disturb her mother whose room was on the same floor. She had altered the furniture in the room somewhat, in order to be closer to the television set, and there were two lounge chairs, one of which she used, the other one close by, near the television set, so that another person could sit in it and also view the screen. She was just watching television, when she sensed the stranger come up the stairs again and walk into the living room. Next he sat down in the empty chair close to Reba, but this time the atmosphere was different from that first encounter at the door of her room. He seemed more relaxed and comfortable and Reba was almost glad that he was there, keeping her company. Somehow she felt that he was glad to be in the room with her, and to be less lonely because of her. He was no longer angry, he just wanted to visit.

Reba looked at the stranger's face and noticed his rather high-bridge nose and she had a chance to study his clothes. He was wearing a brown suit, rather modern in style. Even though the house was quite old, this man was not from the early years, but his clothes seemed to indicate a comparatively recent period. As she sat there, quietly studying the ghost, she got the feeling that he had owned the house at one time and that their living room had been the sitting room where the ghost and his wife had received people. And Reba somehow knew that his wife had been very pretty—a fair-complexioned blonde, and she was shown a fireplace in the living room with a small love seat of the French Provincial type next to it, drawn up quite close to the fireplace. She saw this in her mind's eye as if the man were showing her something from his past. At the same time, Reba knew that some tragedy had occurred between the ghost and his wife.

Suddenly, panic rose in Reba, as she realized she was sharing the evening with a ghost. Somehow her fears communicated themselves to her phantom visitor, for as she looked close, he had vanished.

As much as she had tried to keep these things from her mother, she could not. Her mother owned an antique covered casserole, made of silver, which she kept at the head of her bed. The bed was a bookcase bed and she used to lift the cover and put in receipts and tickets and papers whenever she wanted to.

One day Reba and her mother found themselves at the far end of her bedroom on the second floor. Her bed was up against the wall without any space between it and the wall. As the two ladies were looking in the direction of the bed, they suddenly saw the silver casserole being picked up, put down on the bed, turned upside down and everything spilling out of it. It didn't fly through the air, but moved rather slowly, as if some unseen force were holding it. Although her mother had seen it, she did not say anything, because she felt it would be unwise to alarm her daughter; but later on she admitted having seen the whole thing. It was ironical how the two women were trying to spare each other's feelings—yet both knew that what they had witnessed was real.

The ghost did not put in any further appearances after the dramatic encounter in the living room. About a year later, the two ladies moved away to another old house far from this one. But shortly before they did, Reba's mother was accosted on the street by a strange, middle-aged lady who asked her whether she was living in the house just up the street. When Reba's mother acknowledged it, the lady informed her the house had once belonged to her parents. Were they happy in it? Reba's mother wanted to know. "Very happy," the stranger assured her, "Especially my father." It occurred to Reba that it might have been him who she had encountered in the house; someone so attached to his home that he did not want to share it with anyone else, especially flesh and blood people like her mother and herself.

The new home the ladies moved into proved "alive" with unseen vibrations also, but by then they didn't care. Reba realized that she had a special gift. If ghosts wanted her company there was little she could do about it. Years before, she had had a friend who worked as a motorcycle patrolman, by the name of John H. He was a young man and well liked on the force. One day he chased a speeder—and was killed in the process. They were friends, although not really close ones, and she had been out of touch with him for some time prior. One morning she suddenly sensed his presence in the room with her; it made no sense, yet she was positive it was John H. After a while, the presence left her. She remarked on this to her mother and got a blank stare in return. The young man had been killed on the previous night, but Reba could not have known this. The news had come on the radio just that morning, but apparently Reba had had advance news of a more direct kind.

Reba B. shared her interest in the occult with an acquaintance, newscaster Bill G. In his position as a journalist he had to be particularly careful in expressing an opinion on so touchy a subject as extra-sensory perception. They had met at a local restaurant one evening and somehow the conversation had gotten around to ghosts.

When Mr. G. noticed her apprehension at being one of the

"selected" ones who could see ghosts, he told her about another friend, a young medium who had an apartment not far away. One evening she walked out onto her patio, and saw a man in old-fashioned clothes approach her. The man tried to talk to her, but she could not hear anything. Suddenly, he disappeared before her eyes. The young lady thought she was having a nervous breakdown and consulted a psychiatrist; she even went into a hospital to have herself examined, but they found nothing wrong with her. When she returned to her home, and went out onto the patio again, she saw the same ghostly apparition once more. This time she did not panic but studied him closely. When he disappeared, she went back into her apartment, and decided to make some inquiries about the place. It was then that she discovered that a long time ago a man of that description had been hanged from that very tree in her garden.

"These things *do* happen," Bill G. assured Reba, and asked her not to be ashamed or afraid of them. After all, ghosts are people too. After that, Reba came to terms with her ghostly encounters. She even had an experience with a ghost cat—but that is another story for another time.

HENNY FROM BROOKLYN

Clinton Street, Brooklyn is one of the oldest sections of that New York City borough, pleasantly middle-class, and still amongst Brooklyn's best neighborhoods, as neighborhoods go. The house in question was in the 300 block, and consists of four stories. There was a basement floor, then a parlor floor, a few steps up as was the usual custom with brownstone houses, and a third and fourth floor above it. If one preferred, one could call the third floor the fourth floor, in which case the basement becomes the first floor; but no matter how one called it, there were four levels in this brownstone, all of them capable of serving as apartments to those who wished to live there. The house was more than one hundred years old at the time the events herein described happened, and the records were somewhat dim beyond a certain point.

In the 1960's, the house was owned by some offbeat people, about whom little was known. Even the Hall of Records isn't of much help, as the owners didn't always live in the house, and the people who lived in it were not necessarily the owners, not to mention tenants sharing a part of the house with people legitimately entitled to live there. However, for the purpose of my story we need only concern ourselves with the two top floors; the third floor contained two bedrooms and a bath, while the fourth or top floor consisted of a living room, dining room, kitchen and a second bath.

At the time when my account begins, the first two floors were rented to an architect and his wife, and only the two top floors were available for new tenants. It was in the summer of 1970 when two young ladies in their early 20's, who had been living at the Brooklyn YWCA decided to find a place of their own. Somehow they heard of the two vacant floors in the house on Clinton Street and immediately fell in love with it, renting the two top floors without much hesitation. Both Barbara and Sharon were 23 years old at the time, still going to college, and trying to make ends meet on what money they could manage between themselves. Two years later, Barbara was living in San Francisco with a business of her own in independent merchandising of clothing, and Brooklyn was only a hazy memory. But on August 1, 1970 it was very much her world.

Immediately after moving in, they decided to clean up the house, which needed a good deal of cleaning up indeed. The stairway to the top floor was carpeted all the way up, and it was quite a job to vacuum clean it because there were a lot of outlets along the way and one had to look out for extension cords in order to clean it. Sharon got to the top floor and was cleaning it and removed the extension cord to plug it in further up. Instead she just used the regular cord of the vacuum cleaner, about 12 feet long, using perhaps 3 feet of it which left 9 feet of cord lying on the floor.

All of a sudden the plug was just pulled out of the wall. Sharon couldn't believe her eyes; the plug actually pulled itself out of the socket, and flew out onto the floor. She shook her head and put it back in, and turned the vacuum cleaner on again. Only then did she realize that she had turned the switch on the cleaner back on, when she had actually never turned it off in the first place. She couldn't figure out how that was possible, how was it turned off. But she had a lot more work to do, so she continued with it. Later she came downstairs and told her roommate who thought she was out of her mind. "Wait till something happens to you," Sharon said, "there is something strange about this house."

During the next five months the young women heard strange noises all over the house, but they attributed it to an old house settling, or to the people living downstairs in the building. Five months of "peace" were rudely shattered when Sharon's younger brother came to visit from New Jersey. He was still in high school and liked to listen to rock music at night, especially when it was played as loud as possible. The young people were sitting in the living room, listening to music and talking. It was a nice, relaxed evening. All of a sudden the stereo went off. The music had been rather loud rock and roll, and at first they thought the volume had perhaps damaged the set. Then the hallway light went out, followed by the kitchen light. So they thought a fuse had blown. Barbara ran down four flights of stairs, into the basement to check. No fuse had blown. To be on the safe side, she checked them anyway, and switched them around to make sure everything was fine. Then she went back upstairs and asked the others how the electricity was behaving.

But everything was still off. At this point Sharon's brother decided to go into the kitchen and try the lights there. Possibly there was something wrong with the switches. He went into the hallway where there was an old Tiffany type lamp hanging at the top of the stairway. It had gone off, too, and he tried to turn it on and nothing happened. He pulled again, and suddenly it went on. In other words, he turned it off first, then turned it on, as it had been on in the first place.

This rather bothered the young man, and he announced he was going into the kitchen to get something to eat. He proceeded into the kitchen and when he came back to join the others he was as white as the wall. He reported the kitchen was as cold as an icebox, but as soon as one left the kitchen the temperature was normal in the rest of the house. The others then got up to see for themselves and, sure enough, it was icy cold in the kitchen. This, despite the fact that there were four or five radiators going and all the windows were closed.

That night they realized that they had a ghost, and for want of a better name they called her Hendrix—it happened to have been the anniversary of Jimi Hendrix's death, and they had been playing some of his records.

Shortly afterward, another young woman named Toby joined the other two roommates in the house. Toby moved in on April 1, 1971. It had been relatively quiet between the incident in the kitchen and that day. But somehow Toby's arrival was also the beginning of a new aspect of the haunting.

About a week after Toby moved in, the women were in the living room, with friends, talking. It was about 11:00 o'clock at night and they had dimmers on in the living room. Toby was sitting on the couch, with Barbara and some friends sitting on the other side of the room, when all of a sudden she felt a chilly breeze pass by her. It didn't touch her, but she felt it nonetheless, and just then the lights started to dim, back and forth, back and forth, and when she looked up, she actually saw the dial on the dimmer moving by itself. As yet, Toby knew nothing about the haunting, so she decided to say nothing to the others, having just moved in, and not wishing to have her new roommates think her weird.

But things kept happening night after night, usually after 11:00 o'clock, when the two women and their friends sat around talking. After a couple of weeks, she could not stand it any longer and finally asked the others whether they could feel anything strange in the room. Barbara looked at Sharon and a strange look passed between them; finally they decided to tell Toby about the haunting, and brought her up to date from the beginning of their tenancy in the house.

Almost every day there was something new to report: cooking equipment would be missing, clothing would disappear, windows were opened by themselves, garbage cans would be turned over by unseen hands. Throughout that period, there was continued walking of an unseen person in the living room located directly over the third floor bedroom. And they heard it at any hour of the night and once in a while even during the day. Someone was walking back and forth, back and forth. They were loud, stomping footsteps, more like a woman's than a man's, but the steps sounded as if someone were very angry. Each time one of them went upstairs to check if anyone was there, they found absolutely nothing.

The three women held a conference and decided that they had a ghost, make no mistake about it. Toby offered to look into the matter and perhaps find out what might have occurred at the house at an earlier age. Barbara kept hearing an obscure whistling, not a real tune or song that could be recognized, but a human whistling nevertheless. Meanwhile, Toby heard of a course on witchcraft and the occult being given at New York University, and started taking an interest in books on the subject. But whenever there were people over to visit them and staying in the living room upstairs past eleven o'clock at night, the ghost would simply run them out of the room with all the tricks in her ghostly trade.

"She" would turn the stereo on and off, or make the lights go on and off. By then, they were convinced it was a woman. There were heavy shutters from the floor to the ceiling, and frequently it appeared as if a wind were coming through them and they would clap together, as if the breeze were agitating them. Immediately after that they heard footsteps walking away from them, and there was an uncomfortable feeling in the room, making it imperative to leave and go somewhere else, usually downstairs into one of the bedrooms.

As yet, no one had actually seen her. In June 1971, Bruce, Toby's boyfriend, was staying in the house with her. They had the master bedroom, and off the bedroom was a bathroom.

Since Barbara would frequently walk through in the middle of the night, they left the light in the bathroom on all night so that she would not trip over anything. That particular night in June, Toby and her boy friend had just made love and she was looking up, not at the ceiling, but at the wall, when suddenly she saw a girl looking at her.

It was just like an outline, like a shadow on the wall, but Toby could tell that she had long hair arranged in braids. Somehow she had the impression that she was a Native American, perhaps because of the braids. Toby looked up at her and called the apparition to her boyfriend's attention, but by the time he had focused on it, she had disappeared.

He simply did not believe her. Instead, he asked Toby to go upstairs to the kitchen and make him a sandwich. She wasn't up there for more than five or ten minutes, when she returned to the bedroom and found her boy friend hiding under the covers of the bed. When she asked him what was wrong, he would shake his head, and so she looked around the room, but could find nothing unusual. The only thing she noticed was that the bathroom door was then wide open. She assumed that her boy friend had used the bathroom, but he shook his head and told her that he had not.

He had just been lying there smoking a cigarette, when all of a sudden he saw the handle on the door turn by itself, and the door open. When he saw that, he simply dived under the covers until Toby returned. From that moment on he no longer laughed at her stories about a house ghost. The following night, her boyfriend was asleep when Toby woke up at two o'clock in the morning. The television set had been left on and she went to shut it off, and when she got back into bed she happened to glance up at the same place on the wall where she had seen the apparition the night before. For a moment or two she saw the same outline of a girl, only this time she had the impression that the girl was smiling at her.

Two weeks after that, Toby and her boy friend broke up, and this rather shook her. She had come back home one day and didn't know that he had left, but, then she found a note in which he explained his reasons for leaving, and that he would get in touch with her later. This, of course, very much upset her, so much so that her two roommates had to calm her down. Finally, the two other women went upstairs; Toby was lying on her bed trying to compose herself.

In the quiet of the room, she suddenly heard someone sob a little and then a voice said, "Toby." Toby got up from bed and went to the bottom of the stairs and called up, demanding to know what Barbara wanted. But Barbara hadn't called her. She went back to the room and lay down on the bed again. Just then she heard a voice saying "Toby" again and again. On checking, she found that no one had called out to her—no one of flesh and blood, that is.

Toby then realized who had been calling her, and she decided to talk to "Henny," her nickname for Hendrix, which was the name given by the others to the ghost since that night when they were playing Jimi Hendrix records. In a quiet voice, Toby said, "Henny, did you call me?" and then she heard the voice answer, "Calm down, don't take it so hard, it will be all right." It was a girl's voice, and yet there was no one to be seen. The time was about five o'clock in the afternoon, and since it was in June, the room was still fairly light.

Toby had hardly recovered from this experience, when still another event took place. Sharon had moved out and another young woman by the name of Madeline had moved in. One day her brother came to visit them from Chicago, and he brought a friend along who had had some experience of a spiritual nature. His name was Joey, and both young men were about 20 years old.

Madeline and her brother were much interested in the occult, and they brought a Ouija board to the house. On

Saturday, December 19, 1971, while it was snowing outside and the atmosphere was just right for a seance, they decided to make contact with the unhappy ghost in the house. They went upstairs into the living room and sat down with the board. At first, it was going to be a game, and they were asking silly questions of it, such as who was going to marry who, and other romantic fluff. But halfway through the session, they decided to try to contact the ghost in earnest. The three women and Madeline's brother sat down on the floor with their knees touching and put the board on them. Then they invited Henny to appear and talk to them, if she was so inclined. They were prepared to pick up the indicator and place their hands on it, so it could move to various letters on the board.

But before their hands ever touched it, the indicator took off by itself! It shot over to the word yes on the board, as if to reassure them that communication was indeed desired. The four of them looked at each other, dumbfounded, for they had seen only too clearly what had just transpired. By now they were all somewhat scared. However, Toby decided, since she was interested in psychic research, she might as well ask the questions. She began asking why the ghostly girl was still attached to the house. Haltingly, word for word, Henny replied and told her sad story.

It was a slow process, since every word had to be spelled out letter by letter, but the young people didn't mind the passage of time—they wanted to know why Henny was with them. It appears that the house once belonged to her father, a medical doctor. Her name was Cesa Rist and she had lived in the house with her family. Unfortunately she had fallen in love with a boy and became pregnant by him. She wanted to marry him and have the baby but her father would not allow it and forced her to have an abortion. He did it in the house himself, but she died during the abortion.

Her body was taken to Denver, Colorado and buried in the family plot. The ghost realized that her boy friend would be dead now also, because this all happened a long time ago. Her reason for staying on in the house was to find help: she wanted her remains to be buried near her lover's, in New York.

"Do you like the people who live in this house?" "Yes," the ghost replied. "Is anyone who lived here ever in any danger?" "Yes, people who kill babies." This struck the young people as particularly appropriate: A close friend, not present at the time, just had an abortion. "Will you appear to us?" "Cesa has," the ghost replied, and as if to emphasize this statement, there suddenly appeared the shadow of a cross on the kitchen wall, for which there was no possible source, except of course from the parapsychological point of view.

The girls realized they did not have the means to go to Denver and exhume Cesa's remains and bring it to New York, and they told the ghost as much. "Is there anything else we can do to help you?" "Contact Holzer." By that time, of course, Toby had become familiar with my works, so she decided to sit down and write me a letter, telling me of their problem. They could not continue with the Ouija board, or anything else, that night, they were all much too shaken up.

On Monday Toby typed up the letter they had composed, and sent it to me. Since they were not sure the letter would reach me, they decided to do some independent checking concerning the background of the house, and if possible, try to locate some record of Cesa Rist. But they were unsuccessful, even at the Hall of Records, the events having apparently transpired at a time when records were not yet kept, or at least not properly kept.

When I received the letter I was just about to leave for Europe and would be gone for two and a half months. I asked the women to stay in touch with me and, after my return, I would look into the matter. After Toby had spoken to me on the telephone, she went back into the living room and sat down quietly. She then addressed Henny and told her she had contacted me and it would be a couple of months before I could come to the house because I had to go to Europe.

Barbara decided not to wait, however; and one night she went upstairs to talk to Henny. She explained the situation to her, and why she was still hanging around the house; she explained that her agony was keeping her in the house, and that she must let go of it in order to go on and join her boy friend in the Great Beyond. Above all, she should not be angry with them because it was their home now. Somehow Barbara felt that the ghost understood, and nothing happened, nothing frightening at all. Relieved, Barbara sat down in a chair facing the couch. She was just sitting there smoking a cigarette and wondering whether Henny really existed, or whether perhaps she was talking to thin air.

At the moment an ethereal form entered the room, standing near the couch. It looked as if she were leaning on the arm of the couch, or holding on to the side of it. She saw the outline of the head and what looked like braids around the front of her chest. For half a minute, she was there, and then she suddenly disappeared. It looked to Barbara as if the girl had been 5'4", weighing perhaps 120 pounds. Stunned, Barbara sat there for another ten or fifteen minutes, trying to believe what she had seen. She smoked another five cigarettes and then walked downstairs to try to go to sleep. But sleep would not come; she kept thinking about her experience.

At the time Sharon moved out, they were interviewing potential roommates to replace her. One particularly unpleasant woman came over and fell in love with the house. Both Barbara and Toby didn't want her to move in, but she seemed all set to join them, so Toby decided to tell her about the ghost. She hoped it would stop the girl from moving in. As Toby delineated their experiences with Henny, the would-be roommate became more and more nervous.

153

All of a sudden there was a loud crash in the kitchen, and they went to check on it. The garbage can had turned itself over and all the garbage was spilled all over the kitchen even though no one had been near it. The would-be roommate took one look at this and ran out as fast as she could. She never came back.

But shortly afterward, Toby went on a vacation to California. While she was there, she made arrangements to move there, and found employment in the market research department of a large department store. Under the circumstances, the women decided not to renew the lease, which was up in July, but to move to another apartment for a short period. In September 1972, they all moved to California. The women did not contact me any further, and I assumed that matters had somehow been straightened out, or that there had been a change in their plans. It was not until a year later that we somehow met in California and I could fill in the missing details of Henny's story.

On the last day of their stay at the house on Clinton Street, with the movers going in and out of the house, Toby went back into the house for one more look and to say goodbye to Henny. She went up to the living room and said a simple goodbye, and hoped that Henny would be all right. But there was no answer, no feeling of a presence.

For awhile, the house stood empty, then it was purchased by the father of an acquaintance of the young women. Through him, they heard about the new people who had moved in after the house was sold. One day when the new tenants had just been in the house for a few days, they returned to what they assumed to be an empty house.

They found their kitchen flooded with water: There were two inches of water throughout the kitchen yet they knew they had not left the water taps on. Why had Henny turned the water on and left it run? Perhaps Henny didn't like the new tenants after all. But Henny had little choice, really. Being a ghost, she was tied to the house.

Following her friends to San Francisco was simply impossible, the way ghosts operate. But since the new tenants on Clinton Street didn't call for my services, there was really nothing I could do to help Henny.

HOW THE LITTLE GIRL GHOST WAS SENT OUT TO PLAY

*I*n the 1960s, Ed Harvey ran a pretty good talk show called "The Talk of Philadelphia" on WCAU radio. It was the sort of program people listened to in their homes and cars, and they listened in large numbers. I know, for the telephone calls came in fast and furious in the show's final half hour, when calls from the public were answered on the air.

One day in April, 1965, Ed and his charming wife, Marion, went to a cocktail party at a friend's house. There he got to talking to Jack Buffington, who was a regional director of a world-wide relief organization and a pretty down-to-earth fellow, as Ed soon found out. Somehow the talk turned to ghosts, and Mr. Buffington had a few things to say on that subject since he lived in a haunted house. At that point, Ed Harvey asked permission for medium Sybil Leek and me to come down and have a go at the house.

We ended up arriving at the Buffington's house on Lansdowne Avenue, in Lansdowne, a Philadelphia suburb, around 10 o'clock. It was a little hard to find in the dark, and when we got there it did not look ghostly at all, just a nice old Victorian house, big and sprawling. Jack Buffington welcomed us at the door.

As I always do on such occasions, I asked Sybil to wait in another room where she could not hear any of the conversation, while I talked to those who had had experiences in the house.

After Sybil had graciously left, we seated ourselves and took inventory. What I saw was a tastefully furnished Victorian house with several wooden staircases and banisters, and lots of fine small antiques. Our host was joined by his dark-haired Italian-born wife, and two friends from his office.

The Buffingtons, who had a four-year-old daughter named Allegra, had come to the house just nine months before. A lot had happened to them in those nine months.

"We came home from a trip to Scranton," Jack Buffington began, "and when we got back and I inserted the key in the front door, the hall light went on by itself. It has two switches, one on the upstairs level, so I raced upstairs to see who was in the house, but there was no one there. Periodically this happens, and I thought it was faulty wiring at first, but it has been checked and there is nothing wrong with it. The cellar light and the light in the third floor bathroom also go on and off by themselves. I've seen it, and so have my wife and our little girl."

"Anything else happening here?" I asked casually.

"There are many things that go bump in the night here. The first noise that happened recurrently was the sound of an old treadle sewing machine, which is heard on the average of once every month. This happens in a small room on the second floor, which we now use as a dressing room, but which may well have been a sewing room at one time."

I walked up the narrow stairs and looked at the little room. It had all the marks of a Victorian sewing room where tired servants or a worried mother worked at the clothes for her child.

"It's always around three in the morning, and it awakens us," Mr. Buffington continued, "and then there are footsteps and often they sound like children's footsteps."

"Children's footsteps?"

"Yes, and it is rather startling," Mr. Buffington added, "since we do have a small child in the house and inevitably go and check that it isn't she who is doing it. It never is."

"Is it downstairs?"

"All over the place. There are two stories, or three flights, including the basement. And there are a front and back stairway. There is never any pattern about these things. There may be a lot of happenings at the same time, then there is nothing for weeks, and then it starts again."

"Outside of the child's footsteps, did you ever have any indication of a grown-up presence?" I asked.

"Well, I saw the figure of a woman in the doorway of the dining room, walking down this hall, and through these curtains here, and I heard footsteps in conjunction with it. I thought it was my wife, and I called to her. I was hanging a picture in the dining room at the time. No answer. I was getting annoyed and called her several times over, but there was no response. Finally she answered from the second floor—she had not been downstairs at all."

"What happened to the other woman in the meantime?"

"I walked in here—the hall—and there was no one here."

"How was she dressed?"

"She had on a long skirt, looking like a turn-of-the-century skirt, and she did have her hair on top of her head, and she was tall and slender. "

Mrs. Buffington was not very tall, but she did wear dark clothes.

"It was a perfectly solid figure I saw—nothing nebulous or

transparent," our host added. "The spring lock at the entrance door was locked securely. "

"Did anyone else see an apparition here?"

"My brother met a woman on the stairway—that is, the stairway leading to the third floor. He was spending the night with us, around Thanksgiving time. There was a party that evening and he mistook her for a guest who had somehow remained behind after all the other guests had gone home. She passed him going *up* while he was coming *down*, and she walked into his room, which he thought odd, so he went back to ask if he could help her, but there wasn't anybody there!"

Jack Buffington gave a rather nervous laugh.

I took a good look at the upstairs. Nobody could have gotten out of the house quickly. The stairs were narrow and difficult to negotiate, and the back stairs, in the servants' half of the house, were even more difficult. Anyone descending them rapidly was likely to slip and fall. The two brothers hadn't talked much about all this, I was told, since that time.

"Our little girl must be seeing her, too, for she frequently says she is going up to play with her lady friend," Jack Buffington said.

I started to wander around the house to get the feeling of it. The house was built in 1876 to the specifications of George Penn, a well-known local builder. Although it had been made into a duplex, it was originally a townhouse for one family.

The upper stories contained several small, high-ceilinged rooms, and there was about them the forbidding atmosphere of a mid-Victorian house in a small town. The Buffingtons had furnished their house with taste, and the Italian background of the lady of the house was evident in the works of art and antiques strewn about the house.

As I soon discovered, tragedy had befallen the house on Lansdowne Avenue at least twice as far was known. The original builder had a sister who suffered from mental illness and was hospitalized many times. She also spent many years in this house. Then a family named Hopkins came to live in it, and it was at that time that the house was divided into two parts. Incidentally, no manifestations had been reported from the other half of the house. About six years before—the exact time was none too clear, and it may be further back—a family named Johnson rented the half now occupied by the Buffingtons. They had a retarded child, a girl, *who was kept locked up in a room on the third floor.* She died in her early teens, they say, in a hospital not far away. Then the house stood empty, looking out onto quiet Lansdowne Avenue with an air of tragedy and secret passion.

Three years went by before the Buffingtons, returning from Italy, took over the house.

"Have there been any unusual manifestations on the third floor?" I asked Mr. Buffington.

"Just one. Something carries on in the trunk up on the third floor. The trunk is empty and there is no reason for those frightful noises. We have both heard it. It is above where the child sleeps."

Mr. Buffington added that a book he read at night in bed often disappeared and showed up in the most peculiar spots around the house—spots that their little four year old couldn't possibly reach. On one occasion, he found it in a bathroom; at least once it traveled from his room upstairs to the top bookshelf downstairs, all by itself.

"My impression of this ghost," Mr. Buffington said, "is that it means no harm. Rather, it has the mischievousness of a child."

I now turned my attention to Mrs. Buffington, who had been waiting to tell me of her own most unusual experiences in the house.

"On one occasion I was on the second floor with the child," she began. "It was about eleven in the morning, and I was taking some clothes out of a cabinet. The back staircase is very close to this particular cabinet. Suddenly, I very distinctly heard a voice calling 'Mammi,' a voice of a person standing close to the cabinet, and it as a girl's voice, a child's voice and quite distinct—in fact, my daughter, Allegra, also heard it, for she turned to me and asked 'Mammi, who is it?'"

"What did you do?"

"I pretended to be nonchalant about it, looked all over, went up the stairs, opened cabinets—but, of course, there was no one there. "

"And your daughter?"

"When we did not find anyone, she said, 'Oh, it must be our lady upstairs.'"

"Any other experiences you can recall?"

"Yes, tonight, in fact," Mrs. Buffington replied. "I was in the kitchen feeding the child, and I was putting something into the garbage container, when I heard a child's voice saying 'It's lower down'—just that, nothing more."

"Amazing," I conceded.

"It was a young girl's voice," Mrs. Buffington added. "I looked at Allegra, but it was obvious to me that the voice had come from the opposite direction. At any rate, Allegra was busy eating. I've been very nervous the past few days and about a week ago, when my husband was away in Washington, I spent the night alone, and having had some strong coffee, could not find sleep right away. I had moved the child in with me, so I did not have to stay by myself. I switched the light off, and the door to the landing of the second floor staircase was open. Just on that spot I suddenly heard those crashing noises as if somebody were rolling down. I was terrified. As soon as I switched the light back on, it stopped. There was nothing on the stairs. I sat on the bed for a moment, then decided it was my nerves, and turned the light off again. Immediately, the same noise returned, even louder. There was no mistaking the origin of the noises this time. They came from the stairs in front of the room. I switched the light on again and they stopped, and I left the lights burning the rest of the night. I finally fell asleep from sheer exhaustion."

"One more thing," Jack Buffington broke in. "On the back staircase, there is an area about four feet long which is a terribly frigid area sporadically. My little girl wouldn't walk up that staircase if she could possibly help it. Both my wife and I felt the cold spot."

"Is this in the area of the room where the little child was kept?" I asked.

"It is one floor below it, but it is the area, yes," Mrs. Buffington admitted.

I had heard enough by now to call in Sybil Leek, who had been outside waiting patiently for the call to lend her considerable psychic talents to the case.

After she had seated herself in one of the comfortable leather chairs, and we had grouped ourselves around her in the usual fashion, I quickly placed her into trance. Within a few minutes, her lips started to quiver gently, and then a voice broke through.

"Can't play," a plaintive child's voice said.

"Why not?" I asked immediately, bringing the microphone close to Sybil's entranced lips to catch every word.

"No one to play with. I want to play."

"Who do you want to play with?"

"Anyone. I don't like being alone."

"What is your name?"

"Elizabeth."

"What is your family name?"

"Streiber."

"How old are you?"

"Nine."

"What is your father's name?"

"Joseph Streiber."

Now Sybil had no knowledge that a child's ghost had been heard in the house. Nor had she overheard our conversation about it. Yet, the very first to manifest when trance had set in was a little girl! I continued to question her. "Your mother's name?"

"Mammi."

"What is her first name?"

The child thought for a moment, as if searching, then repeated:

"Mammi."

With sudden impact, I thought of the ghostly voice calling for "Mammi" heard on the steps by Mrs. Buffington and her little daughter.

"Do you go to school?"

The answer was almost angry.

"No! I play."

"Where do you live in this house?"

"Funny house . . . I get lost . . . too big."

"Where is your room?"

"On the stairs."

"Who else lives in the house?"

"Mammi."

"Anyone else?"

"No one."

"Where were you born?"

"Here."

"What is your birthday?"

"Eight . . . Eighteen . . . Twenty-One."

"What month?"

"March."

Did she mean that she was born in 1821? The house was built in 1876 and before that time, only a field existed on the site. Or was she trying to say: March 8th, 1921? Dates always confuse a ghost, I have found.

"Are you feeling well?"

A plaintive "no" was the answer. What was wrong with her, I wanted to know.

"I slip on the stairs," the ghost said. "I slipped down the stairs. I like to do that."

"Did you get hurt?"

"Yes. "

"What happened then?"

"So I sit on the stairs," the little girl ghost said, "and sometimes I run down one staircase. Not the other. Then I have fun."

"Is there anyone else with you?"

"Mammi."

Again I thought of the apparition in the Victorian dress Jack Buffington had seen in the hall.

"Do you see her now?" I asked.

An emphatic "no" was the answer.

"When have you seen her last?"

She thought that one over for a moment.

"Two days."

"Is she living?"

"Yes . . . she goes away, and then I'm lost."

"Does she come back?"

"Yes."

"What about your father?"

"Don't like my father. Not very nice time with my father. He shouts."

"What floor is your room on?"

"At the top."

I recalled that the retarded little girl had been kept in a locked room on the top floor.

"Do you ever go downstairs?"

"Of course I go downstairs. I play on the stairs. And I'm going to sit on the stairs all the time until somebody plays with me!"

"Isn't there any other little girl or boy around?" I asked.

"I don't get at him . . . they take him away and hide him."

"Who does?"

"People here."

"Do you see people?"

"Yes."

"Do people see *you*?"

"They think they do . . . they're not very nice, really."

"Do you talk to them?" She seemed to nod. "What do you tell them?"

"I want to play."

"Do you call out for anyone?" I asked.

"Mammi."

"Is there anyone else in this house you can see? Any children?"

"Yes, but they won't play."

"What sort of children are there in this house?"

"They won't play."

How do you explain to a child that she is a ghost?

"Would you like to meet some other children like yourself who do want to play?" I asked. She liked that very much. I told her to imagine such children at play and to think of nothing else. But she wanted to play in this house.

"I live here."

I persisted in telling her that there were children outside, in a beautiful meadow, just waiting for her to join them.

"My father tells me not to."

"But he is not here."

"Sometimes I see him."

"Come outside now."

"I don't go outside in the daytime."

"What do you do in the daytime then?"

"I get up early and play on the stairs."

She was afraid to go outside, she said, but preferred to

wait for "them" in the house, so she would not miss them. I explained things to her ever so gently. She listened. Eventually, she was willing to go, wondering only—"When do I come back?"

"You won't want to come back, Elizabeth," I replied, and asked if she understood these things now.

She thought for a moment, and then said:

"Funny man . . ."

"You see, something happened to you, and you are not quite the same as before," I tried to explain. "People in this house are not like you and that's why you can't play with them. But outside in the meadow there are many like you. Children to play with all your life!"

And then I sent her away.

There was a strange, rapping noise on the staircase now, as if someone were saying good-bye in a hurry. Abruptly, the noise ceased and I recalled Sybil, still entranced, to her own body.

I asked her to describe what she saw on her side of the veil.

"The child is difficult," she said. "Doesn't want to leave the house. She's frightened of her father. She's about ten. Died here, fell."

I instructed the medium to help the child out of the house and across the border. This she did.

"There is also a woman here," Sybil said. "I think she followed the child. She is tied to this house because the child would not go."

"What does she look like?"

"Medium fair, full face, not thin—she wears a green dress in one piece, dark dress—she comes and goes—she worries about the child—I think *she left the child*."

Guilt, I thought, so often the cause of a haunting!

"When she came back, something had happened," Sybil continued. "The child had been injured and now she keeps coming back to find the child. But the child only wants to play and sit on the stairs. "

"Can you contact the woman for us?" I asked.

"The woman is not a good person," Sybil replied slowly. "She is sorry. She listens now."

"Tell her we've sent the child away."

"She knows."

"Tell her she need no longer haunt this house; her guilt feelings are a matter of the past."

"She wants to follow the child. She wants to go now."

"She should think of the child with love, and she will join her."

"She doesn't love the child."

"She will have to desire to see her family again, then, to cross over. Instruct her."

In a quiet voice, Sybil suggested to the ghost that she must go from the house and never return here.

"She won't upset the house, now that the child is gone," Sybil assured us. "The search for the child was the cause of it all."

"Was the child ill?" I asked.

"The child was difficult and lonely, and she fell."

Again I heard rapping noises for a moment.

"Was there anything wrong with this child?"

"I'm not so sure. I think she was a little *fou*. She was florid, you know, nobody to look after her, looking for things all the time and frightened to go out."

"Did she die in this house or was she taken somewhere?"

"She died here."

Sometimes the ghost reattaches himself to the last refuge he had on the earth plane, even though the body may expire elsewhere, and instantly returns to that place, never to leave it again, until freed by someone like myself.

"The woman is gone now," Sybil mumbled. "The child went a long way, and the woman is gone now, too."

I thanked Sybil and led her back to consciousness, step by

step, until she woke up in the present, fully relaxed as if after a good night's rest, and, of course, not remembering a thing that had come through her entranced lips the past hour.

Mr. Buffington got up, since the spell of the foregoing had been broken, and motioned me to follow him to the next room.

"There is something I just remembered," he said. "My daughter, Allegra, took a fall on the staircase on the spot where those chills have been felt. She wore one of her mother's high heels and the likelihood of a spill was plausible—still, it was on *that* very spot."

The next morning, I called a number of people who knew Lansdowne history and past residents well enough to be called experts. I spoke to the librarian at the Chester County Historical Society and the librarian at Media, and to a long-time resident Mrs. Susan Worell, but none of them knew of a Joseph Streiber with a little girl named Elizabeth. The records back into the twenties or even earlier were pretty scanty in this area and research was almost hopeless. Quite conceivably, the Streibers were among the tenants who had the house in a transitory way during the years of which Jack Buffington had no records—but then again, there are certain parallels between fact and trance results that cannot be dismissed lightly.

Jack Buffington thought the description of the woman he saw and that given by the medium did not fully correspond, but then he did not see the specter long enough to be really sure.

The retarded child Sybil Leek brought through had an amazing similarity to the actual retarded girl of about ten who had lived in the house and died in a nearby hospital, and the word "Mammi" that Mrs. Buffington had heard so clearly was also what the ghost girl said she kept calling her mother.

There was some mystery about the dates—and even the longtime residents of the area I interviewed could not help me pin down the facts. Was there a man by that name with a little girl?

Records were not well kept in this respect and people in

America could come and go far more easily than in European countries, for instance, where there was an official duty to report one's moves to either the police or some other government office.

A day or two after our visit, Jack Buffington reported that the noises were worse than ever! It was as if our contact with the wraiths had unleashed their fury; having been told the truth about their status, they would naturally have a feeling of frustration and resentment, or at least the woman would. This resentment often occurs after an investigation in which trance contact is made. But shortly after, things quieted down and I had the feeling that the woman's guilt feelings would also cease. That the little girl ghost had been sent out to play, I had no doubt. Perhaps that aftermath was the mother's fury at having her no longer in her sight. But then I never said that ghosts are the easiest people to live with.

GOINGS-ON IN MARYLAND

Norma Martin's family had been psychic all the way back, usually on the female side. There was a great-grandmother who ran a boarding house for the brakemen and motormen who worked on the trolley line to Owings Mills, Maryland. One foggy night a motorman was killed in an accident. Her great-grandmother had forgotten all about the unfortunate fellow when she got off a trolley a year later to walk home. Who would join her but the dead motorman? Since she had befriended him in life she assumed he wanted to protect her on a foggy and rainy night. Every anniversary since she saw the dead fellow walking with her.

Norma was a young woman living near Baltimore. She liked to spend her summer holidays at her aunt's house in Harford County. Although Norma was aware of her family's background in the occult, she was herself not exactly a believer. At least she wasn't until her cousin complained to her about seeing a ghost. Now Norma had been in her aunt's house before and had not experienced anything, so she questioned her cousin further. Since the other girl was an excellent student and a very logical person, Norma felt that her testimony might be of value.

Apparently the cousin had gotten into the habit of staying up very late at night to do her homework. That was in the summer of 1966. In the still of the night she would look up and see a white form go past her toward the bedroom door. Startled, she would turn around but the figure was gone. Not much later she was asleep in the living room when she felt herself awakened by the sound of someone breathing very hard near her. She opened her eyes slightly, and to her bewilderment a strange little man with white hair and a long beard stood next to her bed. A moment later the apparition had vanished. When Norma came back to her aunt's house she wondered about the experience her cousin had reported to her. She was still doubtful and wondered if the whole thing might have been a dream. Shortly after her arrival she woke up in the middle of the night because she had the feeling of a human presence in the room. She looked up and there was the figure of a little man. The sound of his breathing came to her consciousness at the same time. A moment later he had disappeared. It occurred to Norma then that certain spots in her aunt's house had been unusually chilly all along even though it might be very hot outside. Finally convinced that there was something uncanny in her aunt's house, Norma made some inquiries. The little man had been a long-time servant and he had died here, although on the grounds, not in the house direct-ly. Perhaps he had no other place to go than to return to his master's house, still trying to serve.

When I was lecturing on extrasensory perception in Baltimore in October of 1968 a pleasant-looking woman came up to me and asked to speak to me quietly. "We have an earth-bound restless spirit in our home," she explained and looked around as if she had said something no one else should hear. I assured her that there were thousands of people with similar problems and not to be ashamed of being overheard, especially not in an audience that had come to hear me speak on that very same subject. After the lecture I questioned her further. The Schaefers had moved into their home in Baltimore in November of 1967. They knew that the home was very old but had no idea as to its background or prior tenants. The man who had sold them the house was of very little help except to say there had been many tenants before them. Much later Mrs. Schaefer discovered that no tenant had ever stayed there more than three months and that the list of those who had moved in and out of the house was very long indeed. The owner of the house lived out of town and would not come down to be present at the sale. The Schaefers had never met him, and that too seemed unusual. But at the time they moved in they were excited and happy with their new old home and did not worry about such matters as prior problems, or, heaven forbid, ghosts. As a matter of fact, between November of 1967 and the early spring of 1968 there was nothing in the atmosphere of the house suggesting anything out of the ordinary.

One Sunday evening the Schaefers had the visit of a young artist and his wife. In the course of the evening the conversation turned to psychic phenomena and the increased interest the subject seemed to find these days among college people. More as a lark than for serious reasons the young man suggested the use of an Ouija board. He added that he had a feeling there were spirits present in the atmosphere and that they should contact them and find out who they were and why they were present. The Schaefers went along more for amusement's sake than because they felt there was anything haunted about their house. A board was found and immediately the four of them put their hands on it. To their amazement the board came alive instantly. Messages came from it spelled at a rapid pace far more speedily than they could have spelled them even if these messages had originated in their own minds, consciously or unconsciously. What the Ouija kept telling them was that a spirit communicator named David wished to speak to Sara. He identified himself as the son of

Elmer and, in a pointed move toward Mrs. Schaefer, kept repeating over and over that he wanted to be her friend. At this point the young artist rose quickly from the board and pointed to one end of the room. His face was pale and sweat pearls appeared on his forehead. Staring toward that end of the room, he said he saw someone standing there and would have no more truck with the Ouija board. Suddenly what had started as light entertainment became heavy with forbidding silence. The Schaefers put the board away with great haste and tried to dismiss the incident with light banter.

Mrs. Schaefer did not really feel that way, for she was aware of the existence of things beyond the pale of the material and had had some interest in research of this kind. She too felt strange at that moment, but thanks to their conversation the young man regained his composure and a moment later was back to his old self. However, so strong had the impact been on him that he refused to discuss the incident then or at any time thereafter. All he would explain to the Schaefers was that something of this kind had happened to him once before and he did not wish to have it happen again. Neither one of the Schaefers had seen anything in the corner of the room to which the young artist had pointed.

After their guests had left the Schaefers went up the stairs to bed. As she went up Mrs. Schaefer had a strange feeling of a human presence. Before she realized what she was saying she heard herself speak aloud, "You are welcome." There was no fear in her at neither that time nor ever since, but she had within her the certainty that their home had a spirit resident and that the spirit had made himself known to them through the Ouija board that evening. From that moment on they became increasingly aware of a presence. Their two-year-old grandson would play on the stairs and point at something they couldn't see, describing "the man" standing there. They would hear footsteps crossing the living room, ascending the stairs, and were quite sure that someone was coming up. On one occasion Mr. Schaefer was so sure that a flesh-and-blood person had invaded their home that he came downstairs with a revolver. The phenomena increased in frequency both in the daytime and at night. Knockings would come from all parts of the house—knocking for which there was no natural explanation. Finally Mrs. Schaefer wondered about the original communicator. Since her given name is Sara she thought that he had tried to contact her, but she knew no David who would fit into a close relationship with her. She decided to search the title of their old home and with some effort found the original land grant which was dated 1836. To her amazement she discovered it had been given to a certain David Patterson. David Patterson had four children, three sons and a daughter. The daughter was named Sara. After her discovery things quieted down. Then they would pick up again. On such occasions she would ask the spirit to please leave and not disturb the house. This would always work for a few days but eventually the noises returned. Mrs. Schaefer then realized that David Patterson was still concerned with his old house and liked to continue living in it.

The Gridiron Club in Baltimore was an up-to-date establishment belying its unusual past. If you looked closely, you would realize that the house itself was very old and its colonial origins, though fixed up, were nevertheless still in evidence. There was even a swimming pool now where the old slave quarters used to be. And thereby hangs a ghostly tale. The house went back about two hundred years and was originally known as the Hillen House. If it weren't for a psychically oriented young lady by the name of Linda Merlo I would never have heard of the Gridiron Club or the Hillen House. Fortunately, for posterity, Miss Merlo lived about a mile away and knew all about it. In the colonial period a Mrs. Hillen owned much of the land around it. In her later years she fell sick and had a nurse in attendance twenty-four hours a day. One day the nurse went out into the hallway for a moment. When she returned her patient was gone. The nurse realized that the slaves might have abducted her patient in order to blackmail her into concessions of freedom, but how could she have disappeared from the room? If there was a secret passage leading down into the slave quarters, it was never found. She could not have been kidnapped through the window since the room was on the third floor of the house. The door was impossible, too, since the nurse had not left the hallway long enough for people to pass through it, and there was no other door to the room. Whichever way the owner of the house was spirited down into the slave quarters, it appears, according to the tradition which may very well be true, that the slaves tried to make her come to terms with them. In the excitement of the moment, the sick woman died.

In the course of time the house changed hands often. Eventually it became the property of a family who owned it just before it became the Gridiron Club. They were the first ones to realize that something very unusual was going on in their home. The noise of people talking downstairs when no one was about was only one of the phenomena they had to get used to. One of the sons, Ralph, liked to work on motorcycles and cars and frequently went downstairs to wash up. He would walk smack into a party going full blast although he could not understand a single word the voices were saying. As soon as he entered, the noise stopped abruptly. When he left the basement and shut the door behind him he heard the noise resume immediately in what he knew was an empty basement. He would put his working tools carefully away and lock them up. The next day he would find them scattered all over the floor, with some of them missing and never found again. Yet he was sure that no burglar had come into the house. Because of the goings-on, Ralph took to always securely locking all doors and windows. Nevertheless, whenever he did so he would find them wide open the next morning. On one occasion the owner of the house was in the basement locking the windows one by one. As he locked the first window and went on to the second to continue his task he saw the first window open itself again. He locked it again and went on but the phenomenon repeated itself. At that point he said, "All right, Mrs. Hillen, I give up," and up he went.

Two of the owner's sons, Ralph and Billy, were sitting in the kitchen when they saw a window open by itself right in front of their very eyes. They jumped to their feet when they heard someone approaching wearing chains dragging behind him. During the days of slavery, many slaves were chained at the ankles to prevent them from running away. But it wasn't just the noises that kept reminding the owners of the history of their house. Ralph's fiancée, Barbara, once saw a woman's face in the window and, on turning around, realized there was no one there who could have caused a reflection. Not much later the figure of a person holding a candle was seen walking down the hall. The owners had the house checked out for any defects, whether structural or electrical, to account for the many strange noises. That, however, was before the apparition. They realized then that the restless spirit of Mrs. Hillen was still about and that those who had tormented her hadn't found rest either. It is difficult to say whether the patrons of the Gridiron Club were much bothered by these goings-on. If they saw the ghost of Mrs. Hillen or of some of the slaves passing by, they might think that the club was putting on a floor show for them. There is no telling what the ghostly slaves thought of the swimming pool that now occupied the area where they had to live in those far-off days.

Joseph P. Rosinski was a professional radio announcer in Baltimore, Maryland. When I knew him, he was in his early forties and had had some interest in the occult, but not to the point of pursuing it deeply or in great detail. As an avocation,

Mr. Rosinski was interested in working with the blind. It was on an autumn night in 1965 that he happened to be reading aloud a textbook to his friend Ed Maff at the Maryland School for the Blind in Overlea, which is a suburb of Baltimore. About eight o'clock in the evening the supervisor of the institution came into the classroom where Rosinski and the blind man were sitting, apparently in great agitation. A blind student by the name of Mike Moran was faced with an emergency and had telephoned for help. Apparently the young man had lost his talking book needle. It had rolled somewhere on the rug in his room and he just couldn't find it. Would Mr. Rosinski be kind enough to help out? The radio announcer gladly volunteered to go to Mike Moran's place and read him the text.

That place turned out to be the cupola of an old gingerbread house built in the 1870s located at the corner of the thirteen-hundred block of North Calvert Street in Baltimore. The house seemed unusually quiet on the outside, somewhat neglected, but still showing its once proud exterior, built in a period when houses were far more solid than they are today. There was a proprietor by the name of O'Malley, a white-haired Irishman who spoke with a thick brogue. Somewhat gruffly he pointed toward the stairs to indicate that the blind man lived up there. Rosinski started to walk up. Leaving the dimly lit vestibule he suddenly found himself wondering who he really was. He didn't quite feel like himself at that point. Suddenly he found himself transported back into the gaslit area. Walking up the stairs, he arrived at the top floor and rang the bell to Mike Moran's room. Passing through heavy mahogany doors, he saw that the entire cupola was occupied with one large room. There was an old bedstead with a menacingly high headboard which was about a foot shy of hitting the ceiling. Nearby were a candle stand, an antique marble washstand and other authentic period pieces all done in dark mahogany. Somehow the room seemed frightening to Rosinski. He realized that the room and the furniture had been untouched for years. The room was filled with cigar smoke and an undefinable aroma of the past. However, Rosinski didn't wish to let the strange atmosphere of the room prevent him from doing the job he had come to do. He immediately proceeded to read the text to the young man and then prepared to go home, but the hour was late, and it was decided he should spend the night and return home in the morning. The bed was large enough to accommodate both of them, so they turned in for the night. Even though Rosinski was very tired from his efforts, he couldn't sleep. As he lay there on the old bed he suddenly felt a female softness under him. In surprise he sat up, thereby awakening Mike Moran also. Rosinski could not see anything but he felt sure there was someone else with them in bed. Mike was blind, yet he immediately "saw" the figure of a young woman on the bed. He was glad Rosinski had come to stay with him, for he was frightened. Rosinski looked toward the head of the bed and what he saw was not very reassuring. There on the bed was the form of a young woman surrounded by an aura of green and blue-gray mist. Somehow he felt that the girl had suffered in the room, and he also had the impression that a baby was connected with the woman in some dramatic way. But the most disturbing feeling of all was *the fact that he no longer felt that he was himself.* He knew for sure now that he was a nineteenth-century doctor visiting a patient in this cupola room. He felt he had to help the poor woman and suffered her agonies with her. Even the way he walked about the room was not his usual gait. It seemed to him that he walked straighter and with a firmer, lighter step than was his usual custom. There was nothing he could do to change this transformation, yet at the same time he was able to observe it clinically and to wonder about it.

After a sleepless night Rosinski returned to his own home. He implored me to go to the house on Calvert Street and do something about the ghostly woman on the bed. I tried to as soon as I was able. I found the house on Calvert Street near

Mount Royal without trouble. It is situated just opposite the old Mount Royal Hotel. But I looked in vain for O'Malley. In fact, the house gave every impression of being abandoned or pretty nearly so. The vestibule was dirty and dark. No one opened the door for me and I began to feel I had come too late. Time was of the essence and I did not want to hang around and see whether a living soul might eventually turn up and let me in. Regretfully I started to walk down the stairs that led from the vestibule to the street outside. Once more I turned and looked back. I had the distinct impression that I was not alone. I could not see anything, but somewhere in the murky dark of the vestibule I felt two outstretched arms. I went back and said in a soft voice, "You are over now and must find peace. Ask for your loved ones to come and get you and take you away from this house where you have found so much unhappiness. There is no need to stay. Everyone you once knew, everyone you once loved, has gone on. You too must go on." I turned and went back to the street. When I looked back once more, the arms were no longer reaching out to me.

THE OCTAGON REVISITED

*B*ack in 1965 I published a comprehensive account of the hauntings and strange goings-on at one of Washington's most famous houses. Frequently referred to as "the second White House" because it served in that capacity to President Madison during the War of 1812, the Octagon still stands as a superb monument to American architecture of the early nineteenth century. Most people hear more about the Pentagon than about the Octagon when referring to Washington these days, but the fact is that the Octagon, or eight-sided house, is still a major tourist attraction, although not for the same reasons that brought me there originally. As a matter of fact, The American Institute of Architects, who own the building, were and are quite reluctant to discuss their unseen tenants. It took a great deal of persuasion and persistence to get various officials to admit that there was something amiss in the old building.

After my first account appeared in *Ghosts I've Met*, I received a number of calls from people in Washington who had also been to the Octagon and experienced anything ranging from chills to uncanny feelings. I also found that the executives of The American Institute of Architects were no longer quite so unfriendly towards the idea of a parapsychologist investigating their famous old headquarters. They had read my account and found in it nothing but truthful statements relating to the history and psychic happenings in the house, and there really was nothing they could complain about. Thus, over the years I remained on good terms with the management of The American Institute of Architects. I had several occasions to test the relationship because once in a while there seemed to be a chance to make a documentary film in Washington, including, of course, the Octagon. It didn't come to pass because of the difficulties involved not with The American Institute of Architects but the more worldly difficulties of raising the needed capital for such a serious-minded film.

Originally I became aware of the potential hauntings at the Octagon because of a *Life* magazine article in 1962. In a survey of allegedly haunted houses, *Life* claimed that some visitors to the Octagon had seen a shadow on the spot where a daughter of Colonel Tayloe, who had built the house, had fallen to her death. As far as I could ascertain at the time, there was a tradition in Washington that Colonel John Tayloe, who had been the original owner of the Octagon, had also been the grieving father of a daughter who had done the wrong thing marriage-wise. After she had run away from home, she had later returned with her new husband asking forgiveness from her stern father and getting short shrift. In desperation, so the tradition goes, she then flung herself from the third-floor landing of the winding staircase, landing on a spot near the base of the stairs. She died instantly. That spot, by the way, is one of those considered to be the most haunted parts of the Octagon.

A somewhat different version is given by Jacqueline Lawrence in a recent survey of Washington hauntings published by the *Washington Post* in October of 1969. According to Miss Lawrence, Colonel Tayloe had more than one daughter. Another daughter, the eldest one, had fallen in love with a certain Englishman. After a quarrel with her father, who did not like the suitor, the girl raced up the stairs and when she reached the second landing, went over the banister and fell two flights to her death. This, then, would have been not a suicide but an accident. As for the other daughter, the one who had brought home the wrong suitor according to tradition, Miss Lawrence reports that she did not marry the man after all. Her father thought of this young Washington attorney as a man merely after his daughter's money and refused to accept him. This was especially necessary as he himself had already chosen a wealthy suitor for his younger daughter. Again an argument ensued, during which he pushed the girl away from him. She fell over that same ill-fated banister, breaking her neck in the fall. This also according to Miss Lawrence was an accident and not suicide or murder.

In addition to these two unfortunate girls, she also reports that a slave died on that same staircase. Pursued by a British naval officer, she threw herself off the landing rather than marry him. According to Miss Lawrence, the young man immediately leaped after her and joined her in death.

It is a moot question how easily anyone could fall over the banister, and I doubt that anyone would like to try it as an experiment. But I wondered whether perhaps the story of the two girls had not in the course of time become confused into one tradition. All three deaths would have had to take place prior to 1814. In that year Washington was taken by the British, and after the burning of the White House President Madison and his family moved temporarily into the Octagon. They stayed there for one full year, during which the Octagon was indeed the official White House.

Only after President Madison and his family had left the Octagon did accounts of strange happenings there become known. People in Washington started to whisper that the house was haunted. Allegedly, bells could be heard when there was no one there to ring them. The shade of a girl in white had been observed slipping up the stairway. The usual screams and groans associated with phantoms were also reported by those in the know. According to Miss Lawrence, seven years after the Civil War five men decided to stay in the house after dark to prove to themselves that there was nothing to the stories about the haunting. They too were disturbed by footsteps, the sound of a sword rattling, and finally, human shrieks. Their names, unfortunately, are not recorded, but they did not stay the night.

After some correspondence with J. W. Rankin, Director of the Institute, my wife, Catherine, and I finally started out for Washington on May 17, 1963. The beautiful Georgian mansion greeted us almost as if it had expected us. At the time we did not come with a medium. This was our first visit and I wanted to gain first impressions and interview those who actually had come in contact with the uncanny, be it visual or auditory. First I asked Mr. Rankin to supply me with a brief but concise rundown on the history of the house itself. It is perhaps best to quote here my 1965 report in *Ghosts I've Met.*

Mr. Rankin received us with interest and showed us abound the house which was at that time fortunately empty of tourists and other visitors. It was he who supplied some of the background information on the Octagon, from which I quote:

The White House and the Octagon are relations, in a way. Both date from the beginning of government in the national capital; the White House was started first but the Octagon was first completed. Both have served as the official residence of the President.

It was early in 1797 that Colonel John Tayloe of Mount Airy, Virginia, felt the need for a town house. Mount Airy was a magnificent plantation of some three thousand acres, on which the Colonel, among many activities, bred and raced horses, but the call of the city was beginning to be felt, even in that early day; Philadelphia was the Colonel's choice, but his friend General Washington painted a glowing picture of what the new national capital might become and persuaded him to build the Octagon in surroundings that were then far removed from urbanity.

Dr. William Thornton, winner of the competition for the Capitol, was Colonel Tayloe's natural selection of architect.

On April 19, 1797, Colonel Tayloe purchased for $1000 from Gustavus W. Scott—one of the original purchasers from the Government on November 21, 1796—Lot 8 in Square 170 in the new plot of Washington. Although, as the sketch of 1813 shows, the site was apparently out in a lonely countryside, the city streets had been definitely plotted, and the corner of New York Avenue and Eighteenth Street was then where it is today.

Obviously, from a glance at the plot plan, Colonel Tayloe's house derived its unique shape from the angle formed at the junction of these two streets. In spite of the name by which the mansion has always been known, Dr. Thornton could have had no intention of making the plan octagonal; the house planned itself from the street frontages.

Work on the building started in 1798 and progressed under the occasional inspection of General Washington, who did not live to see its completion in 1800. The mansion immediately took its place as a center of official and nonofficial social activities. Through its hospitable front door passed Madison, Jefferson, Monroe, Adams, Jackson, Decatur, Porter, Webster, Clay, Lafayette, Von Steuben, Calhoun, Randolph, Van Rensselaer, and their ladies.

Social activities were forgotten, however, when the War of 1812 threatened and finally engulfed the new nation's capital. On August 24, 1814, the British left the White House a fire-gutted ruin. Mrs. Tayloe's foresight in establishing the French Minister—with his country's flag—as a house guest may have saved the Octagon from a like fate.

Colonel Tayloe is said to have dispatched a courier from Mount Airy, offering President Madison the use of the mansion, and the Madisons moved in on September 8, 1814.

For more than a year Dolly Madison reigned as hostess of the Octagon. In the tower room just over the entrance President Madison established his study, and here signed the Treaty of Ghent on February 17, 1815, establishing a peace with Great Britain which endures to this day.

After the death of Mrs. John Tayloe in 1855, the Octagon no longer served as the family's town house. That part of Washington lost for a time its residential character and the grand old mansion began to deteriorate.

In 1865 it was used as a school for girls. From 1866 to 1879 the Government rented it for the use of the Hydrographic Office. As an office and later as a studio dwelling, the Octagon served until about 1885, when it was entrusted by the Tayloe heirs to a caretaker.

Glenn Brown, a longtime secretary of The American Institute of Architects, suggested in 1889 that the house would make an appropriate headquarters for the Institute.

When the architects started to rehabilitate the building, it was occupied by ten black families. The fine old drawing room was found to be piled four feet deep with rubbish. The whole interior was covered with grime, the fireplaces closed up, windows broken, but the structure, built a century before, had been denied no effort or expense to make it worthy of the Tayloes, and it still stood staunch and sound against time and neglect.

Miraculously the slender balusters of the famous stairway continued to serve, undoubtedly helped by the fact that every fifth baluster is of iron, firmly jointed to the handrail and carriage. Even the Coade Stone mantels in drawing room and dining room, with their deeply undercut sculpture, show not a chip nor scar. They had been brought from London in 1799 and bear that date with the maker's name.

On January 1, 1899, the Institute took formal possession of the rehabilitated mansion, its stable, smokehouse and garden.

So much for the house itself. I was given free rein to interview the staff, and proceeded to do so. Some of them were white, some black; all displayed a high degree of intelligence and dignity.

I carefully tabulated the testimony given me by the employees individually, and I checked the records of each of them for reliability and possible dark spots. There were none.

In view of the fact that nobody was exactly eager to be put down as having heard or seen ghosts, far from seeking publicity or public attention, I can only regard these accounts as respectable experiences of well-balanced individuals.

The building itself was then in the care of Alric H. Clay. The museum part of the Octagon, as different from the large complex of offices of The American Institute of Architects, was under the supervision of Mrs. Belma May, assisted by a staff of porters and maids, since on occasion formal dinners or parties took place in the oldest part of the Octagon.

Mrs. May was not given to hallucinations or ghost stories, and in a matter-of-fact voice reported to me what she had experienced in the building. Most of her accounts were of very recent date.

Mrs. May saw the big chandelier swing of its own volition while all windows in the foyer were tightly shut; she mentioned the strange occurrence to a fellow worker. She also heard strange noises, not accounted for, and mostly on Saturdays. On one occasion, Mrs. May, accompanied by two porters, Allen and Bradley, found tracks of human feet in the otherwise undisturbed dust on the top floor, which had long been closed to the public. The tracks looked to her as "if someone were standing on toes, tiptoeing across the floor." It was from there that the daughter of Colonel Tayloe had jumped.

Mrs. May often smelled cooking in the building when there was no party. She also felt "chills" on the first floor landing.

Caretaker Mathew reported that when he walked up the

stairs, he often felt as if someone were walking behind him, especially on the second floor. This was still happening to him then.

Ethel Wilson, who helped with parties, reported "chills" in the cloakroom.

Porter Allen was setting up for a meeting on the ground floor in the spring of 1962 when he heard noises "like someone dragging heavy furniture across the floor upstairs." In March 1963 he and his colleague saw the steps "move as if someone was walking on them, but there was no one there." This happened at 9:30 A.M.

Porter Bradley had heard groaning, but the sound was hard to pin down as to direction. Several times he had also heard footsteps.

Alric H. Clay, then in charge of buildings, was driving by with his wife and two children one evening in the spring of 1962, when he noticed that the lights in the building were on. Leaving his family in the car, he entered the closed building by the back door and found everything locked as it should be. However, in addition to the lights being on, he also noticed that the carpet edge was flipped up at the spot where the girl had fallen to her death in the 1800s.

Clay, not believing in ghosts, went upstairs; there was nobody around, so he turned the lights off, put the carpet back as it should be, and went downstairs into the basement where the light controls are.

At that moment, on the main floor above (which he had just left) he clearly heard someone walk from the drawing room to the door and back. Since he had just checked all doors and knew them to be bolted firmly, he was so upset he almost electrocuted himself at the switches. The steps were heavy and definitely those of a man.

In February of 1963 there was a late party in the building. After everybody had left, Clay went home secure in the knowledge that he alone possessed the key to the back door. The layout of the Octagon is such that nobody can hide from an inspection, so a guest playing a prank by staying on is out of the question.

At 3:00 A.M. the police called Clay to advise him that all lights at the Octagon were blazing and that the building was wide open. Mr. Woverton, the controller, checked and together with the police went through the building, turning off all lights once more. Everything was locked up again, in the presence of police officers.

At 7:00 A.M., however, they returned to the Octagon once more, only to find the door unlocked, the lights again burning. Yet, Clay was the only one with the key!

Only one prior account of any unusual goings-on at the Octagon had come to my attention before my visit in 1963. The July 1959 issue of The American Institute of Architects' Journal contains a brief account of the long service record of a certain employee named James Cypress. Although Mr. Cypress himself had never seen any ghosts, he did report that there was an unusual occurrence at one time when his wife was ill and in need of a doctor. The doctor had reported that he had seen a man dressed in the clothes of about two hundred years ago coming down the spiral staircase. The doctor looked at the stranger somewhat puzzled. At that instant the apparition dissolved into thin air, leaving the medical man even more bewildered. A short time before publication of *Ghosts I've Met*, Joy Miller of the Associated Press wrote to me about the Octagon ghosts, adding a few more details to the story.

Legend has it that on certain days, particularly the anniversary of the traffic affair, no one may cross the hall at the foot of the stairway where the body landed without unconsciously going around an unseen object lying there.

The story of the bells that ring without due cause also was embroidered in this account.

Once, so a story goes, a skeptic leaped up and caught hold of the wires as they started to ring. He was lifted off the floor but the ringing kept on. To keep superstitious servants, the house was entirely rewired, and this apparently did the trick.

Of course, accounts of this kind are usually anonymous, as a parapsychologist I do not accept reports no matter how sincere or authentic they sound unless I can speak personally to the one to whom the event has occurred.

When I started to assemble material for this book, I wondered what had happened at the Octagon since 1963. From time to time I read accounts of the hauntings that used to be, but nothing startling or particularly new had been added. It became clear to me that most of these newspaper articles were in fact based on earlier pieces and that the writers spent their time in the research libraries rather than in the Octagon. In April of 1969 I contacted The American Institute of Architects again, requesting permission to revisit the Octagon, quietly and discreetly but with a medium. The new executive director, William H. Scheick, replied courteously in the negative: "The Octagon is now undergoing a complete renovation and will be closed to visitors until this work is completed. We hope the Octagon will be ready for visitors in early 1970. I am sorry that you and your guest will not be able to see the building when you are in Washington."

But Mr. Scheick had not reckoned with the persistence and flexibility of an erstwhile ghost hunter. I telephoned him and after we had become somewhat better acquainted, he turned me over to a research staff member who requested that I let him remain anonymous. For the purpose of this account, then, I will refer to him simply as a research assistant. He was kind enough to accompany us on a tour of the Octagon, when we managed to come to Washington, despite the fact that the house was in repair or, rather, disrepair.

The date was May 6, 1969; the day was hot and humid, as so many days in May are in Washington. With me was my good friend Ethel Johnson Meyers, whom I had brought to Washington for the purpose of investigating several houses, and Mrs. Nicole Jackson, a friend who had kindly offered to drive us around. I can't swear that Mrs. Meyers had not read the account of my earlier investigation of the Octagon. We never discussed it particularly, and I doubt very much that she had any great interest in matters of this kind, since she lived in New York City and rarely went to Washington. But the possibility existed that she had read the chapter, brief as it was, in my earlier book. As we will see in the following pages, it really didn't matter whether she had or had not. To her, primary impressions were always the thing, and I know of no instance where she referred back to anything she had done before or read before.

When we arrived at the Octagon, we first met with the research assistant. He received us courteously and first showed us the museum he had installed in the library. We then proceeded through the garden to the Octagon building itself, which is connected with the library building by a short path. Entering the building from the rear rather than the imposing front entrance as I had in 1963, we became immediately aware of the extensive work that was going on inside the old building. Needless to say, I regretted it, but also realized the necessity of safeguarding the old structure. Hammering of undetermined origin and workmen scurrying back and forth were not particularly conducive to any psychic work, but we had no choice. From noon to one o'clock was the agreed-upon time for us, and I hoped that we could at least learn something during this brief period. I urged Ethel to find her own bearings the way she always does, and the three of us followed her, hoping to catch what might come from her lips clairvoyantly or perhaps even in trance.

Immediately inside the building, Ethel touched me, and I tried to edge closer to catch what came from her. She was quite herself and the impressions were nothing more than clairvoyant descriptions of what raced through her mind. We were standing in the room to the left of the staircase when I caught the name "Alice."

"What about Alice?" asked. "Who is she?"

"I don't know. It just hit me."

"I won't tell you any more than that you should try to find your way around this general area we are in now, and upstairs as far as you feel like."

"Oh yes, my goodness, there's so many, they won't stay still long enough. There's one that has *quite a jaw*—I don't see the top of the face yet; just a *long jaw.*"

"Man or woman?"

"Man."

"Is this an imprint from the past or is this a *person?*"

"From the past."

"Go over to this banister here, and touch the banister and see whether this helps you establish contact."

"I see a *horse face.*"

"Is this part of his character or a physical impairment?"

"Physical impairment."

"What is his connection with this house?"

"I just see him here, as if he's going to walk out that door. Might have a high hat on, also. I keep hearing, 'Alice. Alice.' As if somebody's calling."

"Are there several layers in this house, then?"

"I would say there are several layers."

"Is there anything about this area we're standing in that is in any way interesting to you?" We were now in front of the fatal banister.

"Well, this is much more vivid. This is fear."

She seemed visibly agitated now, gripping the banister

with both hands. Gently, I pried her loose and led her up a few steps, then down again, carefully watching her every move lest she join the hapless Tayloe girls. She stopped abruptly at the foot of the stairs and began to describe a man she sensed near the staircase—a phantom man, that is. Connected with this male ghost, however, was another person, Ethel indicated.

"Someone has been carried down these steps after an illness, and out of here. That's not the man, however. It seems to be a woman."

"What sort of illness?"

"I don't know. I just see the people carrying her down—like on a stretcher, a body, a sick person."

"Was this person alive at the time when she was carried down?"

"Alive, but very far gone."

"From where did she come?"

"I think from down here." Ethel pointed toward the spot beneath the banister. "There is also a Will, but during this time I don't think Will is alive, when this happens. I also find the long-faced man walking around. *I can see through him.*"

"Is he connected with the person on the stretcher?"

"I would say so, because he follows it." Then she added, "Someone comes here who is still alive from that. Moved around."

"A presence, you mean?" She nodded. "This man with the horse face—what sort of clothes did he wear?"

"A formal suit with a long coat. Turn of the century or the twenties?"

"The *nineteen*-twenties?"

"Somewhere in here, yes."

"And the person on the stretcher—do you see her?"

"No, she's covered up. It is the woman I still see in here."

"Why don't you go up those stairs, to about the first landing."

"I am afraid of that, *for some reason or other.*"

"Why do you suppose that is?"

"I don't like it."

"Did something happen in that area?"

"I don't know. I'm just getting a feeling as if I don't want to go. But I'll go anyway."

"See whether you get any more impressions in doing that!"

"I'm getting a cerebral heaviness, in the back of the head."

"Was somebody hurt there?"

"I would say. Or—stricken."

"What is the connection? Take one or two steps only, and see whether you feel anything further in doing this. You're now walking up the stairs to the first landing."

"Oh, my head. Whew!"

"You feel—?"

"Numb."

"We're not going further than the first landing. If it is too difficult, don't do it."

"No. I'll take it for what it is." Suddenly, she turned. "Don't push me!"

"Somebody's trying to push you?"

"Yes."

I didn't feel like testing the matter. "All right, come back here. Let us stand back of the first landing."

"I get a George, too. And Wood, and something else. I'm holding onto my head, which hurts, very badly."

"Do you know who is this connected with, the injury to the head?"

"It sounds like Jacques."

"Is he connected with this house in any official capacity?"

"Well, this is a definite ghost. He's laughing at me. I don't like it!"

"Can you get any name for this person?"

"Again I get Jacques."

"Did anything tragic ever happen here?"

"I would say so. I get two individuals here—the long-faced man, and a shorter-faced man who is much younger."

"Are they of the same period?"

"No."

"Where does the woman on the stretcher fit in?"

"In between, or earlier."

"What is this tragic event? What happened here?"

"I can hardly get anything. It feels like my brains are gone."

"Where do you think it happened? In what part of the building?"

"Here, of course, *here.*"

"Did somebody die here? Did somebody get hurt?"

"According to my head, I don't know how anybody got through this. It is like blown off. I can't feel it at all. I have to put my hand up to find it."

"Are the presences still here?"

Instead of replying, Ethel put up her hands, as if warding off an unseen attack. "Oh, no!"

"Why did you just move like this? Did you feel anyone present?"

"Yes—as if somebody was trying to get hold of me, and I don't want that. I don't know how long I can take the head business, right here . . ."

"All right, we'll go down. Tell them, whoever might be present, that if they have to say something, they should say it. Whatever information they have to pass on, we are willing to listen. Whatever problem they might have."

Ethel seemed to struggle again, as if she were being possessed.

"There's something foreign here, and I can't make out what is being said."

"A foreign language?"

"Yes."

"What language is it?"

"I'm not sure; it's hard to hear. It sounds more Latin than anything else."

"A Latin language? Is there anything about this house that makes it different from any other house?"

"There's a lot of foreign influence around it."

"Was it used in any way other than as a dwelling?"

"There were séances in this place."

"Who do you think held them?"

"Mary."

"Who is this Mary?"

"She parted her hair in the middle. Heavy girl. I've got to put my hand up, always to my head, *it hurts so.*"

"Do you get the names of the people involved in this horrible accident, or whatever it is that you describe, this painful thing?"

"That has to be Mary who's taken down the steps. I think it's this one."

"The tragedy you talk about, the pain . . ."

"It seems like it should be *here,* but it could have been somewhere else. I don't understand. There are two layers here."

"There may be many layers."

"There are so many people around here; it's so hard to keep them separate."

"Do you get the impression of people coming and going? Is there anything special about the house in any way?"

"I would say there is. *The highest people in the land have lived here.* I'm positively torn by the many things. Someone married here with the name of Alice. *That* has nothing to do with the head."

"Alice is another layer?"

"That's right."

"Mary has the injury to her head. Is the marriage of Alice later or earlier?"

"Much later." Then she added. "This house is terribly psychic, as it were—it is as if I have been able to find the easiest possible connections with a lot of people through what has been done here, psychically. There's a psychic circle around this place. From the past."

"Do you feel that these manifestations are still continuing?"

"I would say there are, yes. I don't know what all this rebuilding is doing to it, particularly when the painting starts. Has Lincoln had anything to do with this house? I feel that I see him here."

"What would be his connection with the house?"

"Nothing at all, but *he's been here.*"

"Why would he be here?"

"I see an imprint of him."

"As a visitor?"

"I would say, yes. Some other high people have been here, too."

"As high as he?"

"That's right."

"Before him or after him?"

"After."

"What about before? Has anybody been as high as he here?"

"I would say so." Ethel, somewhat sheepishly, continued. "The man with the long face, he looks like Wilson!"

At that I raised my eyebrows. The mention of President Lincoln, and now Wilson, was perhaps a little too much name-dropping. On the other hand, it immediately occurred to me that both of these dignitaries must have been present at the Octagon at one time or other in their careers. Even though the Octagon was not used as a second White House after the disastrous War of 1812, it had frequently been used as a major reception hall for official or semiofficial functions. We do not have any record as to President Lincoln's presence or, for that matter, Wilson's, but it is highly likely that both of these men visited and spent time at the Octagon. If these occasions included some festivities, an emotional imprint might very well have remained behind in the atmosphere and Ethel would, of course, pick that up. Thus her mention of Lincoln and Wilson wasn't quite as outlandish as I had at first thought.

For several minutes now I had noticed a somewhat disdainful smile on the research assistant's face. I decided to discontinue questioning Ethel, especially as it was close to one o'clock now and I knew that the assistant wanted to go to lunch.

I wondered whether any of the foregoing material made any sense to him. Frankly, I didn't have much hope that it did, since he had been honest enough to communicate his lack of faith in the kind of work I was doing. But he had been kind enough to come along, so the very least I could do was use his services such as they might turn out to be.

The name Alice meant nothing to him, but then he was tuned in on the history of the Octagon rather than Washington history in general. Later, at the Wilson House I realized that Ethel was in some peculiar way catapulting her psychic readings. It appeared that Alice meant a good deal in the history of President Wilson.

What about Lincoln? The assistant shook his head.

"The family left the house about eighteen fifty-four, and I guess Lincoln was a Congressman then. He could have been here, but . . ."

"You're not sure?"

"I mean, he's not on the list that we have of people who have been here. I have no knowledge of it."

Colonel Tayloe died in 1854, and the house was owned by the family until after 1900 when the Institute bought it. But it was not occupied by the Tayloe family after the Colonel's death. I wondered why.

As to the names of the Tayloes' daughters, the research assistant wasn't very helpful either. He did have the names of some of the daughters, but he couldn't put his hands on them right now. He did not remember Mary. But, on reflection, there might have been.

I turned to Ethel. It was clear to me that the noise of the returning workmen, who had just finished their lunch hour, and the general tone of the conversation did not help to relax her. I thanked the assistant for his presence, and we left the building. But before we had walked more than a few steps, Ethel stopped suddenly and turned to me and said, "Somebody was murdered here, or badly wounded at least." She felt it was the woman on the stretcher. She was not completely sure that death had been due to murder, but it was certainly of a violent kind. I pointed at a portrait on the wall; the picture was that of Colonel Tayloe. Did Ethel recognize the man in the picture, I asked, without of course indicating who he was. Perhaps she knew anyway. She nodded immediately.

"That's the man. I saw him."

He was one of the men she had seen walking about with a peculiar tall hat. She was quite sure. The face somehow had stuck in her mind. Ethel then pointed at another portrait. It was a photograph of Mrs. Wilson. She too had been at the Octagon. Ethel felt her presence.

"Would this be nineteen fifty-eight?" she asked somewhat unsure. The date seemed possible.

In evaluating Ethel's performance, I kept in mind that she had rarely if ever been wrong in pinpointing presences in haunted houses. Under the circumstances, of course, there was no possibility of Ethel going into full trance. Her contact with the entities was at the very best on the surface. Nevertheless, if three lady ghosts mentioned by Jacqueline Lawrence in her article had been present, then Ethel would surely have felt, seen, or otherwise indicated them. I am quite sure that Ethel never saw the article in the *Washington Post*. I am also equally sure that had she seen it, it would have made no difference to her, for she is a dedicated and honest medium. In the building itself she found her way to the psychic "hot spot" without my help, or in any way relying on my guidance. Had she been there before it would have made no difference, since the renovation had completely altered the impression and layout of the downstairs. I myself was hard put to find my way around, even though I had been to the Octagon on two previous occasions.

Thus, Ethel Johnson Meyers tended to confirm the original contention published by me in 1965. One girl ghost and one male ghost, daughter and father, would be the logical inhabitants of the Octagon at this time. Whether or not the entities themselves are aware of their plight is a moot question.

It appears to be equally difficult to ascertain the true nature of the girl's problem. Had she merely brought home a suitor whom her father did not like, or had she actually gotten married? Strange as it seems, the records are not clear in this case. What appears to be certain, at least to me, is her death by falling from the upper story. Ethel Johnson Meyers would not have picked up the "passing condition" had she not genuinely felt it. Furthermore, these impressions were felt by the medium on the very spot where traditionally the girl landed. Thus, Ethel was able to confirm the continuous presence of an unfortunate young woman in what used to be her father's house. Since the two Presidents whom the medium felt in some way attached to the house are hardly of the ghostly kind, it remains for Colonel Tayloe himself to be the man whose footsteps have been identified by a number of witnesses.

The American Institute of Architects no longer considers the Octagon the kind of museum it was before the renovation. It prefers that it be known primarily as their headquarters. In fact, the AIA has built a larger building behind it to be the actual headquarters.

If you are a visitor to the nation's capital and are bent on unusual sights, by all means include the Octagon in your itinerary. And as you walk about the Octagon itself and look up at the staircase perhaps wondering whether you will be as fortunate, or unfortunate as the case may be, as to see one of the two phantoms, remember that they are only dimly aware of you if at all.

You can't command a ghost to appear. If you manage to wangle an invitation to spend the night, perhaps something uncanny might happen—but then again, it might not. What you can be sure of, however, is that I haven't "de-ghosted" the Octagon by any means even though a medium, Ethel Johnson Meyers, was briefly almost on speaking terms with its two prominent ghosts.

THE GHOST CAR

*W*hen I met her, Marlene S. was a thirty-seven-year-old housewife leading a typical American housewife's life—which is to say she was neither given to explorations into the unknown nor particularly involved in anything out of the ordinary. After two years of college, she found that her married life took up most, if not all, of her time, but she was still hoping to get her teacher's degree after which she would like to teach English literature on a secondary level. But with four youngsters—ranging in age from eleven to fifteen—and a husband around the house, time for study was limited. Her husband, Mr. S., was a district manager for a shoe company.

Marlene came from an average Nebraska family and nothing particularly unusual or shocking ever happened to her, that is, until she, her husband and children moved into a house in Kansas City that will forever be etched in her memories. The house itself was nothing special: about seven years old, inexpensive looking, with four bedrooms, built ranch-style all on one floor.

They moved into this house in 1958 when the children were still quite young. A few weeks after they had settled down in the house and gotten used to the new surroundings, Marlene was lying awake in bed, waiting to fall asleep.

She never could go to sleep right away, and lying awake trying to sort things out in her mind was her way of inviting the sandman.

Because the children were still young, ranging in age from one to five, she had to be always alert for any moves or noises in case something was wrong. Perhaps this contributed to her light sleep, but at any rate, she was not yet drowsy at this point and was fully cognizant of what might transpire around her.

Suddenly, she felt pressure at the foot of the bed as if one of the children was trying to climb into bed to sleep with the parents.

Marlene sat up quickly but quietly, leaned toward the foot of the bed, made a grab, at the same time saying, "Got you!"—only to find herself grabbing thin air.

She assumed the little culprit had quickly scuttled back to his own bed, and got up and went across the hall to the boys' bedroom. After that, she inspected the girls' room, but all four were sound asleep, tucked in precisely the way she had earlier tucked them in and it was clear that none of her children had caused the pressure at the foot of her bed.

She decided she had imagined the whole thing and went back to bed. But the following night, the pressure was back again and again; she grabbed nothing but a fistful of thin air.

It got to be such a common occurrence she quit checking on the children whether or not they were doing it. She then decided that it had to be caused by her husband's moving his foot in a certain way. Somehow she reasoned that his moves gave the feeling the covers were drawn up against her foot, creating the impression of an outside pressure. Far-fetched though this explanation was, she accepted it gladly. But she kept her foot against his for several nights after this to find out what move of his caused all this to happen.

As her husband slept, she observed, but it got her nowhere: the pressure was still present, but there was no connection with her husband's foot or his movements.

She had hardly accepted the strange pressure in her bed when still another phenomenon caused her to wonder about the house. Near the doorway to the bedroom she heard someone breathe deeply and heavily when there was no one but her around. When this recurred several times she decided to tell her husband about it. He shook his head and said he had heard nothing. She did not tell him about the pressure on the bed, thinking it just too absurd to discuss. That night she heard the crackling of what sounded like someone stepping on cellophane just before she felt the pressure at the foot of the bed again. She knew she had left a cellophane bag at the foot of the bed on the floor and she was sure one of her children had come out and stepped on it. Again she grabbed but again her hands held only air and the children were all soundly asleep in the respective rooms.

By now a little bit of fear crept into her mind when she came to realize that there wasn't really any rational explanation for the strange noises and especially the heavy breathing. But she pulled her knees up at night and thus avoided coming in contact with whatever was causing the pressure at the foot of the bed.

For a while, nothing untoward happened, and the family was busy getting on with the problems of daily living. The strange occurrences drifted into the background.

Then one night, several weeks later, Marlene was awakened from sleep by a most incredible sound. It was as if a giant vat of water was being poured on the house. The swooshing sound of water cascading down upon them reverberated for several seconds afterward. Her immediate thought, being just awakened from deep sleep, was a logical one—one of the kids had not been able to make it to the bathroom and what she was hearing was the result! But no: they were all fast asleep in their rooms.

The next morning, she examined the floor. In the boys' room she found a strange liquid spot. It was like water, except much thicker and did not ooze out, as water would, but lay there on the floor, perfectly cohesive and round. It had neither odor nor color and when she removed it with tissue paper, it left no trace. Her husband explained that probably the liquid had oozed up from the ground or dropped from the ceiling but her logical mind refused to accept what was obviously not likely.

There was absolutely no rational explanation for either the swooshing noise or the presence of the thick liquid in the boys' room. Several months afterward, a similar spot appeared in the girls' room. Especially since they had no animals in the house, the matter remained a puzzle. The house was so new that any thoughts of ghosts were furthest from Marlene's mind. But strange things began to occur. One day, a car securely parked across from the house on a slanting driveway, came downhill and crashed into the boys' bedroom. Luckily no one was hurt.

Not much later, another car from across the street did the same thing, only this time the car went into the girls' room. The owner swore he had put the car into parking position on leaving it. Just as he got out, he saw his car roll down the driveway *by itself!*

This wasn't too reassuring to Marlene. Was some unknown force trying to "get" them? Was there a connection between the spots of liquid in the childrens' bedrooms and the two car crashes?

Somehow the atmosphere in the house was different now from the time they had first moved in. It seemed heavy, as if some sort of tragic pressure was weighing upon it. Her husband did not notice anything unusual, or if he did, he did not discuss it with her. But to her there was an ominous presence in the house and she didn't like it.

One night her husband was working late. She had gone to bed and had just turned the lights out. No sooner had she lain down, than she began to hear the heavy breathing again. Next came the pressure at the foot of the bed. With the breathing so close to her, she was absolutely terrified and did not dare move. Whatever it was, it was very near and she realized now that all her reasoning had not explained a thing. Someone other than herself shared her bed and that someone was not friendly.

But what was she to do? The children were asleep in their

beds and her husband was at work. She decided that under the circumstances the best thing was to play possum. She lay there as if asleep, barely breathing and not moving a muscle.

She did not know how much time had passed, when she heard the car drive up to their door. The headlights shone through the bedroom window and she heard the motor being turned off.

"Thank God, Don is home," she managed to say under her breath.

Even though the presence was still close by, she somehow managed to get enough courage to jump out of bed and race to the window. Turning on the lights on the way to the living room as she went by, she reached the window and looked out to the driveway.

Instead of seeing her husband and the family car, she was greeted by the blackness of the night. Nothing. No car.

"This is the last straw!" she almost cried and ran back to her bed. Pulling the covers over her she lay there in terror, not knowing what to do next. When her husband finally returned after what seemed hours upon hours, she managed to sob out her story.

"There, there," he said, soothingly, taking her head in his hands. "You've been having nightmares."

"He doesn't believe a word I've said," she thought, between sobs, but she preferred being consoled by a nonbeliever than not being consoled at all.

The next few weeks passed somehow. They had requested a transfer to another location. When it came, she was a new person. The prospect of moving into another house where nothing would disturb her sleep was just too wonderful.

Her husband had rented a big, old mansion in Wichita, where they were transferred by the company, and it was filled with antiques and fine furniture of a bygone era.

When Marlene first saw the house, she thought, "Oh my God, if any house ought to be haunted, this looks like one!"

But it wasn't, and the house in Wichita proved as peaceful

and serene as a house can be, if it isn't inhabited by a restless ghost.

The house was full of memories of its past fifty years but none of them intruded upon her and she lived a happy, relaxed life now. The experiences in Kansas receded into her memory and she was sure now that it had all been the fault of the house and not something connected with her—least of all, her imagination, for she knew, no matter what her husband had said, that she had seen and heard that ghost car drive up to the house.

She sometimes wonders who the new owners of that house in Kansas were and whether they can hear the heavy breathing the way she did. But then she realizes that it was her own innate psychic ability that allowed the phenomena to manifest themselves when they did. Another person not so endowed might conceivably not feel anything at all.

What was the horrible accident that was being reenacted—from the sound of the water being poured down, to the rushing up of the ghost car? And whose heavy breathing was disturbing her nights?

Many times, her curiosity almost made her inquire but then she decided to let sleeping dogs lie. But in later years while living in California, her psychic ability developed further until she was able to hear and see the dead as clearly and casually as she could commune with the living. It frightened her, and she thought at first she was having waking nightmares. All through the night she would be aware of a room full of people while at the same time being able to sleep on. Her observation was on several levels at the same time, as if she had been turned into a radio receiver with several bands.

Clearly, she did not want any of this, least of all the heavy breathing she started to hear again after they had moved to California.

But then it could be the breathing of another restless soul, she decided, and not necessarily something or someone she had brought with her from Kansas. She read as much as she could now on the subject of ESP, and tried her hand at automatic writing. To her surprise, her late father and her grandparents wrote to her through her own hand.

She noticed that the various messages were in different hands and quite clearly differed from her own. Yet her logical mind told her this might all come from her own subconscious mind and she began to reject it. As she closed herself off from the messages, they dwindled away until she no longer received them.

This she regretted, for the presence of her father around her to continue the link of a lifetime and perhaps protect her from the incursions of unwanted entities of both worlds, was welcome and reassuring.

By now she knew of her psychic powers and had learned to live with them, but also to close the psychic door when necessary.

Meanwhile the house in Kansas still stood, but very few tenants stayed for long.

THE HOUSE ON PLANT
AVENUE

*P*lant Avenue was a charming suburban boulevard running through Webster Groves, Missouri, a better-than-average small town, near St. Louis. Plant Avenue was not known for anything in particular except perhaps that it did have some plants, mainly very old trees that gave it a coolness other streets lack, even in the heat of summer when this part of the country can be mighty unpleasant.

Webster Groves wasn't much of a landmark either until *Life* magazine published an article on its high school activities, and then it had a short-lived flurry of excitement as the "typical" American upper-middle-class town with all its vices and virtues. But now the town had settled back to being just one of many such towns, and the people along Plant Avenue sighed with relief that the notoriety had ebbed. They were not the kind that enjoyed being in the headlines and the less one paid attention to them, the happier they were.

In the three hundred block of Plant Avenue there were mainly large bungalow type houses standing in wide plots and surrounded by shrubbery and trees. One of these houses was a two-story wood and brick structure of uncertain style, but definitely distinguished looking in its own peculiar way. The roof suggests old English influences and the wide windows downstairs were perhaps Southern, but the overall impression was that of a home built by an individualist who wanted it his way and only his way. It does not look like any other house on the block, yet it fit in perfectly and harmoniously. The house was somewhat set back and there was a garden around it, giving it privacy. From the street one walks up a front lawn, then up a few stairs and into the house. The downstairs contains a large living room, a day room, and a kitchen with a rear exit directly into the garden. From the living room, there was a winding staircase to the upper floor where the bedrooms were located.

The house was built in the final years of the nineteenth century by a man of strange character. The neighborhood knew little enough about this Mr. Gehm. His business was the circus and he seems to have dealt with various circus performers and represented them in some way. He was not a good mixer and kept mainly to himself and ultimately died in the house he had built for himself.

This much was known around the neighborhood, but to tell the truth, people don't much care what you do so long as you don't bother them, and the real estate agent who took on the house after Mr. Gehm passed away was more concerned with its wiring and condition than Mr. Gehm's unusual occupation. As the house had a certain nobility about it, perhaps due to the German background of its builder, it seemed a good bet for resale and so it turned out to be.

In 1956 the house passed into the hands of Mr. and Mrs. S. L. Furry, who had been married twenty years at the time, and had two young daughters.

Mrs. Furry had worked for the Washington University medical school in St. Louis, and she had been a major in psychology in college. Thus, she found herself more than shaken when she discovered some peculiarities about the house they had moved into—such as being awakened, night after night, at precisely two A.M. with a feeling of having been shaken awake. On one occasion, she clearly heard a heavy hammer hit the headboard of her bed, turned on the lights only to discover everything intact where she was sure she would find splinters and a heavy indentation. Soon this was amplified by the sound of something beating against the windows at night. "It sounds just like a heavy bird," Mrs. Furry thought, and shuddered. There was nothing visible that could have caused the sounds.

One morning she discovered one of the heavy wall sconces, downstairs, on the floor. Yet it had been securely fastened to the wall the night before. On examination she discovered no logical reason for how the piece could have fallen.

By now she also realized that the footsteps she kept hearing weren't simply caused by overwrought nerves due to fatigue or simply her imagination. The footsteps went up and down the stairs, day and night, as if someone were scurrying about looking for something and not finding it. They always ended on the upstairs landing.

At first, she did not wish to discuss these matters with her husband because she knew him to be a practical man who would simply not believe her. And a woman was always vulnerable when it comes to reporting the psychic. But eventually he noticed her concern and the problem was brought out into the open. He readily remarked he had heard nothing to disturb his sleep and advised his wife to forget it.

But shortly after, he sheepishly admitted at the breakfast table that he, too, had heard some odd noises. "Of course, there must be a logical explanation," he added quickly. "It is very likely only the contraction and expansion of the old house. Lots of old houses do that." He seemed satisfied with this explanation, but Mrs. Furry was not. She still heard those scurrying footfalls and they did not sound to her like a house contracting.

Eventually, Mr. Furry did not insist on his explanation, but had no better one to offer and decided to shrug the whole thing off. One night he was awakened in the bedroom adjoining his wife's boudoir because of *something strange:* he then noticed a filmy, white shape *go through the door* into the hall and proceed into their little girl's room. He jumped out of bed and looked into the room, but could see nothing. "Must have been the reflection of car lights from the street," he concluded. But it never happened again, and cars kept passing the house at all hours.

The years went on and the Furrys got somewhat used to their strange house. They had put so much money and work into it, not to say love, that they were reluctant to let a ghost dislodge them. But they did become alarmed when their three-year-old child kept asking at breakfast, "Who is the lady dressed in black who comes into my room at night?" As no lady in black had been to the house at any time, this of course upset the parents.

"What lady?" Mrs. Furry demanded to know.

"The lady," the three-year-old insisted. "She's got a little boy by the hand."

Some time later, the child complained about the lady in black again. "She spanks me with a broom, but it doesn't hurt," she said. Mrs. Furry did not know what to do. Clearly, there was something in the house the real estate people had failed to tell her about. After nine years, they found a better house— one more suitable to their needs—and moved. Again, the house on Plant Avenue was for sale. It wasn't long until a new tenant for the handsome house appeared.

In the middle of November 1965, the Walshes rented the house and moved in with two of their three children, ten-year-old Wendy and twenty-year-old Sandy. They had of course not been told anything about the experiences of the previous owners and they found the house pleasant and quiet, at least at first.

A short time after moving in, Mrs. Walsh was preparing dinner in the kitchen. She was alone except for her dog. The time was six-thirty. Suddenly, she noticed the dog cringe with abject fear. This puzzled her and she wondered what the cause was. Looking up, she noticed a white cloud, roughly the shape and height of a human being, float in through the open door leading into the living room. The whole thing only lasted a moment but she had never seen anything like it.

"A ghost!" she thought immediately, for that was exactly what it looked like. Clare Walsh was not a simple-minded believer in the supernatural. She had a master's degree in bio-chemistry and had done research for five years. She was a trained scientist. But what she saw was, indeed, a ghost! She wasn't frightened. In fact, she felt rather good, for her sneaking suspicions had been confirmed. On the day she first set foot into the house, when they had not yet taken it, she had had a deep feeling that there was a presence there. She dismissed it as being a romantic notion at the time, but evidently her intuition had been correct. With a sigh Mrs. Walsh accepted her psychic talents. This wasn't the first time that they had shown themselves.

At the time her husband's ship was torpedoed, she dreamed the whole incident in detail. When she was a child, her aunt died, and she saw her aunt's apparition before anyone in the family knew she had passed on. As time went on, she had developed a good deal of telepathy, especially with her daughters.

She dismissed the apparition she had seen in the kitchen, especially since nothing similar followed. But the nights seemed strangely active. At night, the house came to life. Noises of human activity seemed to fill the halls and rooms and in the darkness Mrs. Walsh felt unseen presences roaming about her house at will. It wasn't a pleasant feeling but she decided to brave it out and wait for some kind of opening wedge, whereby she could find out more about the background of her house. In February of 1966, her neighbors next door invited them to dinner.

Over dinner, the question of the house came up and casually Mrs. Walsh was asked how quiet the house was. With that, she confessed her concern and reported what she had seen and heard. The neighbors—a couple named Kurus—nodded to each other with silent understanding.

"There seems to be a pattern to these noises," Mrs. Walsh said, "it's always at 4 A.M. and upstairs."

The Kurus had almost bought the house themselves but were dissuaded from it by the experiences of another neighbor who lived across the street. This man had been a frequent houseguest at the house and while there, had encountered ghostly phenomena sufficient to convince him that the house was indeed haunted. The Kurus then bought the house next door instead. When Mrs. Walsh obtained the name of the man across the street, she called him and asked what he knew about their house.

"The original owner has hidden some valuables in a number of places, niches, all over the house." the gentleman explained, "and now he's looking for his treasures."

One of those secret hiding places apparently was the fireplace downstairs. Upon putting down the receiver, Mrs. Walsh started to examine the fireplace. There was a strange hollow sound in one spot, but unless she took tools to pry it open, there was no way of telling what, if anything, was hidden there.

The vague promise of hidden treasure was not sufficient to outweigh the pride of ownership in a handsome fireplace, so she did not proceed to cut open the fireplace, but instead went to bed.

About midnight, she was awakened by a peculiar, musty odor in the room. She got up and walked about the room, but the musty odor lingered on. It reminded her of the smell of death.

The next morning she told her husband about it.

"Ridiculous," he laughed, but the following morning the same odor invaded his bedroom and he, too, smelled it. Since Mr. Walsh worked for a large chemical concern, odors were his business, in a manner of speaking. But he could not classify the peculiar odor he was confronted with in his own house.

After that, not much happened beyond the 4 A.M. noises that kept recurring with strict punctuality—almost of Germanic character.

But Mrs. Walsh noticed that the door to the attic was always open. The stairs leading up to the attic from the second story have a stair whose tread lifts. Underneath the stairs she discovered a hollow space! So the tales of hidden treasure might have some basis of fact after all, she mused. The secret space was once completely closed, but the catch had long disappeared.

On one occasion, when Mr. Walsh was down with the flu, he used an adjoining bedroom. While Mrs. Walsh was resting she heard the attic door open and close again four times, and thought it was her husband going to the bathroom. But he had only been up once that night. The other three times, it was another person, one they could not see.

As time went on, Mrs. Walsh kept notes of all occurrences, more as a sport than from fear. Both she and her husband, and soon the children, kept hearing the footsteps going up to the attic, pausing at the now empty hiding place. Each following morning the attic door, securely closed the night before, was found wide open. It got to be such a routine they stopped looking for *real* people as the possible culprits. They knew by now they wouldn't find anyone.

One morning she went up to the attic and closed the door again, then continued with her breakfast work in the kitchen. Suddenly she had the strange urge to return to the attic once more. Almost as if led by a force outside of herself, she dropped the bread knife and went up the stairs. The door was open again, and she stepped through it into a small room they had never used for anything but storage. It was chock-full of furniture, all of it securely fastened and closed.

To her amazement, when she entered the little room, things were in disorder. The heavy chest of drawers at one side had a drawer opened wide. She stepped up to it and saw it was filled with blueprints. She picked one of them up, again as if led by someone, and at the bottom of the blueprint she saw the name "Henry Gehm."

She had been looking in the attic for a supposedly hidden doorway and had never been able to locate it. Was it after all just gossip and was there no hidden door?

At this moment, as she held the blueprints of the house in her hands, she received the distinct impression she should look in a certain spot in the attic. As she did, she noticed that the furniture against that wall had recently been moved. No one of flesh and blood had been up there for years, of course, and this discovery did not contribute to her sense of comfort. But as she looked closer she saw there was now a door where before a large piece of furniture had blocked the view!

Who had moved the furniture?

She felt a chill run down her back as she stood there. It wasn't the only time she had felt cold. Many times a cold blast of air, seemingly out of nowhere, had enveloped her in the bedroom or in the kitchen. As she thought of it now, she wondered why she had not investigated the source of that air but taken it for granted. Perhaps she did not want to know the results.

The events in the attic occurred on March 1, 1966. The following day, she was awakened quite early by incessant footsteps in the hallway. Someone was walking up and down, someone she could not see.

She got up. At that moment, she was distinctly impressed with the *command* to take out an old music box that had belonged to her mother. The box had not played for many years and was in fact out of order. She opened the box and it started to play. It has remained in working order ever since. Who had fixed it and was this a reward for having looked at the blueprints for "someone"?

On March 5, she was roused from deep sleep once more at the "witching hour" of 4 A.M., but the house was quiet, strangely so, and she wondered why she had been awakened. But she decided to have a look downstairs. In the dining room, the breakfront that she had left closed the night before, stood wide open. Unseen hands had rearranged the teaspoons in one of the drawers! A plant had a shoot broken off and the twig lay on the table nearby. Since the dog had not been in the room, there was no one who could have done this.

The next morning, her sleep was again interrupted at 4 o'clock. This time the drawer containing her underclothes was all shaken up. Suddenly it dawned on her that her ten-year-old daughter might have spoken the truth when she reported "someone" in her mother's bedroom opening and closing the dresser when Mrs. Walsh knew for sure she had not been in the room.

She realized now what it was. The bedroom she occupied had been Henry Gehm's room. If he had hidden anything in it, he might be mistaking her dresser for his own furniture and still keep looking.

On March 8, Mrs. Walsh was in the basement, and her ten-year-old girl, Wendy, was in the garden playing. The house was quite empty.

Suddenly, she heard the sound of a child running at a mad pace through the dining room and kitchen. It must be Sandy, she thought, and called out to her. She received no reply. She went upstairs to investigate and found the house empty and quiet. Yet the footsteps had been those of a child, not the same footfalls she had so often heard on the stairs and in the attic. So there were two of them now, she thought, with a shudder.

It was then also that she recalled the baby hair she had found under the couch shortly after they had first moved in. At the time she had dismissed it as unimportant, even though no one with *blond* hair lived in the house. The hair was very fine, clearly blond and seemed like the hair of a very young child.

"Like angel's hair," she thought, and wondered.

Five days later, all but Mr. Walsh were out of the house, in church. He was still in bed, but after the family had left for church he came downstairs, and fixed himself breakfast in the kitchen. At that moment, he thought he heard Wendy running upstairs.

He assumed the child was not well and had been left behind, after all. Worried, he went upstairs to see what was the matter. No child. He shook his head and returned to his breakfast, less sure the house didn't have "something strange" about it.

Upon the return of the others, they discussed it and came to the conclusion that the house was haunted by at least two, possibly three, people. It was a large enough house, but to share one's home with people one could not see was not the most practical way to live.

A few days later, Mrs. Walsh was again in the basement, doing the laundry. A sweater hanging from the rafters on the opposite side of the basement suddenly jumped down from the rafters, hanger and all, and landed in front of her. The windows were firmly closed and there was no breeze. What amazed Mrs. Walsh even more was the way the sweater came down. Not straight as if pulled by gravity, but in an ark, as if held by unseen hands.

"Mrs. Gehm," she heard herself exclaiming. "What did you do that for?"

There she was, talking to a ghost.

What is your first name, anyway? she heard herself think.

Instantly, a counterthought flashed into her mind. *My name is Mary.*

On March 16, she woke again early in the morning with the sure sensation of not being alone. Although she could not see anyone, she knew there was someone upstairs again. However she decided to stay in bed this time. First thing in the morning, as soon as it was *light,* she ventured up the stairs to the attic. In the little room the furniture had been completely reshuffled! She then recalled having heard a dull thud during the night.

A trunk had been moved to the center of the room and opened; a doll house had been placed from one shelf to a much lower shelf, and a tool box she had never seen before had suddenly appeared in the room. There were fresh markings in the old dust of the room. They looked like a child's scrawl . . .

Mrs. Walsh looked at the scrawl. It looked as if someone had made a crude attempt to write a name in the dust. She tried to decipher it, but could not. The next day she returned to the room. No member of the family had been there. The children were by now much too scared to go up there.

The scribbled signature was still there, and not far from it, someone had made a handprint in the dust. *A small child's hand!*

As Mrs. Walsh stared at the print of the child's hand, it came back to her how the month before she had heard a child's voice crying somewhere in the house. None of her children had been the cause of the crying, she knew, and yet the crying persisted. Then on another occasion, a humming sound such as children like to make, had come to her attention, but she could determine no visible source for it.

Two days later, still bewildered by all this, she found herself again alone in the house. It was afternoon, and she clearly heard the muffled sound of several voices talking. She ran up the stairs to the attic—for it seemed to her that most of the phenomena originated here—and sure enough the door to the attic, which she had shut earlier, was wide open again.

Early the next morning Mrs. Walsh heard someone calling a child up in the attic. Who was up there? Not any of the Walshes, she made sure. Slowly it dawned upon her that a family from the past was evidently unaware of the passage of time and that the house was no longer theirs. But how to tell them?

A busy family it was, too. At 5 A.M. one morning a typewriter was being worked. The only typewriter in the house stood in Wendy's room. Had she used it? *She* hadn't, but that morning she found her typewriter had been used by someone. The cover had been put back differently from the way she always did it. A doll she had left next to the machine the night before, was now on top of it.

That night, while the family was having dinner in the kitchen, the lights in the living room were turned on by unseen forces. Pieces of brightly wrapped candy disappeared from a tray and were never seen again.

The dog, too, began to change under the relentless turn of events. She would refuse to sleep in the basement or go near certain spots where most of the psychic phenomena had occurred. The seven-year-old dog, once the very model of a quiet suburban canine, soon turned into a neurotic, fear-ridden shadow of her former self.

It got to be a little too much for the Walshes.

The treasure Mr. Gehm was hunting had no doubt long ago been found and taken away by some earlier tenant or stranger. As for the house itself, the ghosts could have it, if they wanted it that much. The Walshes decided to build a new home of their own, from scratch. No more old homes for them. That way, they would not inherit the ghosts of previous owners.

They notified the owner of their intent to move and as soon as the new home was ready, they moved out.

Even on the last day, the sounds of footsteps scurrying up the stairs could be heard.

Plant Avenue gossips can add another chapter to the lore of the Gehm house, but the sad little girl up in the attic lost her playmates. Even if they couldn't see her, the children knew she was *there*.

And that's all a ghost can hope for, really.

CHARLOTTESVILLE AND THE REVOLUTION

*W*hen people think of the times of the American Revolution, they think primarily of Boston and the Tea Party, Paul Revere and his uncle, and Philadelphia and its Liberty Bell. Very few people realize that Charlottesville, Virginia, was the focal point of the emerging United States for a while—that it was at the small, conveniently situated town in northern Virginia where much of the early planning of the Revolution took place. That was so because some of the leaders of American independence, such as Thomas Jefferson and James Monroe, made their homes in and around Charlottesville. Tourists who are eager to see Washington, D.C., and cannot get enough of its majestic government buildings should take an extra hour to fly down to Charlottesville to see where it all began.

It had been years since I had been to Charlottesville, when Horace Burr, professor of speech and director of drama at Madison College in Harrisonburg, and Virginia Cloud, the noted librarian and historian, had invited me. At that time, however, my main interest was in ferreting out some of the local ghosts and discussing them in a book I was then writing.

Professor Burr was instrumental in prearranging my visit in early February 1973, knowing what I was hoping for, and clearing permission for me and a mediumistic friend to visit some private homes of the area. Virginia Cloud was on hand too, and it felt like old times revisited when my friend Ingrid Beckman and I emerged from the jet plane at the little Charlottesville airport. We were going to stay for two days, which had been tightly planned by Professor Burr and Ms. Cloud. Even a television interview with a crew from nearby Richmond, Virginia, had been penciled into the schedule, and I gave it while standing on the historical staircase of the Burr house, Carrsgrove.

Immediately upon arriving, we checked in at the Monticello Hotel in downtown Charlottesville. In retrospect, it seems odd that such a patently third-rate provincial hotel should bear the illustrious name of Monticello. The rooms weren't at all what we had ordered, the service and food were below standard, and it occurred to me how Jefferson would have felt had he been forced to put up some of his friends at this hostelry. Fortunately, it didn't exist during Jefferson's lifetime.

Promptly at two o'clock, Professor Burr picked us up at the hotel and, together with Ms. Cloud, who had arranged our visit, drove us to Foxhill Farm, then the home of Mrs. Isabelle Palmer, a prominent society leader in Charlottesville. The house was somewhat on the outskirts of the town, on a knoll set back from the street. Although of pre-Revolutionary origin, it had been nicely fixed up and contained the latest comforts. Its dozen or so rooms were distributed on two floors, with a large kitchen downstairs and an imposing dining room to the right of the entrance. Upstairs, there were mainly bedrooms. Behind the house was the loveliest of gardens, enclosed by a brick wall behind which extended the rolling hills of Virginia's horse country, as far as the eye can reach.

Mrs. Palmer received us with much cordiality, and, as she

had been briefed beforehand not to divulge anything about the house while Ingrid and I were inspecting it, only formalities and generalities were exchanged between us at first. As in my custom, I let my mediumistic associate go about the house as her intuition commanded her. Immediately on entering the large room to the right of the entrance, Ingrid stopped. She found herself then in the left-hand corner of what was obviously a dining room.

"What's the matter?" I asked, realizing that she was picking up some imprint from the past.

"I have a generally heavy feeling here. I can't describe it as yet, but the area is loaded with impressions," Ingrid replied, still trying to get her psychic bearings.

Ever since I had started to work with mediums, my own ESP ability also sharpened, and on occasion I was able to sense things along with them. Thus I heard myself say, "Walk around and see whether you feel anything. I get the feeling of a meeting of some importance having taken place here." I had no idea why I said it, but both Ingrid and I agreed that a meeting of some importance had taken place in that very room, that someone had been arguing and had gotten up to leave in order to warn someone about a matter of importance.

"I feel there is a series of meetings here, not just one," Ingrid added, and then we walked over to the kitchen area. Since Ingrid felt nothing particularly strong in that area, we proceeded upstairs.

As soon as Ingrid walked into the bedroom to the left of the stairs, she stopped. "Guests on government business stayed here," she said, touching the bed to receive stronger psychometric impressions. "I 'get' a woman here; she is the wife of someone who has gone away, and I think she is very anxious for him. I get the feeling that she is worried for the man to get through the lines, and she is sitting up in an all-night vigil."

While Ingrid was speaking, I received the impression of

the name Margaret, followed by the initial L. I have no idea why, but the imprint was quite strong.

"I have the feeling a lot of people went up and down the front stairway in the middle of the night," Ingrid said, "and that this is in a sense like a refuge."

I turned to Mrs. Palmer and Horace Burr, asking them to comment on the psychic impressions received by Ingrid and myself.

"Well," Professor Burr began, "this house, Foxhill Farm, stood halfway between Brown's Cove and the new village of Charlottesville at the time of the Revolutionary War. Our civilization came in through this part, through the valley, along the river. So this was actually a very important location; people who lived here were well-to-do, and it was a huge plantation. The owner was a certain John Rodes, and his son David was made sheriff of the county in 1775. During Colonial days, the post of sheriff was a very important government position, and Rodes had his own son filling that office.

"Since this house was a place halfway between the Revolutionary lines and the British, I felt it would be interesting to see what your psychic friend would get from the vibrations in the house," Burr added.

"What about the important meetings both Ingrid and I felt in the dining room downstairs?" I asked.

Professor Burr nodded emphatically. "Yes, if there were meetings they would undoubtedly have been held here."

At this point, Mrs. Palmer explained that the corner of the dining room where Ingrid had felt such strong vibrations had always puzzled her. It was on that spot that she had felt chills and had a sense of presence. Not being a medium, however, she could do very little with it. Nevertheless, she felt that whatever psychic activities might be present in her house would center around that corner of the dining room. I then questioned her about the room upstairs where Ingrid had had such a vivid impression. It turned out that the room was exactly above the library and not far from the area where the meetings had been held in the dining room. The house itself consisted originally of two separate houses that were joined together in the middle. The area where Ingrid had felt the strongest impressions had been built in 1765; the other, where she had felt nothing special, had been built in 1807.

I then directed a question to Burr. "Was there any particular meeting where people were sitting down at a long table, wearing a kind of severe dark brown coat, with lots of buttons running down the middle? Somebody at the end of the meeting would be getting up with a rather serious face, saying, 'I'll let him know,' and then take some papers and leave the assembly. This would have been very late at night or early in the morning, and someone would have had to ride quite a distance to notify someone of a decison taken here for some area to join up with some other forces." As I finished speaking, I wondered where I had gotten all that information; it seemed to me that it was simply coming out of me, as if I had been *impressed* with it by some external source. I could tell by the took on Ingrid's face that she felt pretty much the same but that I had somehow expressed it first.

Burr thought this over for a moment. "It sounds very reasonable, since it was the time when they were recruiting and the sheriff would have had his hands in it, of course."

Again I followed a hunch. "Has anyone ever left here who was connected with this house and whose life was in jeopardy if he were caught?"

"Well, okay," Burr replied, "then let us go into the bloodstain on the floor, which you can see plainly even now." Sure enough, in the door jamb between the library and the next room there was a bloodstain deeply soaked into the wood.

Isabelle Palmer took up the explanation from this point on. "This has some connection with a Revolutionary person," she explained. "That is why when you mentioned refuge it hit home with me. Tradition has it that a wounded man came here during the Revolution and sought refuge. But we don't know who he was or whether he died here."

We walked back into the sumptuous library and sat down, surrounded by eighteenth-century oil paintings of great historical value. I asked about the men dressed in the reddish brown long coats which I had been impressed with a little while earlier. Could it have any meaning in terms of historical fact?

"Well," Burr replied, "that was the most typical homespun yarn that you could have in the 1770s in Piedmont, which is where we are. The material was produced on a loom and dyed with tobacco dyes, so the colors were dark brown."

Since the old pre-Revolutionary houses were once the centers of large plantations, they were not clustered in or around the town of Charlottesville but stood in lonely majesty in the countryside, even though much of the land had long since been sold off. Such was the case with Castalia, an imposing three-story manor house with red brick at the bottom, a veranda going around most of the house, and a portico dressing up the rest. The tall red brick chimneys, which supplied the fireplaces with outlets in the days before central heating, looked like imposing flagpoles peering out into the Virginia hills. Castalia was surrounded by tall, old trees and was reached by a driveway from a dirt road which in turn branched off the main highway. Even in its reduced size, Castalia was the center of an estate which took a full fifteen minutes to drive through.

As we were halfway between the town of Charlottesville and the estate, Virginia Cloud, who had been chatting incessantly, as was her custom, happened to say something about a ghost. Now, don't get me wrong. Virginia Cloud had a lot to say, and nothing she ever tells you was without interest. She probably knew more about motion pictures and stars than any living soul, and nearly everything there was to know about Charlottesville and the American Revolution.

"About that ghost," I said, and turned around. I was seated next to Horace Burr, and Ingrid and Virginia were in the rear seats.

"Well," Virginia said, "this very road we are riding on is the road where my friend Mrs. Emily Money Kelly had a remarkable experience with a ghost."

"Tell me more," I coaxed her, as if that were necessary.

"Emily lived nearby because her father was Colonel Money, an Englishman who worked for John Armstrong Chanler, a very famous gentleman of the area. One night Emily and her sister were on this long road which, as you know, connects Castle Hill with Castalia."

I knew that fact very well. In 1964 I had visited Castle Hill, where there was a haunted bedroom, allegedly visited at times by a lady ghost who appears only to people she doesn't like so she can tell them to leave "her" bedroom. At the time of my visit to Castle Hill, I had questioned the owner, Colonel Clark Lawrence, about any psychic occurrences. Politely, he informed me that he had none to report.

"Emily and her sister were turning into the driveway of their house, when they saw a rider very clearly—so clearly, in fact, that upon arriving at the door they asked one of their servants, 'Who was right in front of us when we came here?' The man seemed surprised. 'Why, Miss Emily, I've been out here all evening and I didn't see anybody.' Other people living in the area have also reported seeing a lonely rider ahead of them, heading up the road from Castle Hill to Castalia. Nobody knows who he is, or where he goes."

I thanked Virginia for her contribution to the local ghost lore, and just then the sleek blue car turned into the driveway leading up to Castalia. There we were welcomed by the owners, the Boocock family. We were exactly eighteen miles from Charlottesville and in the very heart of the Virginia horse country. The several ladies and gentlemen assembled to greet us in the large parlor downstairs were all members of the family, eager to contribute their experiences to the investigation. As I had requested that nothing be said about the house or the occurrences therein, only polite chitchat was exchanged at first. Ingrid took a look at the downstairs part of the house, and explained how pleasing it was to her artistic taste. But within a matter of minutes, she was on her way upstairs and I followed her, tape recorder and camera in hand. Behind me came Horace Burr and Virginia Cloud, followed at a respectful distance by the lady of the house.

The house was living proof that the Southern gentry still knows how to furnish homes. Elegantly decorated in the proper style, without so much as a single intrusion of modernism or so-called improvements, the interior of Castalia was a joy to the eye. Four-posters, heavy drapes, thick carpets, early nineteenth-century furniture, beautifully carved staircases and, above all, rooms upon rooms, space upon space, and all of it deep in the country, far away from pressures and the onrushing traffic.

As soon as we reached the second-floor landing, Ingrid made an immediate dash for a corner room, later identified as the chintz room. It had windows on both outside walls, giving a person an excellent view of the drive and thus of anyone coming up to the house. There was a period bed, or rather a double bed, in the center, and heavy drapes at the tall windows, reaching almost to the floor in the French manner. Opposite the bed stood a dresser with a large mirror. Horace and I kept back, close to the entrance door, while Ingrid walked slowly around the room.

"There is an impression here of an older woman; I get the feeling of an all-night vigil," she said finally. "I think she is worried about someone at a distance." I queried her about the person this woman worried over. "It is a man," Ingrid replied. "He's away on a war campaign. I think he is either a general or some other high-ranking officer; a leader and a patriot."

"Try to see what he looks like," I instructed her, "what his name is, what his connection is with this house, anything you can get on him."

Ingrid closed her eyes, breathed deeply for a moment, then reopened them again and said, "He is at a great distance right now, a hundred miles or more. She is worried that he may never return."

"Is he in any kind of action at the moment?"

"Yes. There is a decision, a turning point in the war, and she is worried that he may not come back from it. I get 1760 or '70. Her name is Margaret."

"What happened to this man? Does he come back?"

Ingrid's face took on a sad expression, almost as if she were feeling what "Margaret" must have felt at the time. "I don't think he comes back."

"What happens to her?"

"She stays here in great sadness."

"Is she still attached to this house, or do you merely feel her imprint?"

"Oh, I think she comes here. I think this is the room where she did most of her worrying. She comes back in the hopes that *he* will return."

"Did he die in battle?"

"Yes."

"How did she hear of it?"

"A carrier came with the news."

"How is it connected with this house?"

"He owned it; he was in the family."

"When the news came to her, was she in this room?"

"Yes, she was ill."

"As you speak, do you sense her close to you? Is she in some way telling you this? What was she dressed like?"

"I think she wore a nightgown," Ingrid replied, closing her eyes again to better describe what her psychic senses told her. "She wears perfume, her hair is pulled back, it is of dark brown color. She's a woman of perhaps forty-five. She likes to wear flowered clothes, gauzy material, and beads around her neck."

"What keeps her in this house?"

"He never returned and she is *still waiting*."

"Is she aware of his death?"

"She's confused."

"Does she realize that her own death has occurred?"

"I don't think so."

Next, we entered the so-called lavender room, also on the second floor of the house. It was situated opposite the chintz room, on the right of the stairwell, but also facing toward the road so that one could observe it from the window. The lavender room was considerably smaller than the chintz room we had just left. I decided to leave Ingrid and Virginia alone in it for a few moments, to see whether they could gather up some impressions from the past. Meanwhile, I went outside to change film and tape.

When I returned, both ladies seemed agitated and said they had news for me. "I think a woman was brought in here. She was very ill and stayed here until her death," Ingrid said firmly. "I think it is the same woman I felt in the chintz room except that she actually stayed in this one. I think she received the shock when she was in the other room, and then her condition became hopeless and she was moved in here. I don't know whether it was because of drink, but she never recovered emotionally. She was in here for several years, and eventually she died here. In this room I feel only sadness and the long-drawn-out period of her suffering. I think she wants to tell her story, she is so lonely and sad."

I instructed Ingrid to try and contact the entity, in trance if possible. Ingrid sat back in a deep, comfortable chair in the corner, closed her eyes and waited. Although full trance did not occur, she seemed very much under the influence of an outside entity. "David," Ingrid said, her voice barely audible. "David or Davis," she added, "I think that is the man. She is very confused and still waiting for him." I instructed Ingrid to inform the lady that the man had passed on and that she herself was no longer in the flesh. Did the spirit understand her condition? "She understands what I am saying," Ingrid replied, "but I don't think she pays attention."

I decided to follow a different route of questioning. "Ask her to reveal more about herself."

"I think she was a very delicate lady, with lots of perfumes and fineries and beads; she catered to herself. She was a socially prominent woman."

"Was there anything among her habits that was particularly outstanding, such as a hobby or interest of some sort?"

"I think she liked to read a lot. Poetry. Especially Emerson, I think. But she didn't do any more reading after her loss; she was too confused. She thinks she is still here. *She is afraid to leave.*"

As was my custom under such circumstances, I explained to the entity that she could join her loved one merely by calling out to him and displaying a sincere desire to join him. Did the spirit lady understand what I was saying to her? "She listens," Ingrid explained. "She is showing herself to me with a shawl now, a white shawl bordered with fringes. Maybe she does needlework. She is always watching out the windows. *But the news does not come.* She grows old in this room."

"Does she understand why the man she is waiting for is not returning?"

"No. She is very stubborn."

But eventually, Ingrid and I persuaded her that there was

no point in waiting any longer, and with our blessings we sent her away to the man who had also been waiting for her on *his* side of the road.

We continued our inspection of the large house, walking down half a flight of stairs and up another half on the other side of the house, which apparently had been built at a different time. The house presented a fascinating pattern of staircases and corridors, not laid out in a perfectly straight pattern but allowing for unexpected corners, turns, and hidden nooks. The master bedroom was located at the other end of the house, its windows looking down onto the land and toward the main road in the distance. It was a bright, large, and well-appointed room, beautifully decorated and well kept. Again, I let Ingrid step into it first by herself to pick up whatever she could in the way of psychic impressions.

"I don't feel anything here," Ingrid announced with a determined tone of voice. I had learned to respect her judgment, for whenever she felt nothing in the atmosphere of a room, there usually was nothing to be felt. On the other hand, whenever I had taken her to allegedly haunted rooms, she had picked up the scent without fail. I thanked her, and we descended to the ground floor, where the members of the family awaited us with great curiosity. Briefly, I filled them in on what Ingrid had discovered and in turn asked them to brief us on the house and make comments about Ingrid's discoveries.

Horace Burr was the first to speak. "The grandson of the famous Dr. Thomas Walker of Castle Hill, about whom you have written in *Ghosts I've Met,*" he said, "had a grandson named Lewis. The house, as it stands then , was built around 1850, but there was an older house here before that time." Burr got up and showed me the dividing line where the old part ended and the newer portion began. About two-thirds of the living room was in the older section, while the frontal third actually occupied the newer part of the house. "So the first part, that is, the first room we were in, wasn't standing when the phenomena occurred," Burr explained. "Yet the apparition of a woman which had been observed by many of the people around here always occurred in the chintz room, the room where Ingrid correctly identified her. This was Mrs. Sally Lewis, the wife of Robert Lewis."

"Who saw her?" I asked.

"Mrs. Lila Boocock, the present Mrs. Boocock's sister-in-law. It happened prior to her marriage when she, her mother, and her intended were visiting here from New York. In the middle of the night she was awakened by a little woman with dark brown hair, pulled back, wearing a shawl and a striped taffeta dress. The woman was in her bedroom busying herself with a briefcase which Lila had brought with her and which contained some real estate papers. *The ghostly lady tried to go through it as if she were checking things out.* As Lila sat in bed, amazed at what she saw, she heard a sound reminding her of crisp onions being cut while the woman was going through her papers. Finally the woman walked straight over to the bed, with a faint smile on her face, and leaned over as if she wanted to say something. The next moment she was gone."

Mrs. Lila Boocock lived in Florida then. The experience occurred in 1926.

I turned to my hostess, Mrs. Elizabeth Boocock. "Have you yourself had an experience along these lines?"

"Yes," she replied. "Before we actually lived here, we used to come down to visit, and we would take the bedroom in the left part. That was in 1929. One morning I woke up around five o'clock because I heard footsteps with a regular rhythm to them. It sounded like, one-two-three-stop. At first I thought that my husband was ill. He hadn't been very well and was in the bed next to me, so I turned on the lights. But he was sound asleep. After that, I heard the same footsteps again and again, always at five o'clock in the morning. Finally I asked my mother-in-law what it all meant, and she replied, 'Oh, that's Mrs. Lewis.' But I never heard it again after we moved into the house."

I turned to the lady to her right, Gwendolyn Goss, Mrs. Boocock's daughter, asking for any first-hand experiences.

"When I was at school in 1943, I brought a roommate home for Thanksgiving weekend," she began. "My friend, Marie de France, and I stayed in the chintz room, and it was a very cold, windy night, so we had a fire going in the fireplace. We put our clothes over a chair near the fireplace and went to bed. Sometime after midnight I heard some noise, as if someone were moving around the room, and I assumed Marie had gotten up. At the same time, Marie thought I had gotten up, so we both got out of bed and turned on the lights. Imagine our surprise when we found all our clothes on the floor *and the chair turned toward the fireplace with an open book on it!* Neither of us had put the book there. All that time the wind was blowing hard and the room was icy cold."

"Someone must have sat in that chair, reading a favorite book by the fireplace," I interjected. Horace Burr gave me a significant look.

"When we first moved down here, we lived in this house for a while before we moved out to the cottage, which you can see out the window," Gwendolyn continued. "When mother mentioned again and again to me that she had heard footsteps of an unseen person overhead, I finally said, 'Why, that's ridiculous.' But one night I heard the footsteps myself and immediately went upstairs to look. They sounded like four very definite footsteps going in one direction, then turning around and coming back. Immediately I went upstairs to look above the room I was in, and there was nothing."

"What sort of footsteps were they?" I asked.

"It sounded almost as if someone were pacing up and down," Gwendolyn replied.

"But that wasn't all," she continued. "During the 1930s my grandparents had gone to Europe for a while, and the house was locked up. Not only was it closed from the outside but each individual room in the house itself was also locked. When they sent word by cablegram that they were coming home and asked the maid and the farm manager to open the house for them, these people came in. When they got to the lavender room and unlocked the door, they found the bedspread off the bed and on the floor, the bureau scarf off it, and all the silver in a mess. It looked as if someone had gone through it in a fit of temper, yet there had been no one in the house. No one could have gotten in. A mouse couldn't have gotten in.

"On one occasion, Mrs. Boocock and her mother were sleeping in the room next to the chintz room, when she heard a crash in the middle of the night which sounded to her as if someone had jerked off the dresser scarf and everything had gone to the floor. When the two women checked, they found everything in order. This happened two or three times in a row, both in the chintz room and in the lavender room."

"It would seem that somebody was looking for something, wouldn't it?" I said. "But I wonder who the ghost was waiting for?"

"I think I can answer that," Horace Burr said. "Mrs. Lewis's son had been hunting nearby when he shot himself accidentally, or so they say. That was in 1855. Naturally she was upset, pacing up and down, waiting for someone who never came. Ingrid mentioned someone who was part of the family, and she mentioned her reading Emerson. That would fit. George Lewis is buried here on the grounds."

A tall heavy-set man who had been listening to the conversations in patience and silence spoke up then . He turned out to be Gwendolyn's husband, Edward Goss. Since he was an expert in engineering matters, he wanted us to know that important structural changes had taken place in the house.

Both the lavender room and the chintz room had been changed, in 1904 and then again in 1909. He understood that the late Mrs. Sally Lewis was "unhappy" about the changes in her house. He explained that during the Revolutionary period there was a double cabin about two minutes away from the main house, and that this cabin was built in 1747 by a man named Jack, not far from the Castalia spring, which had been named after the legendary spring on Mount Parnassus.

"About two years after Lila Boocock had seen the apparition of Mrs. Lewis in her bedroom," Goss said, "she happened to be introduced to a granddaughter of the late Mrs. Lewis. After describing the apparition in detail, she asked the granddaughter whether she recognized it. 'That is my grandmother,' the granddaughter said firmly. 'She was little and had straight, pulled-back hair. She wore a shawl and a striped taffeta dress.'"

"Did you yourself ever have an experience in the house?"

"Yes, I did. In 1947 the then owner of the house, Mrs. Marmie Boocock, was away in Florida, and the house was quite empty except for myself. One night I noticed a light shining from a distance, and when I went up to investigate, I realized the light was coming from the chintz room. Sure enough, the lights had been turned on in that room. Since I had been the only one in the house and hadn't turned them on, there was no natural explanation for it."

I suddenly recalled that Ingrid had "gotten" the name Margaret when we had first entered the chintz room. Certainly Marmie and Margaret were close enough.

When we had first entered the house, I had asked Virginia Cloud to observe what she could, psychically speaking, and to make notes of her impressions. She too had a very strong impression in the chintz room of a woman named Louise, which could have been Lewis. She "saw" her as a woman with white hair and blue eyes, wearing a kind of filmy nightgown, possibly with a cap on her head, and felt that she had lived quite a long time ago. Virginia senses that the woman had some anxiety about another person *whom she also felt present in the room.* The other person Virginia thought was a very vital individual, and she "got" the name Henry or Alexander. Local tradition had had it that a restless spirit from another century lived on in the patrician rooms of Castalia. Is it a Revolutionary wraith, or indeed Mrs. Lewis, waiting for her beloved son to return from the hunt?

As we were about to leave, I noticed a book on the table in the library downstairs. It was *A Pride of Lions,* by Lately Thomas. The book deals with the life of a local celebrity, John Armstrong Chanler. When Ingrid saw it, she let out a little cry. The book seemed to have been placed there, as if to greet her. You see, it was Ingrid who had designed the jacket for it.

The Farm was a most unlikely name for one of Charlottesville's oldest buildings. Actually, it was a handsome two-story brick house, with a prominent fireplace on one end. The downstairs was then divided into two rooms—a front room very much the way it was in colonial days, and a back room then used by the owner, the postmaster of Charlottesville, as a kind of storage room. Upstairs were two bedrooms. The house stood in a tree studded lot right in the very center of Charlottesville. A little to the left of the house, the postmaster pointed out the spot where the old Kings Highway used to go through. It was here that Ingrid had felt the vibration of many men passing by.

On the outside of The Farm, a simple plaque reminds visitors that this was one of the most historical spots in the area. Carefully avoiding any opportunity for my mediumistic friend to see that plaque, Horace Burr, Virginia Cloud, Ingrid, and I arrived at The Farm at three o'clock in the afternoon and immediately proceeded to the main room downstairs, where

Ingrid stood transfixed in front of the colonial fireplace. To her, the little house looked like any other pre-colonial stone building; there was nothing to indicate that it had been of any significance in the past. As Ingrid stared at the fireplace, another strange thing happened. Almost simultaneously and frequently complementing one another, she and I got impressions from the past, rapidly, as it were; we both said whatever came to our minds.

"I'm getting something about sickness in this room," Ingrid said, while I heard myself say, "I get the feeling of people with long rifles, shooting from the upper story. They are wearing gray jackets and light colored pants, and the rifles are very long. This was in the direction away from the fireplace." Both of us said that men were making plans in the house at one time, and that it had to do with the defense of the building.

"I have the feeling that wounded people are being brought in right down here," Ingrid said. "I get the name Langdon or Langley and the name Nat." She walked around the room and then returned to her position near the fireplace. "I think the people with the light-colored breeches and the brown waistcoats and the long rifles are watching the road nearby for someone to come up that road. This was like a blockhouse, and there was some great anxiety about someone on his way up here. This was a last-ditch defense; there are perhaps five or six men, and they are militia men. I get the feeling of them lying on their stomachs upstairs with those huge rifles pointing with their long barrels and bayonets on top of them. The bullets are homemade, and it is the middle of the night. And then I get the feeling of a skirmish."

"It is like a flank," I said, feeling my way through an indefinite something in the air. "Someone is coming from the *wrong direction* to defend it. They should be coming this way, but they're coming the other way. They are coming up rather than down, and this is a terrible catastrophe for the defenders. I think if they get through, then it is all over."

I asked Virginia Cloud whether she had felt anything in the place. "I had a feeling of sickness here, as if it might be a hospital. I see Redcoats, Tories."

I turned to Horace Burr, asking him to comment on our observations. He seemed plainly delighted. "Well, I thought the most amazing thing that you said was this kind of replay of a group of armed forces, a flank, because there was a very interesting little maneuver that happened down the road, an attempt to cut off the main body of the armed forces coming here. The attempt went awry, though. The American troops were entrenched along the road here, expecting the British to come *this* way. Unfortunately, they came the *other* way, so the British did take Charlottesville for one night. This is a very little known fact of history, and I'm sure you wouldn't have been aware of it. What you said was so interesting because it was one of those little events that are enormously important but did not become generally known because the stratagem didn't work."

"What about the defense outpost here and the men with their rifles upstairs? Do they make any sense?"

"Yes, indeed. From upstairs you could see where this flank should have been down the road, and so they probably were up there looking out for the oncoming troops."

"What about their dress?"

"Of course, they were all colonial, not professional soldiers."

"What about the name Nat?"

"This house was owned at the time by Nicholas Merriweather Lewis. He was a colonel and George Washington's aide. Nat was a colonial nickname for Nicholas."

"What about sick people in here?"

"This was an important center, and the owner's wife, Mary Walker Lewis, was well known for her interest in the public and public affairs. Her father owned Castle Hill. She and her husband were first cousins, both descended from the original Nicholas Merriweather, who had come here from Wales via Jamestown."

Why had Ingrid been so fascinated by the fireplace and the area immediately before it? Although she couldn't pinpoint it in so many words, she insisted that something terribly important had taken place in that very room. To be sure, no ghost had stayed behind in The Farm. But an indelible imprint of an important link with the past was indeed still alive in the atmosphere of the little house.

It was on June 14, 1781, that Colonel Banastre Tarleton, the British commander, had been seen by John Jouett, who then took his famous ride to warn Jefferson and the legislature of the approaching British. About that, anon. When Tarleton finally got to Charlottesville late the same day, proceeding along the old Kings Highway and destroying several wagonloads of Continental supplies on the way, he thwarted the carefully laid plans of the defenders of Charlottesville, two hundred men to whom the defense of the village had been entrusted. They had been planning an ambush in the gorge below Monticello. Captain John Marson, in command of the detachment, was disappointed, but there was nothing to be done. As Tarleton entered Charlottesville, he saw The Farm, with Mrs. Lewis standing at the door, far more curious than frightened. "I think maybe I'll stay here," Tarleton is quoted as saying, and decided to make The Farm his headquarters for the night. Mrs. Lewis had heard all sorts of stories about the handsome Tarleton. The Colonel was twenty-seven and very courteous. "Madam, you dwelt in a little paradise," she quoted him in her diary.

Tarleton spent the night in front of the fireplace which had so attracted Ingrid, leaving the rest of the house to Mrs. Lewis, whose husband was away with the Continental Army.

He spent the night wrapped in his greatcoat, in a chair which once stood in front of the fireplace but which was taken to Carrsgrove, the home of Horace Burr, several years ago.

It had been an unforgettable day, as Horace Burr put it, and the only night Tarleton spent in the area. Evidently the imprint of the expected but never realized ambush and the feelings of the men lying in wait for their feared foe had been left so strongly in the atmosphere of the house that Ingrid and, to some extent, I were able to tune in on it and reconstruct it.

What can one possibly say about Carrsgrove that the owners, Horace and Helen Burr, direct descendants of Aaron Burr, have not said at one time or another, either in person or in print? Carrsgrove was their home, and they lived in it happily and with great style. But it was more than just a home; it was a landmark of great importance, meticulously maintained by Burr and gradually turned into a personal museum. Where else could you find a Gainsborough, a Hogarth portrait of the young King George III, and dozens upon dozens of fine paintings and art works of the seventeenth and eighteenth centuries? Where else could you find a complete blend of antiquities and today's way of life, a little garden with a terra cotta statuette, and, above all, so many important pieces of furniture directly associated with the American Revolution? Not only was Professor Burr the foremost art authority in Albemarle County, as the area is now called, but he can tell you within a fraction of a second who was married to whom two hundred years ago, who their children were, and who they married in turn; his genealogical knowledge was absolutely fascinating, if not frightening. And, all those whose births Horace Burr knows so intimately are the right kind of people, from the Virginia horse country's point of view—the old families. The Randolphs, the Carrs, the Merriweathers, the Lewises, and last but certainly not least, the Burrs.

When I visited the house for the first time in 1964, I was already overwhelmed by its historical atmosphere. People have lived continuously on the spot where Carrsgrove then stands, but the stone house was erected in 1748 by a certain David Reese. This was fourteen years before an Act of Assembly established the town to be called Charlottesville, in honor of Princess Charlotte of Mecklenburg-Strelitz, the wife of the new king, George III. From the Reese family the house passed into the Maury family.

A rising young lieutenant of only twenty years of age by the name of James Monroe, who had been with General Washington at Trenton, visited the house many times during the early years of the Revolutionary War. It was here on April 21, 1779, that the citizens of Albemarle County signed their own "Declaration of Independence." In 1787 the house passed into the hands of Mr. and Mrs. Hudson Martin, probably the first citizens of Charlottesville, except for Thomas Jefferson and the leaders of the Revolutionary War. Martin was George Washington's nephew and Mrs. Martin the daughter of Colonel Nicholas Merriweather Lewis, owner of The Farm in town. Later the house attracted the attention of James Monroe's brother, Joseph Jones Monroe, who purchased it in 1797. Fortunately, James Dinsmore, the famous architect, was then at work at Monticello, the home of Thomas Jefferson, and he was persuaded to design the mantelpiece of the fireplace at Carrsgrove as well.

In 1799 James Monroe was elected governor of Virginia, and the following year he decided to buy Carrsgrove from his brother. For the next nine years Carrsgrove was the home of James Monroe, who was later to become President of the United States. His granite bust done from life then stands in the garden of Carrsgrove.

But Monroe was not the only great American who left his imprint in the atmosphere of Carrsgrove. In 1824, when

Lafayette visited Charlottesville, a party was given in his honor at the house. During the War between the States, the infamous General George A. Custer made the house his head-quarters, renaming it Piedmont, the name often given to that part of Virginia. Some alterations were made in 1896 by the then owner, Price Maury, who united the original stone house with two other buildings which were already standing in 1790. The Burrs acquired the house in 1955.

It had been decided to spend the late morning of our second day in Charlottesville at the Burr house, culminating in a luncheon. Naturally, Ingrid knew nothing whatsoever about the house, and during the television interview I gave to the crew from Richmond I made sure that she did not have a chance to speak to anyone about it. Horace Burr thought we should try the library first, since the downstairs front portion of the house was in the oldest section. He was curious to see what Ingrid might discover in the beautifully appointed library, which would have done any English manor house proud.

It was quiet all around us when we entered the library. As I did so, I felt a strange chill traveling down my spine for which there seemed to be no rational explanation. I had no foreknowledge of any ghostly manifestations in that part of the house, and to the best of my knowledge, the library was simply that. When I remarked upon it, Ingrid cut in to say that she too felt an unusual chill. "There is a lot of malice here, not toward anyone in this house, but there is a plan to execute someone."

I requested that she seat herself in a comfortable chair in the library and try for the semitrance state in which the deeper layers of consciousness might be contacted. After a few moments, Ingrid continued. "I think there are three men, and they are making plans to kill one person in an ambush. This had to do with politics, and we are somewhere in the 1730s or

1740s. *I can hear them talk around the fireplace.* The room was very tiny, not too much furniture in it. The floor was bare. I have a feeling they are killing this person unjustly."

I noticed how Horace Burr was hanging on every word coming from her lips. "Why do they want to kill him?" I asked.

"He is a landowner. It has something to do with importing. They have a private grudge against him."

"Where is this ambush to take place?"

"About five or six miles from here. They're going to shoot him on his way home."

"Do they succeed?"

"Yes."

"Are they ever found out?"

"No." She added that the body was later discovered; it was not a presence she felt, but an imprint from the past.

"What was the explanation given for his death?"

"They said it was a robbery."

"Is there anything else you can find out about this man or the plot?"

"The man is a tradesman, but he is also interested in political office. Like a representative or a seat in the government."

"Can you catch his name?"

"He belongs to a prominent family. Something beginning with A."

Since Ingrid indicated that she could not get any more about the room, I turned to Horace Burr for verification of the material we had just heard.

"I know the family this concerns," he replied, "and since I have the invoice of what was in the house at that time, I know she is correct about the furniture."

"What about this ambush?"

"The builder of this house, David Reese, died only three years after he had moved in. It was a sudden and seemingly unexplained death. Just what happened to this man and why he died after such a short time, all these things make you kind of wonder."

"What about his running for the Assembly?"

"Not to my knowledge. However, a somewhat later owner, Joseph Jones Monroe, did sit in the House of Burgesses."

We decided to go to the upper floor. Walking up the narrow staircase, Ingrid found her way directly to a small bedroom on the other side of the house. I had written about this room in 1965, but Ingrid had no idea where she was or what the room meant to anyone. In addition to a beautiful sixteenth-century bed, there was a hand-carved wooden chair in a prominent position—so prominent, in fact, that Ingrid could not help but sit down in it. I asked Ingrid to tell us about any impressions she might have about the room or the chair. Immediately she said, "I sense a tragedy here, and I think it involves a child."

"Oh, God," Burr exclaimed involuntarily. "Please go on."

"I think that someone may have sat in this chair and watched a child die or that something awful happened. I think it was a boy not older than seven. A disease that couldn't be treated. A lingering death. Something awful, like scarlet fever or cholera."

"What happened to the mother?"

"I sense that it is a woman's presence here trying to hold on to the life of a young child. She is alone somehow. The child is all she has. I think this was her home."

"Do you feel her presence here too?"

"Yes, but I sense the child very strongly. I think this was a child's room. The woman does everything she can with doctors, but nothing can be done. The child is delirious for a long time."

Since I knew from my own recollections of Carrsgrove and from the look Horace Burr gave me while Ingrid was speaking that she had accurately retold the story of the haunting in the room, I decided to test her in relation to the chair in which she was sitting. I pointed out a similar chair on the other side of the room. Evidently, they were a pair, both extremely well carved and at least two hundred or two hundred fifty years old. Ingrid insisted that her feelings concerned not an imprint from the past but an actual presence, something we usually call a ghost. As she was speaking, we all noticed a chandelier move considerably of its own volition. Later, after we had completed the session, we tried unsuccessfully to cause it to move by walking up and down the stairs, walking around the room itself, or doing whatever we could to create vibrations. The chandelier remained immobile.

But Ingrid could not get anything further about the chair. Somehow the overwhelming presence of the woman and the child canceled out any less potent impressions the chair might have carried. I turned to Horace Burr and asked him, as usual, for comments.

"Ingrid was very close to the tragedy which occurred here," he began. "The woman was sitting in this chair, and three feet from it is the spot where she killed herself. It was about her child, which she thought was hopelessly sick. As you know, Hans, we heard her sobbing voice many years after her death and thus discovered the tragedy which had occurred here many years before. But these could not be the chairs she sat in; they came later. The area, however, is correct. Incidentally, these are the oldest documented man-made things in America; they came over from Wales, first to Jamestown, and then to this area. These are the chairs that used to be in The Farm, and in one of them General Banastre Tarleton spent the night wrapped in his cloak in 1781. Incidentally, the unfortunate woman whose presence Ingrid felt here took poison because she felt the child would be deformed. Her dying gasps were heard at the other end of the hall, across the stairwell into the master bedroom, where her father was sleeping, and as he stepped out into the hall and heard her gasps, she died. The child however, grew up to be a perfectly normal and beautiful young woman."

Which proves that a powerful ghostly manifestation from the present time could very well overcome the rambling, though pungent, thoughts of an eighteenth-century British general, especially if he, as Tarleton did, enjoyed the hospitality of his Revolutionary "enemies" far more than was customary under the circumstances.

DOWN IN FLORIDA

*D*r. Rebekah Parker was a long-time resident of Fort Myers. She had taken the occult matter-of-factly all her life, neither being afraid nor shying away from it because of her position. That was because she had had experiences herself. Experiences that can't be explained on so-called rational grounds. Many years ago she was in charge of a children's home in another state. When she took the position she was assigned a certain room. The room seemed cheerful enough at first. Soon, however, she realized that there was something terribly wrong with it. Almost from the start of her residence there she would awake around three o'clock in the morning with the definite impression that someone was trying to choke her. The strange sensation was not of her own doing, she realized; there was nothing physically wrong with her. While she considered asking for another room and at the same time dismissing such a request as outlandish and probably out of place, she also realized that something had to be done about the situation.

One day the grandmother of one of the children under her care called on her and engaged her in conversation. Although the doctor had not brought up the subject, somehow the conversation veered toward the occult. The lady avowed freely that she was psychic. Dr. Parker decided she should test the lady's abilities and she asked her whether she could tell her anything about the room they were in. The lady nodded and closed her eyes and leaned back in the chair. Almost instantly the woman went through the movements of someone being choked to death. In front of the doctor's surprised eyes the woman turned purple in the face and had all she could do to break the spell which had suddenly come on her for no apparent physical or logical reason. As soon as she had regained control over herself she explained what had happened. A bride of six months had been choked to death by her husband in that very room.

Dr. Parker demanded proof and details. Again the lady medium closed her eyes and came up with names and dates. How she could have known so much about the house was a mystery, since she had not been in it before. "What shall I do about this?" the doctor asked. "The husband is earthbound," the lady medium said and suggested that the doctor pray for him. Prayer might very well release him. The doctor nodded and thanked the lady for her help. The following night she prayed in earnest until three o'clock. She had prepared herself for this, determined to rid her room once and for all from its evil connotations. At the stroke of three a figure appeared before her. It was a male wearing what seemed like a long nightshirt and a stocking cap on his head. The doctor did not panic but remained in her bed praying. She observed how the figure passed through the open door and walked down the stairs in his bare feet. She could plainly hear the noise of the feet touching the floor. Then she heard him open the front door and disappear into the rose garden in back of the house. Never again did Dr. Parker have the choking experience from that moment on.

She asked the lady who had given her the key to the psychic experiences in the room to return to the home to inform her of her own experiences. Was the unhappy man really gone? Again the medium leaned back and closed her eyes. She could still see him in the garden at night, she explained, but he was no longer earthbound and could leave at will.

Mrs. A. lived at West Panama City Beach, Florida. She was a lady in her middle years with grown children and came from a family where ESP experiences had been frequent. Probably the most unusual experience she had had happened one day in 1965 when she lived in Kenner, Louisiana. She was waiting for the bus with her four-year-old son when suddenly she felt herself traveling at great speed in the direction of the house of a church member whom she knew and who lived about seven miles away from her. She could see the landscape flying by as if she were traveling on a very fast bus. She was nearly there when she turned around and looked back toward where she had come from. At that point she felt her four-year-old pull her leg, saying, "Mommy, the bus is coming." She found herself back at the bus stop. She did not experience any sensation of riding back to the bus stop. One moment she was near a friend's house, the next moment back at the bus stop. She felt somewhat odd but otherwise all right.

All week long she tried to puzzle out her strange experience. About a week after the occurrence had taken place she ran into a friend by the name of Helen K. Agitated, her friend stopped her on the street. "Hey," she said. "Are you haunting me?" Mrs. A. demanded to know what this was all about. Patiently Helen K.explained that she had been in her trailer home a week before when she had seen her standing outside looking in. Immediately she had told her husband that they were going to have a visitor and to put his shirt back on, for it had been a very warm evening. When she turned around and looked out the window the apparition of her friend was gone. She ran outside to look, assuming that her friend had just wandered off for a moment and would enter the house almost immediately, but there was no one around. Mrs. A. demanded to know what she had looked like, and what kind of clothes she was wearing at the time. Without a moment's hesitation Helen Kenner answered, "A pink blouse and a blue skirt."

Mrs. A. blanched. The description of her dress was entirely correct. Moreover, she had made that pink print blouse herself, had never worn it before, and thus her friend could not have seen it on a prior occasion.

Carolyn M. came from Miami, Florida, though when we spoke, she was living in Ohio. She had had ESP experiences all her life, but the experience that shook her up the most happened to her not long before our speaking. For several nights she dreamed an identical dream. In this dream a casual friend of hers whom we shall refer to as Mrs. B. called her and asked her to come to her house. In the dream Carolyn went to her friend's house and looked at a cold spot in the den. Her friend had asked her to come over and help her figure out why a certain spot was always so cold. The spot, her friend explained, was so cold she could not even put a chair into it. Next Carolyn saw herself walking up to a patio with sliding doors and had the feeling of gravel under her feet. Then she stepped up one step into a den and could plainly see the wooden panels. Then her friend showed her the cold spot and she reached out and felt the cold air herself. Suddenly she was drawn into that cold spot and felt herself coming out of her own body as if someone else were trying to take over her body. Immediately she knew that it was a young woman and that she was crying very hard. The entity said that she did not know where she was and kept calling for someone named Capp, over and over calling for Capp to help her. The words Carolyn heard in her dream were "Capp, Capp, please come and help me. I am lost. It is dark and I cannot see any more. Please, Capp. Please come and help me." Still in the dream, she heard herself ask the woman's name and was told that it was Elaine or something close to that.

At that point the dream ended abruptly and Carolyn M. found herself back in her own bed sitting up shaking and crying. She didn't feel that she had dreamed this but somehow that it had happened to her in reality. The impression was so strong it didn't leave her for days. Finally, after thinking it over, she decided to check on it. She hesitated to call her friend, a casual acquaintance, out of fear of being ridiculed, but she kept on having the same dream over and over. Finally it got to be too much and she decided to telephone the lady in question. Mrs. B. listened quietly as Carolyn M. told her, in a haunting voice, what she had dreamed. When she had finished there was a moment of silence on the other end of the line.

Then Mrs. B. said that she did have a cold spot in her den and that the description given by Carolyn was entirely correct, yet Carolyn M. had never been to Mrs. B.'s house and had no way of knowing what it looked like. As for the sobbing woman Elaine, or something close to that, and for her crying out for Capp, Mrs. B. had an answer for that too. Capp was her husband's uncle. He had been married to a woman named Ellen who had died suddenly two months before.

The ways of the unseen are strange at times. Someone "out there" had evidently decided to have Carolyn serve as a go-between bridging the gulf between a distraught and confused spirit and a husband who would want to know that his wife was still alive in another dimension.

LITTLE MAMA

$\mathcal{M}$ary's mother was a special kind of woman. She had lived with the psychic for so long it had become part of her everyday nature and she took her premonitions and psychic hunches in her stride.

Her family got so used to mother's foretelling every major event affecting them, they were surprised to find other families did not have such a mother. On one occasion the family had assembled and decided to ask mother to read cards once again. Although she had done so many times before, this time she agreed very reluctantly. When the cards had been "thrown," both Mary—who knew a thing or two about the cards also—and her mother knew why. Mother's death and the difficulties that would follow it were in the cards. Within a year, all that Mother had said about her own demise came to pass, but it wasn't the end of mother.

A week after her funeral, a cousin of Mary's by the name of Carrie, was relaxing on her sofa watching television, when her aunt—Mary's mother—stood before her with a smile. Pointing at herself and her radiant countenance, she said, "I'm not dead, see?"

But far from reassuring cousin Carrie, it threw her into a state of shock. Immediately she telephoned another cousin and inquired if her aunt was really dead.

"Indeed she is," the cousin assured her, "We buried her last week." With that, Carrie went back to her sofa, sure she must have dreamed the whole thing. But a moment later, her aunt reappeared, repeating the same message.

Growing up with that kind of psychic awareness made Mary somewhat more tolerant towards the psychic and unknown than other people, but it did not cause her to be unduly interested in the subject either, and she never looked for the thrills of séances, the occult, and the mystic. This was just as well as she married a doctor who had little use for "such foolishness." They had two children, both girls, but after eighteen years of marriage, they broke up and the doctor moved out, leaving the two girls with their mother. Both were then teen-agers and turned out to be bright, knowledgeable youngsters, well-liked in the neighborhood.

Mary was a petite, quiet-looking woman with a slight Southern accent, who tended to be conservative in dress and manner. Even her "little talent" of being able to read cards for her friends was an embarrassment to her: her Methodist religion was a serious matter with her and she really did not want any truck with the occult.

On the day of Halloween, 1962, she and her girls moved into an attractive eighteen-year-old house in Atlanta. The house was in a quiet, suburban neighborhood, and all around were other small homes in little garden plots of the kind that were the backbone of a residential community all over America in those days. Not far from the house ran the tracks of the railroad, then used only for freight, and old Fort McPherson was a short walk away. This may or may not be of importance in the story I am about to tell, but one of the bloodier actions of the Civil War was fought in that valley, on the very ground the house then stood on.

The house was actually on two levels; at street level there was a large living room which one entered first when coming in from the front. There were three bedrooms around it, and, on the right side of the house, a den leading into the kitchen. From one of the bedrooms there was a stairwell, secured by an iron railing, leading into the basement. There was a closet underneath the stairs. In back of the house, there was a large patio and outside stairs also leading into the basement.

The lower level was only partially finished. The rear third was left open for an additional room, and the front third was a dirt area containing the furnace, and slanted toward the front of the house. Only the right-hand third of the basement area was actually used by the family. A laundry room occupied most of the space and a wall sealed it off from the undeveloped dirt area.

Everything about the house was cozy and warm. The furniture was pleasant and functional and if it weren't for the events following their move, Mary and her daughters would be just another genteel Southern family whose man had left, but who carried on nonetheless properly and adequately. Mary had been a topnotch secretary for many years and was respected in the community.

Immediately after they had moved in and gotten settled, Mary knew there was something odd about the house. She woke up in the middle of the night and sat bolt upright in bed: someone was digging downstairs!

Impossible, she thought, but the noise persisted night after night. She wondered whether her neighbors weren't perhaps putting in a water pipe. The sound emanated from beneath the stairs in her bedroom, directly underneath which was the basement.

After a while, she decided she had to know what was behind that scraping, digging sound. She left her bed and went downstairs to see if she could find any reason for the sound. There was nothing. No rats or mice. No freshly turned up dirt either inside or outside the house. The neighbors weren't doing any digging, either. Then, just as suddenly as it had started, the digging stopped. Mary was ready to sigh with relief and hoped that her fears of the house had been unfounded.

But her joys were premature. Night after night, at exactly 2 A.M. she and her daughters heard the sound of someone trying to break into the house, but there was never anyone there, and after they had lost a lot of sleep, they called the police. When the police failed to turn up any clues, Mary installed heavy bolts inside the front and rear doors. That very day she returned from an errand to an empty house and found the heavy bolts of the back door ripped away—from the inside!

When Mary moved into the house, she had been on the verge of a nervous breakdown due to her unhappy marriage. When the phenomena started, she was afraid to discuss them with anyone, even her own girls, out of fear that word would get back to her estranged husband and she would be held mentally deficient. Soon her usual afternoon naps were disturbed by an unseen person entering the house, walking through it as if he or she knew it well, and sometimes even running the water or flushing the toilet. Even the bolted doors did not stop this incursion. Often, when she was doing her laundry in the basement, she would clearly hear footsteps over her head, then the sound of drawers being opened and shut, and water being run. She tried to change her hour of rest to thwart the intruder but no matter how she changed it, the unseen presence found her out and disturbed her rest. It was almost as if someone knew what went on in her mind, someone *inside* the house!

Hiding her fears from her daughters did not work, either. Katie, bright girl that she was, seemed unduly frightened and finally her mother questioned her. That was when the two women realized they had both heard and experienced the same unearthly things. Moreover, Katie had felt a pair of hands upon her during the night when she knew she was alone in the room.

On one occasion, Mary saw a pair of men's slippers before her, and a pair of feet in them, but no other part of the body. Thinking someone had come in to kill her, she was frozen with fear. After a while, which to her seemed eternity, the materialization faded. As soon as she could, she gathered her things and ran to her mother's house.

In plain daylight, such heavy objects as books began to disappear, or reappear at other places and it seemed as if someone were playing a cat and mouse game with them. But who, and why?

When the older girl, then eighteen, came back from school, she did not realize what her mother and sister had gone through. So it was with considerable surprise that she heard someone using a typewriter in the basement when they all knew that there was no one there, and no typewriter.

With a grim sense of humor, Katie explained to her sister that it was "only" a ghost!

Katie had gotten used to the presence in the house. Of course she had no idea that some of the power for the manifestation might come from her, being at the age when poltergeist phenomena are possible. One night she was awakened from heavy sleep by that certain feeling that she was not alone in the room. She was right. There, by her bedside, stood a shadowy figure. Her mother was in the other bedroom, and Katie actually slept in what had been her mother's room, the most haunted part of the house. While the figure vanished, there were other tangible proofs of a presence. Someone was forever pulling Mary's blanket off her as if to rouse her. Katie was luckier. Her blanket was only pulled once in the years they occupied the house. Perhaps the ghost was nonplused by Katie's attitude, which then alternated between contained fear and refusal to be upset by the unseen intruder.

Even Christopher, their cat, became terrified and refused to go outside or to the basement "to do his business," as Katie would call it, unless accompanied by one of them.

Soon Mary and her daughters realized that they weren't dealing with one ghost alone. On several occasions, the quick footsteps of a child were heard by them, along with the heavier footsteps of an adult. Someone seemed to be calling out to them by name. In January of 1968, when they had learned to live with the dreaded powers in the house, Mary awoke to the sound of music, faintly coming from the area of the kitchen ventilator. She investigated but found neither a radio playing nor any reason for this music to be heard. So she returned to bed and tried to ignore it. Just then two sets of footfalls reached her ears through the covers. One set of feet turned toward Katie's room, while the other pair of feet came right toward her bed! There they stopped abruptly. Something icy then seemed to touch her chest. She screamed and jumped from her bed. Apparently this broke the attack and she was able to look into Katie's room. But her daughter was fast asleep.

A peculiar smell then caught her attention, as she returned once more to her own room. It seemed like a mixture of oil, gasoline and dirt and reminded her of some of the filling stations she had bought gas in.

Still critical of her faculties, Mary wanted to make sure she was neither dreaming nor imagining the whole incident.

Prior to her secretarial work, she had been working for a group of psychologists and knew the elementary precautions one must take if one wants to be sure of one's facts. But she was fully awake and had not dreamed it.

About this time Mary began to wonder about the unseen—or, rather, *generally* unseen—presences in the house. How were they, first of all, able to manifest themselves in so forceful a manner. She knew enough about the psychic to realize that someone had to be the medium, but she did not think it was she, at least not alone. Then one night she had her answer. She awakened to the sound of a voice coming from Katie's room. A female voice was saying a phrase over and over again, and Katie was answering by repeating it. As Mary strained her ears, she could clearly hear it. "Golden sand," the voice said in a sweet, kindly voice and "Golden sand," Katie replied in a childish voice totally different from her adult, normal tone. Then she heard Katie clap her hands and say, "Now what can I do?"

By then Mary had tiptoed over to Katie's room and was peeking inside. To her surprise, Katie was fast asleep in bed. She woke the girl and told her to come into her own room. Puzzled and half asleep, Katie obeyed and spent the rest of the night with her mother. The following morning, Mary questioned her about the phrase "Golden sand." Katie did not recall having spoken during the night, but the phrase did seem vaguely familiar to her.

As the days wore on, Katie recalled and finally discussed with her mother an "experiment" she had undertaken a year before, during the Christmas holidays. The two women and a friend had decided to while away the evening with a homemade ouija board more for fun than because of a desire to stir anything psychic into greater activity. Neither of the two women particularly "believed in" ouija boards, but they were curious.

What developed was a communication, allegedly from the ghostly intruders.

A girl by the name of Cathy claimed to have been murdered by her own brother, who lived with her mother and herself on the plot of land adjoining the house. There was an insane stepfather, too, and it was his restless ghost that did the walking, the communicator claimed, along with her mother and herself. The date given was 1949. The spot where the communicator claimed to have been buried was indeed the area where most of the noises, such as the nocturnal "digging" had been heard. But can one trust information obtained from a ouija board? Katie was not too convinced and put little stock into the information at first. One day she saw a fortyish woman "out of the corner of her eye" and felt someone fondling her hair. Was the ghostly woman kind to her because she reminded her of her own unfortunate daughter? Or was Katie's imagination running away with her?

But soon, Mary also became aware of the "Little Mama" as they came to call her. Her own mediumship had evidently gotten to the surface under the attacks of the psychic around her.

Relaxing finally, in an effort to find out what the ghost wanted with her, Mary was able to "hear" with her inner ear the psychic message sent to her from the woman, over and over again.

"I need your help to cross the stream!"

Did she mean she did not know how to cut herself loose from the house and go over to the Other Side? Very likely, Mary thought, but what could she do to help?

Three days later, while she was having her afternoon nap, she heard someone come through the front door. She sat up and yelled at the unseen presence to go away and leave her alone.

A man's gruff voice replied, "She can see me!" But Mary saw no one. A few hours later she heard the then familiar female voice whisper in her ear, "I need your help!"

"Where are you?" Mary said aloud.

"In the basement . . . in the dirt . . ."

Mary went downstairs, unafraid then , and turned on all lights. All was quiet then.

It occurred to her that the evil one, the man, was trying to harass them, while the "Little Mama" was actually attempting to protect them, as best she could.

An emotional relationship resulted from this belief on Mary's part, and she was able to summon Little Mama at will then , or so she thought. She felt her presence at times but never got to actually see her. But the friendlier she got with the female ghost the more threatening the male wraith seemed to get. At one point Mary was sure he was trying to kill her and burn the house down while they were asleep.

By then there was no longer any question that their house was indeed haunted—all they wanted to know was how to get rid of their unwanted guests. Had Mary alone experienced these things, perhaps not much would have come of it, but her girls also felt them and especially Katie, who had had physical contact with unseen hands. Something had to be done or their sanity wouldn't be worth a cent. All the while the voices kept getting louder and bolder and the footsteps more frequent.

Mary felt a "man under the bed with a knife" and the ringing in her ears that preceded actual voices kept getting more frequent each day.

If they were hallucinating all this to make themselves suffer, what was the point? Consciously, Mary wanted nothing more than peace and quiet, and unconsciously, at the very worst, she had deep-seated emotional disappointments, but hardly a desire to hurt herself. Katie's exuberant life force was hardly a hideout for repressed hostilities and her level-headed attitude towards the phenomena at this point indicated no hidden motives for attention: someone as beautiful as she was scarcely needed more attention: both adults and her own teenage friends liked her and made her one of the most popular girls in the community.

And yet, the phenomena in the house were rising in a steady crescendo that could lead only to disaster.

At this point, Mary found her religion once more. Turning to Jesus as a means of driving out "the demons," she managed to hold on by the sheer willpower of her Biblical faith. Not so for the young girls, but their involvement with the psychic was far less total than their mother's.

"These creatures are trying to get into bed with me," Mary complained with a feeling of horror.

She could take it no longer and voluntarily checked herself into the nearest hospital.

After a week and total rest away from the disturbances, she felt stronger again and was ready to face the problem once more. She returned home, but continued her treatments at the hospital as an outpatient.

Then she invited a group of people interested in psychic research to try to exorcise the presences in her home.

The group, headed by a distinguished metaphysician, came and performed the ancient rituals of "casting out the demons," demons meaning not devils but deranged human spirits.

It didn't help very much or for very long, though. The Little Mama no longer communicated with Mary. Instead, the harsh, male voice commanded her to do things, and she obeyed. It dawned on Mary that her mediumship had opened her up to such incursions and there was little she could do to stop them.

She fought, feebly, but was unable to keep herself from doing the unseen tormentor's bidding.

"Get up," he would command, and the voice resounded loudly in her mind, "Get up and do something." So she finally fought her sleepy condition and washed some dishes.

Sleeping pills made it possible for her to find some rest, but the ghostly presences came back as soon as she opened her eyes again.

"I need you," she heard a female voice plead and realized that Little Mama had finally broken through again, "I need you, come to the basement. . . ."

And then, somehow, the voices faded. Whether the work done by the local psychics had loosened the hold the entities had had over Mary and the house, or whether the ghosts simply got bored with it all, no one can say for sure.

But Mary got her strength back and her reason and Katie

turned once more into a good-looking, healthy youngster more concerned with the next dance than with psychic phenomena.

Perhaps Mary's visits to the basement, her genuine affection for the unfortunate woman spirit, had somehow helped her across that stream she had been unable to cross by herself. Once gone, the man's presence would no longer be emotionally motivated.

As the days grew into months, and the months into years, the whole terrible period of their possession becomes less and less real to Mary and her daughters and perhaps that, too, was as it should be, for the line between reality and fantasy was very faint indeed at times, almost as faint as a ghost finally giving up his hold upon his earthly memories and tragedies. The little house by the railroad track has been quiet and pleasant ever since.

LOUISIANA GHOSTS

*J*ean Hatton came from a family in which the psychic had been in evidence for many generations. Precognitive dreams, clairvoyance, foreknowledge of events or places have been rampant on her mother's side of the family, and even as a pre-teenager Jean had some ESP experiences. Around forty years of age then, she and her husband lived in the heart of New Orleans. She was a professional musician for a while and had taught music in high school. Her mother's family was Irish, Dutch, and Indian, while her father's side of the family came from Wales, England, and Ireland. Thus a predominance of Celtic elements in her background may be responsible for her readiness to accept the reality of psychic phenomena. At any rate, when she moved from her childhood home in San Antonio, Texas, to New Orleans she made friends with a married couple living on Decatur Street in the French Quarter. The very first time she tried to enter their apartment she almost tripped. She felt a kind of elastic force trying to keep her out as if she were not welcome. The house in which the couple's apartment was located was a very old house. That one and some of the adjoining ones were among the few that hadn't been destroyed in the fires so common in this part of town. At least two hundred years old, the house in question was one of the finest examples of colonial architecture.

Forcing her way through the invisible curtain, Jean then entered the apartment. She saw an old fireplace against one wall facing a bedroom door. The entrance was to the right. To the left were the living room and a long narrow room probably used as a pantry or wardrobe. The owner of the apartment tried to tell her that something very tragic had occurred in the apartment, but before he could do so Jean herself told him the story. How she could know this was as much a mystery to her as it was to her host. But she pointed at a clock and insisted that it would always stop at three o'clock in the morning because it was then that "something had happened." Before she knew what she was doing, Jean found herself standing by the fireplace looking at the clock. Then she turned toward the door, resting her hands on the mantelpiece. She seemed to be wearing a white gown with full sleeves, probably a nightgown. At this moment she clearly heard steps. A door was opened and through it came the "wrong man." The man she saw now clairvoyantly was tall, had unruly gray hair and a deep-set type face. He wore a silk hat and black cape. She knew then that the woman was trying to express herself through her; that she had been stabbed where she stood and had fallen in front of the fireplace.

At this moment she came out of her semi-trance. It was all she could get, but her host assured her that the impression was not fantasy. He explained that he had seen just such a woman walk at night, her bloody hands crossed on her breasts. Both he and his wife had frequently heard the footsteps of someone coming up the stairs to their third-floor apartment. One night when Sheri, the wife, was home alone playing old English folk songs on her guitar, she looked up and saw the two entities standing there in the door. She was not afraid so she kept on looking at them before they faded away.

It became clear to the owner of the apartment that something very drastic had occurred at a previous time. But they could not figure it out and learned to live with their spectral visitors. One day the husband was up in the attic, above their apartment, clearing up some flooring. To his horror he discovered two human skeletons underneath. Hastily closing the door to the attic behind him, he took the two skeletons and quietly buried them. He decided not to report the matter to the police after all since it might have been something that had occurred a long time ago and calling attention to it then might draw unfavorable publicity to himself and the house. From that moment the psychic phenomena stopped abruptly. But the owner of the apartment was not satisfied until he knew what had caused the two skeletons to be buried in so unusual a place as the attic of the apartment. He started to dig into the past of the house and asked questions around the area. As far as he could figure out, this was what happened. The woman in the nightgown had lived in the apartment, and once while she was waiting for her lover the door had opened and instead of her lover her husband had come through it. He had discovered the relationship and had come to kill her. After he had murdered her he in turn waited until the lover arrived and killed him too, then hid the bodies in the attic.

Silently the host handed Jean a knife to touch and psychometrize, that is to say, read from it what could be gleaned of its past. As if she had been handed a glowing piece of coal, she dropped it immediately. She could not touch it no matter how often she tried. The knife was an old knife of nondescript appearance, with a discolored blade, and of no particular merit. Almost hysterical, with sobs Jean assured her host that it was the knife that had been used to murder the woman. He nodded. He himself had found the blade among the bricks of the fireplace.

GHOSTS IN TEXAS

*W*hen Texas decided to join the union it had the option of becoming five separate states or remaining one large state. As we all know, the new state chose to be one state. If it was larger than states are supposed to be in a federal union, it also had a tendency to aim for bigger and better things. Not necessarily to accomplish them, but to try to interest other states and people in them. So it doesn't come as a great surprise that there were comparatively more psychic occurrences in Texas than there were in a smaller state. Also, its colorful history, during which the area changed hands several times, had contributed to the number of psychic incidents from the past. The psychic occurrences in Texas differ greatly in nature from hauntings in, let us say, the Carolinas or Virginia. In the latter, they were frequently connected with homesteads and very old houses. In Texas, the phenomena take on a more personal note and seem to be tied in with people rather than locations.

Elaine M. was a pleasant woman in her thirties living about 50 miles from Houston. On my last visit to that city I talked to her about two of the many strange experiences she had had. These two shook her up more than anything else that had happened to her and I began to see why.

The first event happened in the fall of 1957. Elaine and her husband had just received word that their two closest friends, Jack and Linda S., with one of their children, had died of asphyxiation in their home in Florida. Apparently Linda had been slated for brain surgery two weeks later and had not been able to face it. The death by gas of three people so close to her depressed Elaine very much. She and Linda had been very close, cared for each other and worried about each other's children. But after several months she began to come out of her depression. In January of 1958 Texas underwent an unusually hard cold spell. It was therefore necessary to use additional heaters, and it was the custom in Mr. and Mrs. M.'s home to leave the gas heat on all night. In the kitchen there was an ordinary open gas stove, but they kept the flame low, and since the windows were all locked there didn't seem to be any danger of any of the flames going out and causing gas to leak into the apartment.

One night, at two o'clock in the morning, Elaine felt herself waking up. Clearly as if she were standing next to her she heard her good friend Linda speak to her. "Elaine," the voice said, "get up and see about the boys." Elaine was terrified and fully awake then. As she was about to jump out of bed she smelled gas. She ran to the boys' room and found the gas jets wide open. In another five or ten minutes the gas would have caused an explosion from the other heaters. Quickly Elaine turned them off. At this moment she felt a cool moist cloud surround her and clearly heard her late friend Linda laugh and say, "I told you." For several days after this Elaine was upset over what had occurred. She was grateful to her late friend for having warned her but at the same time she did not easily accept the communication from the beyond. A few days had passed when she found herself discussing the entire matter on the telephone with a minister. Somehow the conversation drifted from the psychic occurrence to her late friend's personal life and the difficulties she had encountered in adjusting to the world in which she lived. As she was speaking so freely about Linda, being all by herself in the room, she happened to turn her head and saw the flame in the heater slowly die out as if someone had just turned it off, yet no one had been near it. At that point she felt a sense of acute anger and a presence beyond her own. Elaine started to cry into the telephone. Her minister friend urged her to hang up and run for it, but even that she was completely unable to do. She knew that her late friend had come to listen in on the conversation about her and that she resented it. A few moments later her minister friend and his wife came running into the apartment. At that point Elaine was able to let go of the telephone and fall to the floor. Linda was not heard from again. From that time on, Elaine regretted having gossiped about her late friend, especially in view of that friend's help on the previous occasion. She remembers the old adage "de mortibus nihil nisi bonum," meaning when you speak of the dead speak only of good things.

The other experience which Elaine could not forget occurred not long after the first one. She had an increasing feeling that one of her children would pass on soon. This went on for about a year and caused a mental condition which she found hard to cope with. Somehow she managed to live a normal life in spite of it. On April 2, 1958, she happened to be taking a dozen 4-H Club girls to a fabric shop to look for yard goods. It was 5:15 in the afternoon when she suddenly panicked. Without adequate explanation she rushed the girls in her care to the car and drove like a madwoman toward her home. One mile before she reached her home she passed an ambulance going in the opposite direction, and at that instant she knew that her four-year-old son Scott was already dead. She drove into her street, where her neighbors stood in groups crying and talking. Her fears were confirmed. Someone offered to drive her to the hospital. No one had yet told her exactly what had occurred. Later she learned that the boy had been alive but had died shortly after at the hospital. He had drowned. Apparently, she was told by her husband, he had jumped into a creek after their dog to rescue him. When she was told this, Elaine got very angry and did not wish to speak about it. Why were they all lying to her, she wondered, when she knew so much better what had actually happened. For the next three days she stayed in seclusion. Then the evening after her little boy's funeral she gathered up some of his toys and carried them across the street to some of his little friends. As she did so she suddenly knew that a little boy playmate of her son by the name of Warren had pushed her boy into the creek. Returning home, she confronted her husband with the explanation, and he had no choice but to confirm it. Several times later she felt her little boy's presence although she could not see him. She felt no unhappiness with the little spirit yet wondered whether she should tell him that he had passed on in case he was not aware of it. Then a year after his passing, in September, when he was to have started school she felt him very strongly. A school bus was passing the house when she suddenly heard her dead little boy say to her, "I want to go to school."

Without thinking about what she was doing, she heard herself reply, "But you can't, darling, you're dead." After that, all was quiet around Elaine's house. She hoped her little boy had found another school of his own in his new home.

Jeffrey O. was an electrical engineer by profession and because of his training not easily given to the acceptance of occult phenomena. He and his family moved into a newly built house on Sharp View Avenue in Houston on November 15,

1968. He was the first occupant of the house. His professional connection with a large computer company made it necessary for Mr. O. to travel frequently. At such times his wife was
alone with their two children. The chain of events which
made Mr. O. wonder about poltergeists in his new home
began with the sudden appearance of two large stuffed animals belonging to his three-year-old daughter. The animals
had been missing for two weeks and no amount of searching
had turned them up. Suddenly they reappeared in a most conspicuous place where they could not possibly have been over-
looked. While the O. family was still debating this phenomenon something else occurred. Mr. O. was out of town and his
wife and a fourteen-year-old baby-sitter spent the night in the
downstairs bedroom of the house with the two children.
While downstairs they heard a tremendous amount of walking and moving about upstairs. Immediately assuming that
someone had entered the house, they called the police. The
police came and found nothing amiss. As soon as the police
had left, the walking upstairs resumed. Mrs. O. and the sitter
were too frightened to do anything about it during the night,
but as soon as morning came they went directly into the children's bedroom upstairs. There they discovered that a table
with the boy's electric train on it had moved clear across his
large walk-in closet. No one had been upstairs during the
night, nor had any human agency made these changes in the
room. The following day Mr. O. returned from his trip. He
took the report less than seriously and teased his family about
it, but when he awoke the next morning he was not so sure of
the whole thing. In his daughter's room someone had taken
one shelf down from among the three shelves hanging on the
wall. All the small stuffed animals that had been on the shelf
were scattered around the room. Needless to add, the girl had
not done this, nor had anyone else been in the room during
that time. A few days later, Mr. O. had to leave town again for

271

a few days. Thoroughly frightened by now, his wife decided to ask two friends, two fourteen-year-old girls, to stay the night with her. Again they were awakened around two o'clock in the morning by the footsteps of someone walking upstairs. They also heard the boy's window being opened. Since they were all downstairs, including the kids, they decided to barricade themselves in the downstairs bedroom, forcing a heavy dresser in front of the door. Then they went to sleep with somewhat mixed feelings. When they awoke the next morning they discovered that the door to the bedroom was cracked about six inches across.

The following day Mr. O. returned. He listened with somewhat more concern to what had happened in his absence. His wife went to bed early because of a cold. He remained downstairs alone watching television until about 11:30 P.M. Everything was in its proper place. He locked up and went to bed. Awakening the next morning, he noticed that two candle holders and a flower arrangement had been taken off the mantel of the fireplace, along with a ceramic leopard from atop the television, and that all these objects were arranged perfectly on the fireplace. He had not done any such thing nor had anyone else been in the room who could have done this. No one, that is, of flesh and blood. He immediately checked every window in the house, every door and every chain lock; nothing had been tampered with. At this point Mr. O., despite his scientific training, became thoroughly convinced of the reality of the phenomena in his house. As if in response to his open-minded attitude toward the occurrences, they materialized then with greater frequency. An artificial weeping willow four feet high and rather heavy was moved six feet and lifted up to the first stair of the staircase. Mr. O.'s pool balls were scattered and hidden all over his poolroom as if they had been Easter eggs. A flower arrangement was removed from a dresser and found on the floor right next to it. All without the help of human hands. Their clock radio was switched on by itself three times in a way that was different from the time he and his wife would have set it. It was his custom to turn off all lights before going to bed. Nevertheless, more than once Mr. O. found the upstairs lights on when he was quite sure that he had not turned the switch prior to going to bed.

One Sunday afternoon his wife was taking a nap in the middle of their king-size bed. Mr. O. was about ten feet away in another room when he heard the telephone fall off the table next to the bed. He assumed that the telephone had been close to the edge and had somehow fallen off but on checking realized that this could not have happened by natural means. He replaced the receiver and went back to the other room. Five minutes later he heard the telephone being violently knocked off the table again, and he ran into the bedroom only to find it stretched the length of its cord on the floor. During all this commotion his wife had been asleep.

At that point Mr. O. requested my assistance in clearing up the matter. As it happened, his company, one famous for moving its employees, transferred him to California before I could look into the origin of the strange occurrences on Sharp View Avenue. A written request by Mr. O. to the new owners concerning such matters remained unanswered, so one can only assume that the new owners had nothing to report or did not care to discuss it. What makes the case even more puzzling was the fact that no ghosts disturbed the peace of the O. family in their new location in California.

The old Howard home on South Main Street in Henderson, Texas, was a Southern mansion of the kind that was once so numerous throughout the South. In 1851 the mansion was erected by a certain James L. Howard on land he bought for $100. It was the oldest brick home in town. Later, it belonged to the Heritage Association and was maintained as a museum, with visitors coming not only from other parts of Texas but even from abroad. The house had three stories and six rooms; four columns adorn the front of it. Perhaps the most remarkable thing about the house was the fact that every room had a fireplace, some of them very large old-fashioned fireplaces of the kind you rarely see any more. The stairs had banisters made of the highest grade walnut.

When the Howards built this home they stated proudly, to anyone who would hear it, "God Almighty Himself could not tear it down because it was well built." Even the worst storm seemingly could not touch the house. There was the account of a particularly horrifying electrical storm when a streak of lightning hit one of the corner columns, causing only slight damage. One of the Howard brothers ran out into the yard, looked up into the sky and shook his fist and said, "See. I told you that you couldn't tear down my house." With so large and outstanding a mansion in a small town, it was only natural that legends would crop up around it, some of which were true and some were not. One of them making the rounds concerns a murder in the house. The Rusk County Heritage Association checked into it and found that an accident, not a murder, had occurred. The accident concerned a member of the Howard family named Pat Howard, who lost his life in an accident in the home. In fact, the descendants of the Howards went to great length to explain again and again that Pat Howard died of an accident and that the shooting that took his life was not murder in any sense of the word. Of course, where there is smoke there is sometimes fire. Was the family merely trying to kill the story, or were they correcting the facts? I have never been to the Henderson mansion but have talked with people who have been there, so my account must of necessity be second hand. In 1905 Mrs. M. A. Howard and Dore Howard, being alone, decided to sell the house to a certain Mrs. M. A. Dickinson. Mrs. Howard was then in ill health. The sale did not go down well with her children and the rest of the family, who would have preferred to have the house stay family property. It seems incredible today that such an imposing house could be sold for $1500, but, of course, that was a lot more money in 1905 than it is today. Still, even for 1905, $1500 was very little money for a house of this kind. It seems strange therefore that the sale was made in this manner. The sale of the house from the Howard family to an outsider took the town by surprise. No one had surmised that it could be for sale, especially not for such a low price. The house had a reputation as an historical landmark. Sam Houston himself slept there many times, since he was a cousin of the Howards. In 1950 the house passed from the Dickinson family to Hobart Bryce, who in 1961 deeded the property to the Historical Association. One of the townspeople who had spent much effort in restoring the old house and who had been active on behalf of the fund-raising committee was a certain Carl Jaggers. Partly due to his efforts and those of others, the house was in excellent condition again when it opened to visitors as a museum.

My attention was drawn to it when I appeared on a television program in nearby Tyler, Texas. The lady who interviewed me, Jane Lassiter, provided me with much of the material about the Henderson house.

While the controversy among the townspeople concerning the restoration of the house was going on and there was some doubt whether the house could be saved or had to be torn down, no one had the time or inclination to look into any possible ghostly manifestations at the house. But as soon as the matter had quieted down and the house was safe from the wreckers' tools and perhaps because of the renewed quiet in the atmosphere, something did occur that had not been observed before. Maia Jaggers was one of those who served as honorary guides around the house, particularly during the weekends, when there were more visitors than during the week. She would act as hostess to those who came to look at the house. One Sunday afternoon in the winter of 1968, she had just finished showing the house to a group of visitors and was quite alone in it. She found herself downstairs looking toward the stairway leading to the upper stories. At that precise moment she saw a woman materialize before her eyes. Seemingly solid, or almost so, it was clearly a woman of a past age. As she looked closely at the apparition, she realized that it was the ghost of Mrs. Howard herself. As soon as Maia Jaggers and the ghost had come face to face the apparition floated up the stairway and disappeared. She has not been seen since that time. Could it be that a grateful Mrs. Howard wanted the one person directly connected with the salvage of her home made aware of her continued existence in it? Was her presence in what was once her home caused by a belated regret at having sold out to others against the wishes of her family? If you are ever in Henderson, Texas, be sure and drop in on Mrs. Howard's house. Sale or no sale, she seems to be quite at home in it still.

When she contacted me, Grace Trotter lived in Dallas and was in her middle thirties. She was the author of several novels for young girls published by leading publishers. For years, however, she had become more and more interested in the occult, partly because of an experience that opened her eyes to the continuance of life after death. She contacted me after she had read my book of that title to tell me of a visitation that, in a manner of speaking, had changed her outlook entirely. In 1965 Ms. Trotter, who wrote under the professional name of Nancy Paschal, suffered the loss of her father in July, and that of her mother in October. The double passing left a deep imprint on Ms. Trotter. Her mother had died on a Friday and was buried the following Monday morning.

That afternoon, after her friends had left the house, Ms. Trotter lay down to rest in her house and fell asleep. She was awakened from deep slumber about an hour later by something or someone whose presence she felt in the room. She opened her eyes and looked straight into her mother's face. This was no dream but a fully materialized apparition. She noticed that her mother was dressed in white, and while she was observing her in awe her mother came over to her and kissed her. She felt the imprint of her lips quite clearly. At the foot of her bed stood a smaller woman, a brunette, dressed in red. Grace Trotter also recognized the other woman as her mother's mother, her own grandmother, even though she had died many years before Grace was born. She had been familiar with her appearance from a large picture which had been in the house. Not a word was spoken and the entire experience lasted perhaps five or ten minutes. After it was over Ms. Trotter wondered whether she had not been asleep after all when it occurred. There was a certain wish to believe and a deep understanding for the need for this occurrence to have taken place, but at the same time her rational and scientific mind wanted to be sure that that which she had experienced was real. She did not have to wait long for additional confirmation. Two weeks later she awoke one morning and saw her mother again coming from the door. Then Grace Trotter realized that her mother did not look her age, that was to say the age she was when she passed on. Again she wore a beautiful dress. The other woman who had been in the first visitation was along this time too. But what amazed Grace Trotter more was the fact that her mother carried in her arms what appeared to be a six-month-old baby. It came to her in a flash that the baby was she, for she had been six months of age when her mother was twenty-four. The picture of her mother holding her own self as a baby was the additional proof of identity Ms. Trotter needed. The apparitions faded quickly, but the imprint they left behind had stayed with her ever since. As a professional writer and poet she felt herself impelled to put down on paper what the experience had meant to her, and she had asked me to reproduce that beautiful poem called *Safe Passage* in this account. Here it is:

SAFE PASSAGE
By Nancy Paschal
My mother passed on a Friday
Just twenty minutes after Thursday midnight.
I was alone with her when she drew the breath
That was final. And it was right
That it was free from pain and peaceful, dear Lord.
But grief caught me like blinding light.
I couldn't see my way without her—
My counselor, my friend, my own sweet mother.
She was a real young eighty-nine
And I had loved her all of sixty-five years,
But giving her up was so hard
That I couldn't stop the hurting or the tears.
She was buried Monday morning.
That afternoon, after all my friends had left,
I lay on my bed and fell asleep.
In an hour, when I woke up sad and bereft,
Mother was standing beside me.
She bent over and kissed my lips, quick and deft
And loving, as she always was.
I gazed into her smiling face
And it was young—not more than twenty-four.
Her body looked strong, with beauty and grace.

One morning two weeks later I woke early
And saw her again, coming in at the door.

She had a six-months-old baby in her arms.
I had been six months old when she was twenty-four.
So the baby was me.
She brought my baby-self back for me to see,
To prove that she still lived and cared
And that death is only a passageway.
The spirit of life everlasting dared
To show itself as plain as day.
Death is a safe passageway.

One of the most popular legends in American ghostlore is the "hitchhiking ghost story." It had been told to me many times by people in many places. Carl Carmer had immortalized the hitchhiking girl ghost in one of his books and there is no doubt that the legend is part of traditional American folklore. Consequently, I treat further variations of this tale with extreme caution, if not outright skepticism. Basically, the story concerns someone driving at night who is flagged down by a stranger in the road. The stranger is always a woman, always beautiful, and she always wears unusual clothes such as an evening gown or other formal attire. She asks for a lift home, and of course the motorist obliges. The woman then gets in and sits in the back, and when the motorist reaches the destination requested by the woman he turns around, and lo and behold, there is no one in the back seat. His curiosity has been aroused. He rings the doorbell at the house in question, someone opens the door, and when he describes the girl hitchhiker he is told that the lady in question died many years ago, and that this had happened before. So much for the traditional hitchhiking ghost.

I am indebted to Chuck Meegan of the Dallas *Morning*

News and to a reader by the name of Joanne Darr of Dallas for a story which seems to run in a similar pattern but had the ring of truth to it. Ms. Darr moved to Dallas in 1962 and soon after her arrival heard about the ghost of White Rock Lake. Being somewhat interested in the occult, she questioned those who told her of this particular apparition. The lake was man-made and was in a residential area, part of a city park. The alleged ghost lived in that area. In former years there were some very fine homes close to the water, and in the thirties these homes were famous for garden parties and boating excursions on the lake. According to tradition, during one of these parties a boat tipped over and a young woman and her fiancé were drowned. In other accounts it is only the woman who was drowned and her ghost is wandering around looking for her fiancé. She wears evening clothes and tries to hitch a ride back home to Gaston Avenue in the Lakewood area, which is about three miles' distance. But according to local tradition she simply disappears before she gets there. According to some other accounts she disappears immediately after she is given the ride to where she wants to go. Her benefactor then goes to that address and meets her grandfather, who explains the situation to him.

All this seemed terribly ridiculous to Ms. Darr. She discussed it with a local friend, who didn't find it as amusing as she did. Her grandfather had been fishing just after dark not long before, and as he looked out onto the lake he clearly saw a human shape floating above the water. He didn't catch many fish that night.

The story kept bothering Ms. Darr and she did some further research. Through material in the Dallas *Morning News* she made contact with a woman who worked for Neiman-Marcus as the head of the advertising department. The lady was quite obliging in recounting her unusual experience.

This happened in the late thirties or early forties, she explained, and it was in the early morning when she and her boyfriend, who later became her husband, were driving home and passing the lake. Suddenly they noticed a woman crawling up the embankment next to the road. They stopped the car in order to help her. She was dripping wet and wore a blue evening dress. She explained that she lived on Gaston just past Lakewood and that she had been in an accident on the lake. They offered to drive her home and the woman got into the back seat of the car. Since the woman and her boyfriend were rather tired at the end of a long evening, they didn't feel like talking to the stranger, and the woman also remained quiet in the back seat. When they were nearing the Lakewood area the woman turned around to see if the woman was all right. To her amazement the stranger had completely vanished. The car they were driving was a two-door sedan, and no one could have gotten in or out through the windows.

The address where the woman once lived had since been turned into an apartment house. Nevertheless, every year, especially in the spring or fall during the height of the social season, various people claim to have seen her there. The story appealed to one of Ms. Darr's friends, who decided to do a little bit of ghost hunting on his own. He went to the general area where the figure of the woman had been observed in the past and waited. To his surprise he saw a white form standing in the road. When he came closer to her she dissolved. Evidently the woman of White Rock Lake was still trying to hitch a ride home.

At the time she contacted me, Sylvia W. was in her late twenties, had been married twice and had lived a full and normally exciting life. Since the age of eight she had had precognitive experiences, warnings, feelings about impending events, many of which have come true, and psychic dreams. She had always accepted the importance of ESP in her life and never had any fears of the so-called occult. But recently something had happened in her life that had her stumped. She had fallen in love with a widower, Albert, whose wife and infant daughter were killed in a motorcar accident in 1961. Albert's wife herself had had a premonition of the impending accident and had told him so. Moreover, three days after her death she appeared before him and assured him that she would always be with him and take care of him. Before her passing she had requested that should she die he should not remarry. He did not promise this, but she had earnestly requested it.

As soon as Albert had gotten over the shock of his wife's untimely passing he began to mingle socially once again. Despite increased social interest he remained single. However, when he met Sylvia, they became involved with each other in a love relationship. They originally met because her house was rented from his company. They dated for about six months, and the first four months of their relationship were undisturbed and harmonious. But then strange things started to happen and they couldn't help noticing it. Strange noises and movements occurred both in her house and in his house. That was not surprising since they spent time in both. There were knockings on the door and when they opened it there was no one there. This happened mainly late at night. Then there were sounds of someone walking in the next room or heavy objects seemingly dropping to the floor. Upon investigation they found nothing to substantiate the noises. On occasion the blinds would open by themselves or a book would move of its own volition and open by itself to a certain page while the room in which this happened was closed off and no one had access to it. Apparently someone was trying to convey messages to

Albert, for the books were marked at different passages. When they read one of the passages in a particular novel that had been left in a conspicuous spot so that they could not overlook it, they realized who was behind the phenomena. The passage in the book dealt with a female competitor who was domineering; about honest love, and about one partner being "from another world." And one passage referred to someone having seen the light.

Fantastic as it seemed at first, they realized that the dead wife was trying to break up their romance from the beyond. When they were together during the night there was a knocking on the window.

Albert got up to investigate outside. After he had left the bedroom Sylvia rose and looked out onto the patio through the blinds. The lights were on in the patio and she assumed that Albert was checking that area of the house. Also, she clearly heard the door to the kitchen open and close and lock itself. After Albert returned she learned that he had not even been in the back of the house where the patio and kitchen were located. He had been to the front only. Then and there, in the middle of the night, they tried to go over the phenomena and make sense out of them. In listing them, they realized that the disturbances had started just about the time Albert had declared his love for Sylvia.

Moreover, Sylvia had just borrowed an object that had belonged to Albert's first wife. It was a typewriter. She had left it on the floor only to find it moved the following morning from the floor back to the shelf where it had originally been. No one had been near it during the night. That is to say, no one of flesh and blood. What were they to do?

I explained that they must address the deceased woman and explain the facts of life to her or perhaps the facts of "after life." Only by making her understand the error of her ways could they hope to release her from her compulsion and themselves from her interference. I did not hear from Sylvia after that and can only hope that it worked out.

I met Mrs. Ann B. one time when I was lecturing in Houston. She was a middle-class housewife whose husband was an electrician, and she didn't put much stock in her occult experiences. And, he actively discouraged them. Nevertheless, all through the years Ann had had flashes, premonitions and visions, most of which later became objective reality. She was one of those Texans who have the gift of second sight in a very clear way and would like to use it constructively to help others if not herself. Among the most interesting experiences reported by Ann B. was an incident which occurred in 1957. At the time she was living in a small town near Houston. She was having recurrent dreams in which she saw her husband being hurt. Specifically she saw a flash of fire and her husband came rolling out of it across a wooden floor. He seemed to be in terrible pain. Since she had the dream a number of times she decided to discuss it with him, but he would not listen. Then the dream stopped. A few days after she had had this dream for the last time her husband had to go to a nearby town to do some electrical work in a church. While he was doing this, two high-tension wires accidentally touched and her husband was caught by the current. In order to get out of it, he rolled across a wooden floor and his hands and arms were badly burned.

On August 1, 1960, in the evening, she had a vision of her brother-in-law, who lived in another city in Texas. They had not been in touch lately and there really wasn't any emotional reason for her to have the vision at this time. Nevertheless, she suddenly saw his head and shoulders and he seemed to be ascending. The strangest part of this vision was that there were pieces of broken metal floating all around him. She noticed that he had a most peaceful look on his face and knew that he had been killed in an accident. She told her husband so, but it wasn't until the next morning that the telephone rang and they were told that the brother-in-law had been killed in a plane crash.

Some time ago I wanted to go to the Alamo with a reputable professional medium to do some research on the spot where so much history was made. Although I sent letters to the custodians of this shrine twice, and my letters were never returned, I was never given permission to do so, nor did I receive an answer. I received many invitations from Texans to come and visit their haunted houses or to listen to the account of their extraordinary experiences with extrasensory perception, so I can forget the Alamo.

THE HEADLESS GRANDFATHER

*G*rover C. was one of those colorful old-timers you hardly see anymore these days, not even in the deep South. It wasn't that Grover had any particular background in anything special, far from it; he was an untutored man who owed his success solely to his own willpower and an insatiable curiosity that led him places his education—or lack of it—would have prevented him from ever reaching.

He saw the light of day just before the turn of the twentieth century in rural North Carolina. At the age of nineteen he married for the first time, but his wife Fannie and the child she bore him both died from what was then called "childbed fever," or lack of proper medical treatment. He had not yet chosen any particular career for himself, but was just "looking around" and did odd jobs here and there. A year later he was married again, to a lady from Georgia. After their first daughter was born, they moved to Columbus, Georgia, and Mr. C. worked in a local mill for a while. This didn't satisfy his drive, however, and shortly afterwards he and his brother Robert opened a grocery store. The store did right well until "the Hoover panic," as they called it, and then they managed to sell out and buy a farm in Harris County.

Life was pretty placid, and after an accident in which he lost his daughter, Mr. C. moved back to Columbus and tried his hand at the grocery business once more. About this time, the restless gentleman met a lady from Alabama, as a result of which he became the father of an "extracurricular" little girl, in addition to his own family, which eventually consisted of a wife and nine children. When his second-born child died of an infectious disease, Mr. C. had his long-delayed breakdown, and for several years, he was unable to cope with his life. During those rough years of slow, gradual recuperation, his daughter Agnes ran the store for him and supported the family.

As his health improved and he began to return to a happier and more constructive outlook on life, he developed an interest in real estate. With what money he could spare, he bought and sold property, and before long, he did so well he could dispense with the grocery store. Soon he added a construction business to his real estate dealings and was considered a fairly well-to-do citizen in his hometown. This status of course attracted a variety of unattached women and even some who were attached, or semi-detached, as the case may have been, and Mr. C. had himself a good time. Knowledge of his interest in other ladies could not fail to get to his wife and eventually he was given a choice by his wife: it was either her or them.

He picked them, or, more specifically, a lady next door, and for thirteen years he was reasonably faithful to her. Eventually she disliked living with a man she was not married to, especially when he happened to be married to someone else, even though he had bought her a cute little house of her own in Columbus. Mr. C. was not particularly happy about this state of affairs either, for he developed a penchant for drinking during those years. After they separated, the lady next door left town and got married.

Far from returning to the bosom of his family, now that the Other Woman had given him the gate, Grover looked elsewhere and what he found apparently pleased him. By then he was in his late sixties, but his vigorous personality wasn't about to be slowed down by so silly a reason as advancing age!

About 1962 he met a practical nurse by the name of Madeline, who turned out to be the opposite of what the doctor had ordered. After a particularly heavy argument, she kicked him in the nose. When it did not stop bleeding, she became alarmed and took him to the hospital. The family went to see him there even though his wife had not exactly forgiven him. But at this point it mattered little. Mr. C. also complained of pain in his side and the children firmly believed that the practical nurse had also kicked him in that area. Since he died shortly afterward, it was a moot question whether or not she had done so because Mrs. C's abilities no longer corresponded to her amorous expectations. The old gent certainly did not discuss it with his family. He was seventy when he died and Madeline was a mere sixty. Death was somewhat unexpected despite the fact Mr. C. had suffered from various ailments. During the days he had been alone in his room at the hospital. At first, he shared the room with another older man, but several days later a young man was sent in to be with him. The young man's complaint was that he had a lollipop stick stuck in his throat. There probably aren't too many young men with such a predicament in medical annals, and even fewer in Columbus, Georgia. The family found this mighty peculiar, even more so since the young man was a close relative of Madeline, the very practical nurse.

They complained to the hospital authorities and the young man was moved. It is not known whether the lollipop stick was ever removed from his throat, but chances are it was, or we would have heard more of it. At any rate, Mr. C. was then guarded by one of his children each night, the children taking turns.

They were firmly convinced that the practical nurse slipped her erstwhile benefactor some poison and that perhaps the boy with the lollipop stick stuck in his throat might have done her bidding and administered it to the old gent. This was a pretty sticky argument, of course, and hard to prove, especially as no autopsy was ever performed on Mr. C. But it was conceivable that Madeline made a discovery about her friend that could have induced her to speed his failure to recover and do so by any means at her command. She knew her way around the hospital and had ready access to his room. She also had equally ready access to his office and thereby hangs a strange tale.

On one of the infrequent occasions when Mr. C. slept at home, his estranged wife was making up the bed. This was five months before his demise. As she lifted the mattress, she discovered underneath it a heavy envelope, about six by ten inches in size, crammed full with papers. She looked at it and found written on it in Mr. C.'s large lettering, the words:

"This is not to be opened until I am dead. I mean good and dead. Daddy."

She showed the envelope to her daughter, Agnes, but put it back since she did not wish to enter into any kind of controversy with her husband. Evidently the envelope must have been taken by him to his office sometime later, for when she again made his bed two weeks before his passing, when he was still walking around, she found it gone. But there was a second, smaller envelope there, this one not particularly marked or inscribed. She left it there. A short time later Mr. C. was taken to the hospital. When Mrs. C. made the bed she found that the small envelope had also disappeared.

While the C.'s house in Columbus was not exactly a public place, neither was it an impregnable fortress, and anyone wishing to do so could have walked in at various times and quickly removed the envelope. As far as the office was concerned, that was even easier to enter and the family had no doubt whatever that Madeline took both envelopes for reasons best known to herself, although they could not actually prove any of it. At no time did the old gent say an unkind word about his Madeline, at least not to his children, preferring perhaps to take his troubles with him into the Great Beyond.

After his death, which came rather suddenly, the family found a proper will, but as Mr. C. had generously built homes for most of his children during his lifetime, in the 1950s, and there was only a modest amount of cash in the bank accounts, and no great inheritance for anyone.

The will named Mrs. C. as executor, and as there was nothing to contest, it was duly probated. But the family did search the office and the late Mr. C.'s effects at the house for these two envelopes that were still missing. Only the wife and daughter Agnes knew of them, even though "nobody and everybody" had access to the house. The servants would not have taken them, and the safe was empty. As the old gent had occasionally slept in his office on a couch, the family looked high and low in his office but with negative results. The only thing that turned up in addition to the will itself was the neatly typed manuscript of a book of Biblical quotations. Mr. C. had been a serious Bible scholar, despite his uneducated status, and the quotes arranged by subject matter and source represented many thousands of man-hours of work. When his daughter Marie had seen him working on this project in 1962, she had suggested he have the scribbled notes typed up and she had prevailed upon her Aunt Catherine to undertake the job, which the latter did. Somewhat forlornly, Marie picked up the manuscript and wondered whether someone might not buy it and put a little cash into the estate *that* way.

The mystery of the disappearing envelopes was never solved. Even greater than the puzzle of their disappearance was the question about their content: what was in them that was so important that the old gent had to hide them under the mattress? So important that someone took them secretly and kept them from being turned over to the family, as they should have been?

Although there was no evidence whatever for this contention, Marie thinks there might have been some valuables left to Grover C.'s love child, the one he had with the lady from Alabama early in his romantic life.

At any rate, after several months of fruitless searches, the family let the matter rest and turned to other things. Grover C. would have gone on to his just reward, especially in the minds of his family, if it weren't for the matter of some peculiar, unfinished business.

About a year after Grover's death, Lewis C., one of the sons of the *deceased*, as they say in the police records, was busy building a brick flower planter in his home in Columbus. This was one of the houses his father had erected for his children, and Mr. C., the son, had been living in it happily without the slightest disturbance. Lewis was thirty years old and the mystery of his father's disappearing envelopes did not concern him very much at this point. Here he was, at four o'clock in the afternoon, on a brisk March day, working on his planter. Giving him a hand with it, and handing him one brick after another, was a professional bricklayer by the name of Fred, with whom he had worked before. They were in the living room and Lewis was facing the back door, Fred the front door.

"A brick, please" said Lewis, without turning around.

No brick came. He asked again. Still no brick. He then looked up at his helper and saw him frozen to the spot, gazing at the front door.

"What's the matter, Fred?" he inquired. He had never seen Fred so frightened.

Finally, as if awakening from a bad dream, Fred spoke.

"I've just seen Mr. C.," he said, "big as life."

"But Mr. C. has been dead for a year," the son replied.

Fred had worked for Grover for many years and he knew him well.

"What did he look like?" the son inquired.

"White . . . light," Fred replied and then went on to

describe the figure in white pants he had seen at the door. Although it was only the bottom half of a man, he had instantly recognized his late employer. Grover was bowlegged and the white pants facing him surely were as bow-legged as old Grover had been. There was no doubt about whose lower half it was that had appeared and then gone up in a puff again.

Lewis shook his head and went on with his work. But a short time later he began to appreciate what Fred had experienced. In the middle of the night he found himself suddenly awake by reason of something in the atmosphere—undefinable, but still very real. The lights in his bedroom were off, but he could see down the hallway. And what he saw was a man wearing a white shirt, dark pants . . . and . . . with no head. The headless gentleman was tiptoeing down the hallway toward him.

Lewis could only stare at the apparition which he instantly recognized as his late father, head or no head. When the ghost saw that Lewis recognized him, he took three leaps *backward* and disappeared into thin air. Unfortunately, Catherine, Lewis' wife did not believe a word of it. For several months the subject of father's headless ghost could not be mentioned in conversation. Then, in December of 1968, Lewis and Catherine were asleep one night, when at 2:30 A.M. they were both roused by the sound of heavy footsteps walking down the hall from the bedrooms toward the living room. As they sat up and listened with nary a heartbeat, they could clearly hear how the steps first hit the bare floor and then the carpet, sounding more muffled as they did. Finally, they resounded louder again as they reached the kitchen floor. Lewis jumped out of bed, ready to fight what he was sure must be an intruder. Although he looked the house over from top to bottom he found no trace of a burglar, and all the doors were locked.

In retrospect they decided it was probably Grover paying them a visit. But why? True, he had built them the house. True, they had some of his effects, including his old pajamas.

But what would he want with his old pajamas where he *now* was? Surely he could not be upset by the fact that his son was wearing them. They decided then that Grover was most likely trying to get their attention because of those envelopes that were still missing or some other unfinished business, but they didn't like it, for who would like one's headless father popping in in the middle of the night?

But apparently Grover did not restrict his nocturnal visits to his son Lewis' place. His granddaughter Marie, who lived in Atlanta, had come to visit at her grandfather's house in the spring of 1968. The house had no city water but used water from its own well system. It was therefore necessary to carry water into the house from outside. On one such occasion, when she had just done this and was returning with an *empty* basin, Marie stepped into what looked like a puddle of water. She started to mop up the puddle only to find that the spot was actually totally dry. Moreover, the puddle was ice cold, while the water basin she had just carried was still hot. She found this most unusual but did not tell anyone about it. Within a matter of hours eight-year-old Randy reported seeing a man in a dark suit in the bathroom, when the bathroom was empty.

Apparently the old gent liked children, for little Joel was playing the piano in his Atlanta home in February of 1969, when he heard the sound of shuffling feet approach. Then there was the tinkling of glasses and all this time no one was visible. Grover had always liked a shot and a little music.

Soon Marie began to smell carnations in her house when no one was wearing them or using any perfume. This lingered for a moment and then disappeared, as if someone wearing this scent was just passing through the house.

In 1967, her Aunt Mary came to visit her in Atlanta and the conversation turned to the mysterious scent. "I'm glad you mentioned this," the aunt exclaimed, and reported a similar problem: both she and her husband would smell the same scent repeatedly in their own house, sometimes so strongly they had to leave the house and go out for some fresh air. But the scent followed them, and on one occasion "sat" with them in their car on the way to church on Sunday morning!

They weren't too sure whether it was more like carnations or just a funeral smell, but it surely was a smell that had no rational explanation. Then in 1968, Mary informed her niece that a new perfume had suddenly been added to their list of phenomena: this one was a spicy scent, like a man's after-shave lotion.

Not long after this report, Marie smelled the same sharp, men's perfume in her own house in Atlanta, in her den. This was particularly upsetting, because they had shut off that room for the winter and no perfume or anyone wearing it had been in it for months.

In 1969, she had occasion to visit her grandfather's house in Columbus once again. She found herself wandering into her late grandfather's old bedroom. She stopped at his dresser and opened the drawer. There she found her spicy scent: a bottle of Avon hair lotion he had used. None of her husband's eau de cologne bottles had a similar smell. This was it. But how had it traveled all the way to Atlanta? Unless, of course, Grover was wearing it.

She was upset by her grandfather's insistence on continuing to visit his kinfolk and not staying in the cemetery as respectable folk were supposed to do, at least according to the traditional view of the dead. Evidently Grover was far from finished with this life, and judging from the lively existence he had led prior to his unexpected departure from this vale of tears, he had a lot of energy left over.

That, combined with a genuine grievance over unfinished business—especially the missing two envelopes—must have been the cause for his peripatetic visits. Marie decided not to wait for the next one, and went to see a card reader in Columbus. The card reader could tell her only that she had a restless grandfather who wished her well.

Unfortunately, even if the cause for Grover's continued presence could be ascertained, there was no way in which the missing envelopes could be recovered. Marie tried, in vain, to get a local psychic to make contact with her grandfather. Finally, she turned her attention to the manuscript of Bible quotes. Perhaps it was the book he wanted to see published.

Whatever it was, she must have done the right thing, or perhaps all that talk about the headless grandfather had pleased the old gent's ego enough to pry him loose from the earth plane. At any rate, no further appearances were reported and it may well be that he had forgotten about those envelopes, what with the attractions of his new world absorbing his interest.

HAUNTINGS IN VIRGINIA

$\mathcal{V}$irginia, in the rolling hills south of Washington, dotted as they were with magnificent manor houses, many of them dating back to colonial days, seemed to be the kind of atmosphere ghosts prefer. Virginia, which was primarily horse country and was settled originally by people from the Anglo-Saxon countries, was very much like England in many respects. Even the ghosts, such as they are, that continue a shadowy existence in some of the estates and plantation houses were similar in their habits to those found in English stately homes. Almost "the first state in the Union" because of its early connection with the creation of the country and because it was the home of so many of the leaders of the Revolutionary War, Virginia must be considered the closest to an oligarchic state in America. Divided among a small number of illustrious families, Virginia had for a long time been a feudal barony of sorts, and to this very day the great houses attest to the way this first among the thirteen colonies developed. Even though the plantations that were once the life blood of these houses were no longer in existence, the houses themselves continue to flourish because the Virginians have a keen sense of history and tradition. Many of the houses, of course, have been restored. Nevertheless, there were still some which have stood the test of time and survived from their seventeenth- or eighteenth-century origins almost intact to this day.

Foremost among such manor houses was the magnificent estate of Westover on the James River. Built originally in 1730 by William Byrd II, the man who founded Richmond, it stood amid an 11,000-acre working farm. The formal gardens surrounding the house were open to the public, but the house itself was not. A magnificent eighteenth-century ceiling in the entrance hall matched the paneling of the walls. Throughout the manor house there was evidence of grandeur. This was not the home of a country squire but of a statesman of great wealth. William Byrd was killed during the Revolutionary War, and his widow sold the original furniture in 1813.

Eventually, the house passed into the hands of Mrs. Bruce Crane Fisher. Her grandfather had bought the house in 1921 and became the eleventh owner since the plantation had been in existence. Mrs. Fisher had furnished the house with authentic eighteenth-century English and European furniture to restore it as closely as possible to the original appearance.

The Georgian house stood amid tall old trees and consisted of a central portion and two wings. The central portion had three stories of elegant brickwork and two tall chimneys. The two wings were originally not connected to the center portion of the house, but the right wing had to be restored in 1900 since it had been damaged by fire from a shelling during the Civil War. At that time the two wings were also connected to the house and were then accessible directly from the main portion. The main entrance faced the James River and had the original wrought-iron entrance gate with stone eagles surmounting the gateposts. Thus, with minimal additions and restorations, the house presented pretty much the same picture it did when it was first built in 1730.

Colonel Byrd took his beautiful daughter Evelyn, pronounced *Eevelyn* in Virginia, to London for the coronation of King George I. That was in 1717, when the great men of the colonies, when they could afford it, would go to the mother country when the occasion arose. Evelyn, at the time, was eighteen years old and her father decided to leave her in England to be educated. Soon, he received disquieting news from his confidants at the London court. It appeared that Evelyn had been seen with a certain Charles Mordaunt and that the two young people were hopelessly in love with each other. Normally this would be a matter for rejoicing, but not so in this case. Charles was an ardent Roman Catholic and the grandson of the Earl of Petersborough. Colonel Byrd, on the other hand, was politically and personally a staunch Protestant, and the idea of his daughter marrying into the enemy camp, so to speak, was totally unacceptable to him. Immediately, he ordered her to return to Westover; Evelyn had no choice but to obey. As soon as she arrived at the family plantation, she went into isolation. She refused to see any other suitors her father sent her or to consider, or even to discuss, the possibility of marriage.

This went on for some time, and Evelyn quite literally "pined away" to death. Some weeks before her death, however, she had a very emotional discussion with her best friend, Anne Harrison. The two young women were walking up a hill when Evelyn, feeling faint, knew that her days were numbered. She turned to her friend and promised her that she would return after her death. Mrs. Harrison did not take this very seriously, but she knew that Evelyn was not well, and her death did not come as a shock. The following spring, after Westover had somehow returned to a degree of normalcy and the tragic events of the previous year were not so strongly in evidence, Mrs. Harrison was walking in the garden sadly remembering what had transpired the year before. Suddenly she saw her old friend standing near her in a dazzling white gown. The vision then drifted forward two steps, waved its hand at her and smiled. An instant later, it had vanished. At the time of her untimely death, Evelyn Byrd had been twenty-nine years of age, but in the apparition she seemed much younger and lovelier than she had appeared toward the end of her life.

The specter has reappeared from time to time to a number of people, both those who live in the area and those who were guests at Westover. A lady who lived nearby who had been there for nearly three decades saw her in the mid-1960s. She was coming out of the front door one summer day and was walking down the path when she looked back toward the house and saw a woman come out behind her. At first she thought it was a friend and stopped at the gate to wait for her. When the woman came closer, however, she didn't recognize her. There was something very strange about the woman coming toward her. There seemed to be a glow all about her person, her black hair, and the white dress. When the woman was close to her she stopped, and seemed to sink into the ground.

On December 11, 1929, some guests from Washington were staying at Westover, and on the evening of their arrival the conversation turned to ghosts. The house was then owned by Mr. and Mrs. Richard H. Crane, who explained that they themselves had not seen the ghost during their tenancy. One of the house guests retired to the room assigned to her on the side of the house overlooking the great gates from which one had a fine view into the formal gardens. Sometime that night the guest awoke and went to the window. There was no apparent reason for her behavior. It was quite dark outside and very quiet. As she glanced out the window she saw the figure of Evelyn Byrd. She described the apparition to her hosts as filmy, nebulous and cloudy, so transparent no features could be distinguished, only a gauzy texture of a woman's form. The figure seemed to be floating a little above the lawn and almost on the level of the window itself. As she looked at it almost transfixed, the apparition acknowledged her by raising her hand and motioning to her to go back into the room and away from the window. The gesture seemed so imperative that the house guest obeyed it.

When I requested permission to investigate the house I was politely denied access. Perhaps the owners were afraid that I might induce the lovely Evelyn to leave Westover for a better life in paradise, and that would never do, for Westover is, after all, the nearest thing to paradise on earth, at least to an eighteenth-century lass whose lover had gone away. Had I had the opportunity to come into contact with her through some reputable medium perhaps I might have reunited the two in a land and under conditions where her stern father Colonel Byrd could no longer keep them apart.

Another famous Virginia mansion was Blandfield, which had more than one ghost. In the late 1960s the Richmond *Times Dispatch* made a survey of some of the better ghost houses in the area. Tom Howard interviewed a number of people who owned such houses and he also journeyed up to Blandfield to interview the owner. Here was his report: "Blandfield, an eighteenth century mansion in Essex County, has been frequented by a variety of spooks for two centuries. They've come as eerie lights in the night and wispy figures of men and women stalking through the halls.

"Mrs. William Nash Beverley, wife of the owner, related that about five years ago house guests reported apparitions on two occasions. The first was in a long, flowered dress walking across the upstairs hall. Everyone searched the home, but the stranger wasn't found. Two days later, a second guest saw a woman, in a long, dark skirt, cross a downstairs hall, and enter a room. Again an investigation found no one, said Mrs. Beverley.

"The most recent episode came several months before, she said. Mrs. Beverley recounted the experience. She and two dogs were in the downstairs library one afternoon and the only other person in the house was an ill relative who she knew was asleep in an upstairs bedroom. Suddenly, heavy footsteps sounded in the room directly overhead. Startled, she listened. The dogs sprang to their feet, hair bristling.

"First I thought I would take a shotgun and go up," said Mrs. Beverley. "Then I thought how silly that was. But I was uneasy, so I put a leash on each dog and we rushed up the steps. As I went up the steps, the dogs became more excited, and their hair stood straight up."

"She went straight to the bedroom of her relative, who was lying quietly in bed, still asleep. The dogs strained at the leash and pulled toward the room where she heard the heavy footsteps. She opened the door and the dogs bounded in fiercely . . . but there was no one there. She explored every hiding place in the room, but found no trace of a living human being. The dogs quieted down and she decided that, at last, she had heard one of the famed Blandfield ghosts."

There was a rocking chair ghost at Shirley plantation in Chase City and another rocking chair ghost at Ash Lawn, once the home of President James Monroe, and the ghost of Governor Kemper is said to still inhabit Walnut Hill, his erstwhile home. I have reported a number of such cases in an earlier book called *Ghosts I've Met*. In fact, the area around Charlottesville, which I investigated in 1965, abounds with authentic hauntings.

It is just possible that someone who is psychic and who might have passed the building then housing the Health, Education and Welfare Department in Charlottesville might feel peculiar, perhaps a chill or two, perhaps only a sense of displacement in time.

On that spot there was once a magnificent house, built around 1820 in the style of the Roman country houses of Andrea Palladino. James Dinsmore, an architect brought there by Thomas Jefferson, designed the house for Francis B. Dyer, a lawyer. Later it passed into the hands of William B. Fitch, but eventually the house changed hands again and just before the Civil War it belonged to a certain Eugene Davis, a man prominently connected with Episcopal Sunday school work. He was the oldest son of Professor John A. G. Davis, Chairman of the University of Charlottesville. The professor was killed during one of the student riots of those days. Shortly afterwards, when another son, James Maury Morris Davis, occupied the cottage in the yard, the first uncanny experiences took place. Studying late one night, young Davis heard the gate click and footsteps sound along the hall. He opened the door but saw no one out there. This repeated itself numerous times. When the house passed into the hands of Major Horace Jones, who headed a boys' preparatory school in Charlottesville, the phenomena continued. Some of the students who had been assigned the cottage to live in complained of footsteps in the yard. The gate would click open and shut and there never was anyone there. It was assumed that the murdered professor was checking up on his former home. The phenomena continued until after Major Jones died in 1904. When the cottage was eventually pulled down and replaced by the present structure, the noises stopped, but there was no telling what a psychic person might feel standing on the spot where the hauntings used to be.

There was a quietly elegant old frame house at 6321 Monument Avenue in Richmond which belies its violent history. The Richmond *News Leader* of April 7, 1967, told its story for the first time to a broader public. The owner at the time, Donald B. Wiltshire, had seen the ghost of a little old man with a chin beard as he was going to bed. He was so surprised by the apparition that he fell on the top step. Mr. Wiltshire employed the services of a historian, Mrs. Roger Mann, to dig into the past of his house. Mrs. Mann discovered that nineteen bodies had originally been buried in two graveyards somewhere on the Wiltshire property. Moreover, there was good reason to assume that half a million dollars was buried somewhere on the premises. To date that treasure had not been recovered but it had a basis in fact. In 1821 the house on Monument Avenue belonged to a certain Dan Green who worked in a bank. At the time Mr. Green was accused of absconding with $500,000. Since the money was never found the teller was acquitted. The only things remotely relating to the treasure were some coins found by men excavating for a swimming pool a few years ago, but they didn't add up to $500,000.

Andy Wilkins was a ghost fancier of southwest Virginia who kept me informed of some of the goings on in the area, notably of Berry Hill, a magnificent manor house not far from Westover. In fact, it was built on land once part of the Westover estate. Built and owned by the Bruce family, who were related by marriage to the owners of Westover. The estate was then empty. A few years earlier, a certain Fred Watkins bought Berry Hill as a wedding gift for his son, but when the young people tried to spend the night in it they were frightened out of it by footsteps and the uncanny presence of something they could not see. The building was being kept up like a museum, but there was only a caretaker on the grounds. Allegedly, the ghost was the son of the original builder, who died childless but resents that the house passed out of the Bruce family to strangers.

White Marsh in Gloucester County was a magnificent plantation house then owned by Mr. and Mrs. Ingles. In 1654, 3200 acres of land were granted to a certain Lewis Burwell; the house had passed through several hands since the Burwells owned it. The present White Marsh was built in 1798 and enlarged by the Tabb family in 1883. There was a legend that a curse was put on the place at the time when John Tabb bought it, a curse that was to last until the property was returned to its "rightful owners," presumably the sons of Thomas Rootes, who had sold the place to the Tabbs. But apparently the curse was not very effective, for the Tabb family lived at White Marsh undisturbed until 1906, when the place passed into the hands of Willie Buries, who made extensive changes, replacing the Georgian style with Greek revival. When the house passed into the hands of the then-owners, the Ingles, they had to re-do the house to bring it back to its original appearance. Constance Ingles moved into the house in 1948. She made extensive inquiries about anything dramatic that might have transpired in the house in its long history. She discovered no murders or suicides, but apparently several infant children of the Tabb family had died there. There was an account of a ghostly apparition, however, according to which mother Tabb was seen entering a certain room, opening a bureau drawer, removing all the child's clothes, shaking them out and folding them and returning them to the drawer. Mrs. Ingles just knew that this concerned the room where their two oldest sons were living at the time and she always knew that it was young Bill's chest of drawers the ghostly mother Tabb was opening. A neighbor had actually seen mother Tabb passing her on the stairs with her swishing taffeta skirts.

Constance Ingles had a long history of ESP and experiences that can only be classed as memories from a previous lifetime. She had seen her first ghost at the age of sixteen at a small inn near Seneca, New York. At White Marsh Mrs. Ingles had not actually seen any ghosts, but she had shared, with her husband and their little daughter, an auditory experience that had left them very much impressed with the fact that there were unseen presences at their home. Three or four weeks after they had moved into the house Mrs. Ingles was awakened by the sound of heavy footsteps in the attic proceeding from the north side of the house to the center. Reluctant to wake up her husband, Mrs. Ingles wondered who was walking about when she heard her little daughter, then four years old, call "Mommy, who is that walking in the attic?" Now sure that she was not hallucinating, she awakened her husband. Together they decided to investigate. The footsteps were directly over their heads then. A moment later they halted again, and then something seemed to land on the roof of the one-story wing, right under their bedroom window. They dashed to the window and heard a loud thud as something seemed to hit the ground. Seconds after that, there was heard the sound of horses' hoofs going up the lane. The next morning they investigated and found hoofprints under the window. They checked whether one of their horses had escaped from the barn, but none had. Also, the round window in the attic, on the south side where the footsteps had halted, cannot be opened. Mr. Ingles, who was a firm disbeliever in such matters as psychic phenomena, was impressed.

Although she had not seen this herself, Mrs. Ingles, all the children, and some of their friends had frequently reported the appearance of something filmy-white in the gardens. Marguerite Dupont Lee reported some of the traditional legends associated with White Marsh in her books. One of them concerns the sound of a party, music, and dancing going on in the house when there was no one there. Another one deals with a woman rocking in a chair in the northeast bedroom, the room once occupied by General Lee during his visit to White Marsh.

A year after the Ingleses had moved into White Marsh they employed a couple from Philadelphia named Henry and Frances Parker. Mrs. Ingles was quite sure the couple were not aware of these traditions when they first came to the house. Shortly after their arrival the butler came to Mrs. Ingles on a Sunday morning wondering if they had come home unexpectedly the afternoon before. They had not, and she so informed the butler. He then reported that Saturday afternoon, when the children had been sleeping and he and his wife had been in their room, they had heard someone playing the piano. Assuming that Mrs. Ingles had returned home and was playing the piano, he decided to leave the matter alone, but his wife insisted that it didn't sound like Mrs. Ingles playing. So he decided to go out and look. When he reached the stair landing, within perhaps two or three steps of the piano, the music stopped and there was a whooshing sound that moved toward the door to the back hall. Still shaken by this episode, the butler was even more impressed with the presence of something unseen. A few weeks later when he took Mrs. Ingles her morning coffee he explained that he and his wife had not slept all night because something was rocking in their room. When Mrs. Ingles pointed out that there was no rocking chair in that room, he explained that he knew that very well, but that their straight chair seemed to rock as if it had rockers under it.

Later, things quieted down; it was conceivable that the ghosts of White Marsh have taken the Ingleses to their heart and do not wish to interfere with their lives by appearing before them. Ghosts have a way of staying dormant for long times, being unaware of the passage of time and content to relive their own most important moments.

DICK TURPIN, MY LOVE

$\mathcal{D}$uring the summer of 1973, I received a strangely elaborate and pleading letter from a young woman by the name of Cynthia von Rupprath-Snitily. The name itself was fascinating enough to warrant my further interest, but what the lady had to say concerning her strange experiences with the unknown would have attracted me even if her name had been Smith or Jones.

Cynthia had been born in 1948 in Chicago, and lived in the same house until twenty-one years of age, leaving the area only to attend college at Northern Illinois University in De Kalb, Illinois. Immediately I recalled my own visit to Northern Illinois University, a huge college set in a very small town in the middle of the Illinois plains, a school which seemed forever to battle the narrow-mindedness of the surrounding town, while catering to a very large student body bent on exploring the further reaches of the human mind. Cynthia held a Bachelor's degree in both history and art, and was an art historian by profession. "I have dealt with both fictitious legend and concrete fact," she stated, "and therefore I have knowledge of the fine lines that sometimes separate these two entities. I have thus carried over the cognizance to my everyday life and have incorporated it into my style of thinking. In truth, I am my own worst critic."

In 1970 she married a man she had met at the University of Notre Dame and moved to his home town of Seattle, Washington, where he was employed at Boeing Aircraft.

With the termination of the SST project, her husband enlisted in the Air Force and at the time of contacting me they were stationed at the Edwards Air Force Base in California, about an hour's drive from Los Angeles.

Cynthia had always been a serious and sensitive person, perhaps because she was an only child of parents forty years older than herself. As a result she felt more at ease with older people, preferring their company to that of her own age. Due to her sensitivity, she was in the habit of becoming rather emotional in matters of impact to her. In order to offset this strong character trait, she tried very hard to develop a logical and orderly method of approach to things, and to think matters over several times before taking any specific course of action. Thus, when she realized that she had psychic experiences from childhood onward, she decided to analyze and investigate the phenomena in which she was a central element. She realized that her psychic ability had been inherited on her mother's side of the family; her maternal grandparents had come to the United States from Croatia. Deeply embedded in the culture of many Croatian people is the belief in witchcraft and the ability by some countryfolk to do unusual things or experience the uncanny. But Cynthia's attitude towards these phenomena remained critical. "I am not willing to accept such phenomena without further investigation," she explained. One case in particular impressed her, since it involved her personally.

"This case is unusual because it has occurred to three successive generations through the years. In the 1910s my grandmother was living in Chicago performing household tasks, when a neighbor dressed entirely in black came to the door. The latter woman was commonly known as a 'strega' and my grandmother naturally was not too happy to see her. The woman wanted to know what my grandmother was cooking in the pot on the stove. My grandmother refused and told the woman to leave, whereupon the latter reported that she would return that night, 'to find that which she was seeking.' That night while my grandparents, my mother, and my Uncle Bill were all sleeping in the same bed, the door suddenly blew open and my mother recalls seeing my grandmother literally struggling with some unseen force on the bed. Mother remembers quite vividly the movement of the mattress, as if something were jumping up and down on it. Certainly the sensation was stronger than a reclining figure could have inflicted. An aura of evil seemed to have invaded the room and left as quickly as did the 'force.'

"Years later, at the beginning of 1949, a similar event took place. My aunt was sitting in our Chicago home, feeding me a bottle, when this force again entered the scene, causing the two of us to be considerably uplifted from the couch. Again the jumping persisted and the evil presence was felt. The next performance by this 'thing' occurred in the early months of 1971 in Seattle. It was around midnight and I was reading a novel, while my husband, Gary, slept. I suddenly sensed something wicked within the confines of our room. I tossed it off, but then there began that jumping motion. I became quite alarmed as I realized neither my sleeping husband nor my own reclined body could attest to such motion. I woke my husband, who is not psychic, and he, too, became aware of the jumping movement. It was now growing in intensity, but when I called out the Lord's name, the bed suddenly ceased pitching. It wasn't until April, 1971, after moving from Seattle, that I learned of the two previous experiences."

On her father's side, Cynthia was descended from a noble German family, originally from Hanover. Her father had no interest or use for anything psychic. When Cynthia was only a few months old, her Aunt Doris came to live with the family as a temporary replacement for her mother, who was then quite ill and in the hospital. The aunt was sleeping on the living room couch, Cynthia's father in the front bedroom, and Cynthia herself in a crib placed in the back bedroom. Everyone was very much concerned with her mother's health, and her aunt, being a devout Catholic, had been praying almost around the clock. She had only been asleep for a short time, when a cold breeze awakened her and to her amazement, she saw a woman, fairly young and dressed in a nun's habit, walking slightly *above* the floor through the living room and turn down the hall toward Cynthia's room. Concerned for the little girl's safety, the aunt quickly followed the woman into the room. There she saw the nun place her hands on Cynthia's crib, look down at her and smile. She seemed quite unaware of the aunt and, her mission apparently accomplished, turned and walked down the hall. The aunt immediately checked the baby, and seeing that the child was alright, went after the apparition. When she arrived at the living room, the figure had vanished, yet there remained a strong scent of roses in the air which even Cynthia's father noticed the following morning. The scent remained in the house, even though it was winter, until Cynthia's mother came home from the hospital. There were no perfume sachets, fresh flowers, or air fresheners which could have accounted for the strange odor. The unusual scent returned to the house from time to time and can never be satisfactorily explained; it usually coincided with an illness in the family, and often served as a kind of telepathic warning to Cynthia's mother, when Cynthia was ill while at college. This particular event, of course, was told to Cynthia many years later at a family gathering, but it served to underline Cynthia's own awareness of her unusual faculty.

"Perhaps the most vivid and memorable personal experience occurred to me when I was in grade school," Cynthia explained. "I had always heard footsteps in the 1950s and 60s, starting in the aforementioned living room, coming into the front bedroom and stopping at my bed, both during the day and at night. My parents always attributed the noises to the creaking of old floors, but the house was only built in 1947. At times, the footfalls backed away from the bed, thus disputing the 'last footsteps before going to bed' theory. I occupied a twin bed which faced the hallway when the bedroom door was open. On the left side of the bed, my side, was the wall shared by both the living room and front bedroom; Mother slept in the other twin bed adjacent to the driveway wall.

"During one particular night, I had gotten up to go to the bathroom, and upon returning to my bed, snuggled under the covers and shot a quick glance at my sleeping mother. Suddenly, the room became exceptionally cold and on looking toward the door, which I had forgotten to close, I saw four figures coming from the living room *through* the hallway wall and turn into our bedroom. In order to assert that I hadn't unconsciously fallen asleep since returning to bed, I began pinching myself and looking from time to time to the familiar surrounding room and my mother. Thus I know, I was fully awake and not dreaming. The first figure entering the room was dressed, as were all the others, in 19th century Western American clothing. She was a woman in her forties of average height, very thin and dressed in a brown and white calico dress with high-button collar and long sleeves; her dark brown hair was parted in the middle and tied tightly on top of her head in a bun. There was a prim, austere air about her. She moved to the foot of the bed on my far left. Next came a very tall and lanky man, brown hair parted in the middle, wearing a brown three-piece suit, rather shabby. He took his place in the middle, at the foot of my bed. Following him was a woman whom I felt was out of place, even at the time of the vision. She was dressed in the most outlandish purple satin outfit, tucked up on one side as a barroom girl might have worn in the old West. Her blonde hair was curled in ringlets, which were drawn up on one side of her head and cascaded down on the other. I sensed loneliness and a very gentle nature surrounding her as she took her place next to the tall gentleman to my right. Lastly came a very dapper if some-what plump gray-haired gentleman. He carried a small three-legged stool and a black bag, telling me he was probably a medical man. Hatted and wearing a gray three-piece suit complete with gold watch chain, he seated himself on his stool on my righthand side of the bed. They all seemed terri-bly concerned over my health, although I was not ill at the time. When the 'doctor' leaned over the bed and tried to take my hand into his, I decided I had experienced just about all I wanted to with these strangers. My voice quivered as I called out to my mother, who was a very light sleeper, and whose back was facing me, informing her of the unknowns who had invaded our bedroom. 'Mother, there are people in the room!' I called again and again. She reassured me sleepily and with-out turning over that I was only dreaming, and to go back to sleep. During these implorings on my part, the four strangers began backing away from the bed as if they were alamed by my speaking. Whether they actually spoke or I heard them telepathically, I cannot be certain, but I did 'hear' them repeatedly say, 'No, please, we only want to help you. No, no, don't call out.' My cries increased and with that they turned and exited the same way they had entered, through the wall into the living room."

The house in which this vision took place had only been built in comparatively recent times. The land had formed part of a farm in the early 19th century, but the costumes of the fig-ures, Cynthia felt sure, belonged to an earlier period. She wondered whether the land had been part of a western wagon trail, and she was reliving a child's death. On the other hand, she began to wonder whether it referred to a previous existence of her own, since she had very strong feelings about the 19th century West.

Cynthia had had a number of precognitive dreams concerning events that later took place. But the dreams that impressed themselves more than others upon her consciousness had to do with the past. Actually, it was preceded by what she described as "an insatiable interest in England" she developed in early high school, long before the Beatles became the rage of America. This was not a single dream, easily forgotten, but a series of recurrent dreams, all related one to the other, mounting in intensity as if something within her was trying to come to the surface, informing her of a long-forgotten memory.

"At times I noticed myself speaking in a north country British accent and I caught myself using English spellings, drinking tea with milk, and the first time I heard the song, 'Greensleeves,' I felt very moved and certainly melancholy. There is another song, called 'North Country Maid' which has remained my great favorite. I even went so far as to compose a 200-page term paper on England for my sociology class. But long before this project took place, I began dreaming of a cloaked man mounting a horse in the moonlight and riding out of sight into the English countryside. I was in the dream also, dressed in a blue and tan peasant frock, laced up the front. I knew it was me because I remember looking down at the dress I was wearing. In other words, I was actually a participant, not a sleeping spectator of myself, nor recognizing myself as another person. At any rate, I seemed to be coming out of a stable or barn, in which I had been lying on a large pile of hay. I begin running towards the mounting horseman, as if to beg him not to leave. Then I would awaken, only to dream the same dream several nights later.

"One night when I was particularly tired, I managed to continue my dream state after the wench's running, but not for long. In the dream, I uttered between sobs, the name of Dick, and then awoke. The dream continued in this pattern until I, now exasperatedly curious, forced myself to remain sleeping. Finally, one night, I was able to hear the whole phrase—Dick Turpin, my love, wait! Don't go!' Its mission now seemingly fulfilled by giving me a name I had never heard before, the dream never returned again."

At that time, Cynthia had never heard of Dick Turpin. But the dreams had roused her curiosity and she started to research it. Her Encyclopedia Britannica was of very little help, nor did any of the high school encyclopedias contain the name. But in her parents' library she located a 1940 edition of Nelson's Encyclopedia. In it, she found a brief listing of one Richard Turpin, an English highwayman and associate of Tom King, who lived from 1706 to 1739, when he was executed by hanging.

About a year after the dreams had subsided, she was out with a friend, when she suddenly felt a strong urge to return home immediately. Still under a kind of compulsion, she immediately turned on the television set and picked a Walt Disney show, very much to her parents' surprise, since they knew her to dislike the program. At that moment, flashed on the screen were the words, "The Legend of Dick Turpin." Cynthia then proceeded to watch the program, her eyes glued to the set, interrupting the proceedings on screen with comments of her own. "No, that wasn't what happened," she would say and proceeded to correct it. What was remarkable was her ability to relate what was about to happen onscreen and to mention characters' names before this information became available to the viewers. Afterwards, she felt dazed and remembered little of what she had said during the program.

I suggested that Cynthia meet me in Los Angeles so that I could attempt to regress her hypnotically and determine whether her reincarnation memory was factual or merely a romantic fantasy. We met just before Christmas, 1973, at my Hollywood hotel, the Continental Hyatt House. We discussed Cynthia's psychic experiences and I discovered that she had had an accident in 1969 resulting in a brain concussion. Did the accident influence her psychic perceptions in any way? No, she replied, she had had them for years prior to the accident, and they continued after the accident. Had she ever been to England or was she of English background? Both questions she answered in the negative. Her interest in English history and literature at college came *after* the recurrent dream had occurred to her. Having established that neither Cynthia nor her family had any English background nor leanings, I proceeded to regress her hypnotically in the usual manner. It took only a short time before she was under, ready to answer my questions while hypnotized.

After describing life as a Victorian gentleman in New York, and giving the name of John Wainscott, and the year 1872 or 1892, she proceeded back into the 18th century and the year 1703, to a man who had something to do with a Delaware Street. The man's name was Dick, and evidently we had gotten to the subject of her recurrent dreams.

"He is mounting a horse, and he's throwing his cape back so he can take hold of the reins. He's got a hat on with a plume on it, I am standing by the barn."

"What is your relationship with this man? What is your name?" I asked.

"A wench . . . my name is Sally."

"What year is this?"

"1732."

"What happens then?"

"He rides away like he always does."

"What happens to you?"

"I cry."

And that was all I could get out of her through hypnotic regression. But somehow it must have settled this recurrent dream and the urgency connected with it within Cynthia, for I heard nothing further from her after that.

THE GHOSTLY LADY OF NEWBURYPARK

*I*n some of my books I have reported on lady ghosts that roam the realms of the ethereal here and there in the world, but this chapter deals with a phenomenon of a different density: the ghost lady is very much flesh and blood, and her nickname, bestowed upon her for very good reasons as we shall see presently, merely indicates that she is prone to hauntings.

Some people are psychic and see ghosts and all's well; some even see them in more than one place; but my friend in Newbury Park saw them practically everywhere.

I should hasten to add that her ghost experiences were genuine, not the kind produced by an overactive imagination. How do I know this? Because I met the ghost lady and visited the places where she has partaken of the uncanny, with no less a perceiver in matters psychic than Sybil Leek, trance medium extraordinary who never missed a ghost if there was one about, or minces words if there wasn't!

It all started around the beginning of January 1966, when I received a letter from Mrs. Gwen Hinzie of Newbury Park, California. She wished to contribute some material to my research efforts.

"In 1946 I was 26 years old," she wrote. "I spent about four months in New York City working as a secretary. I lived in Brooklyn Heights—at different times in two different rooming houses—and there (in both) was conscious of ghosts.

"One of these old brownstone houses was in the next block south of the St. George Hotel in Brooklyn Heights and the other about a half block distant. It has been so long ago I cannot remember the street names now.

"In the first house mentioned I lived on the ground floor. It was an old firetrap really and even had rats. It was a four-story building in poor repair.

"I lived in a room off the furnace room that had a door leading out to the side of the building. My only heat was from the furnace room itself and there was a small opening in the wall (covered with coarse wire screening) through which the heat was supposed to pass. I lived there for about one month (November 1946).

"My experiences took place over about a two-week period. The first thing that happened was hearing a woman crying in the night. Then another woman spoke to her sharply and she stopped crying. This seemed to be on the other side of the wall in the room or apartment occupied by the only other tenant on that floor. When I asked her later about this, she denied that anyone ever stayed with her!

"Later, one evening I came into the furnace room to go to my room and passed through what seemed to be a pall of black smoke. There was no smoke odor but the furnace was burning. When I told my landlady about it she said she was sure there was nothing wrong with the furnace.

"Another evening, through the wall opening I previously mentioned, there appeared a *thick white mist*—but it looked more like smoke than mist. I got out of my chair and went to the bed to pick up something to flap away this 'smoke' (it was only halfway through the opening) and when I turned back again it was gone.

"At another later time during the day I found *this thick white mist materializing before my eyes*. Then it disappeared. There was also a black mist that had materialized while my back was turned another time—but this was one that frightened me. The other had not. I spoke to 'it' and said to go away but it was several seconds before it did.

"After I had been there about a week I found it necessary to buy a small electric heater since it was becoming cold in there, and I found I had to sit before my little stove with my coat on. It did not even warm my feet. The heat seemed to radiate only about two and a half to three inches from the stove. I became ill while living in that room with a respiratory infection and was so cold that I found by the time I had been there about three weeks that I could not warm up until I had been in our (too) warm office about two hours!

"By that time I believed there were ghosts there and upon inquiring of the landlady found that she had nothing to say. She merely suggested I find another place to live.

"About the first of December I moved into another brownstone. (I should explain here that when I had first arrived in Brooklyn Heights I was visiting friends and stayed in *their* apartment. I had not been there a week before I *occasionally saw strangely dressed people on the street*. I thought this was my imagination as I seemed to get carried away thinking of what the old place must have been like in its heyday. I thought at first there might have been a theatre nearby and that these were actors but later found out this was not the case.)

"I soon was busy going back and forth to work and did not see strange people on the street. One of these people that I did remember was a woman—in her twenties or possibly a little older—who was tall, thin and looked about six months pregnant. She wore a dress that was long and had long sleeves or three-quarter-length sleeves and a bustle. The bodice was very snug and the waist very tight but the bulge below the waist suggested pregnancy. She walked rapidly down the street (across the street) away from me.

"Imagine my shock when I entered my new boarding house and saw *the same woman,* dressed the same, standing in the doorway leading from the foyer to the hallway in the rear of the building! She was standing facing the wall, so was sideways to my view, and when I unlocked the door she distinctly jumped and looked with fear on her face toward the door. *Then she calmly walked into the wall.* I never saw her again there or anywhere else.

"We (my husband and children and I) now live in a small town in Ventura County and are renting a house on farm land. We have a barn—not in sight of the house—and there is some peculiar phenomenon here. There is a road from the house—to the left—that curves around a small hill, at the bottom of which is the barn. You cannot see it until you turn the bend in the road but this barn has a very peculiar atmosphere. It was built no more, I'm pretty sure, than 30 years ago. We have there some rabbits and there is a horse stall though the old horse rarely uses it. Our dog is not afraid to go in there nor are the cats. Yet just before you reach the bend in the road you become aware of this peculiar atmosphere. It is a quiet and solitary feeling in this area and in the barn. The atmosphere is almost the same as you feel in a cemetery but not as peaceful. It is not especially depressing or terrifying—but it is, to me, an uncomfortable place to be. I call it a feeling of discomfiture as *I feel like an intruder.* My husband does not feel it and says I fill my head with all kinds of spooky ideas. I wonder, though, if this might be due to a grave being nearby—*I don't know* that there is one so this may not be it; or could it be the old buggies in the barn, or is it really my imagination? So peculiar—what do you think?"

Well, I thought enough of Mrs. Hinzie's letter to communicate with her further. In the first place, her longhand showed no sign of imbalance, something I can often tell from a person's handwriting or signature. To the contrary, Mrs. Hinzie sounded to me like a pretty level-headed person and her description of the uncanny had clarity and depth. I decided I was going to like the lady and wrote back for more details. For one thing, I detected a peculiar discrepancy between her avowed position of a simple housewife in a small farming community, and the way she expressed herself, so I asked for her background and Mrs. Hinzie was glad to oblige.

"I was born in Los Angeles in 1920 and am of Irish-English descent. I was raised in that city and Beverly Hills, where I attended both public and Catholic schools. I attended the University of Los Angeles and was graduated in 1943 with a Bachelor of Arts degree. I have three sisters and our life was fairly ordinary, I think. We were never poor but not rich. After I was graduated from the University I worked for several years and married in 1952 and now have three children—one of whom is also sensitive.

"I have had clairvoyant experiences many times in my life and until recently did not mention them, as paranormal experiences were considered too 'far out' for ordinary people. Now, of course, there is much interest in the subject.

"When I was 12, in 1932, we rented a house at 3rd Avenue and 12th Street in Los Angeles—the only house on the north side of that short block. When I first went into the house I walked with my mother from the front hall to the breakfast room and looked in while talking to her. I saw (her back was to the door) what I thought was a colored woman bending over a box in that room and, believing mother had hired her to help with the unpacking, greeted her. Then this dark form spread itself over the cardboard box like a coat. As I stared it pulled itself up and became a tall dark form—it appeared hooded but had no face. I called my mother's attention to it and she screamed. It backed out of the room into the kitchen, so tall it bumped its head against the top of the door and went around the corner. We did move in, but never, to my knowledge, did anyone see it again. I cannot explain it at all but it was very loathsome and frightening.

"Across from the breakfast room was a small closet with a door leading to the basement. I and others also did, from time to time, hear footsteps coming up those stairs, but no one had the courage to investigate, as far as I know.

We lived there about five months and then moved away.

"My husband, Don Hinzie, has suggested that I tell you the following, but I believe it is a fairly common experience.

"When I was 21 years old my father passed away from a heart attack. I was in the room at the time of his death. He had been in great pain and was lying on the bed. Emergency hospital attendants were there giving oxygen but he lay with his hands clenched. When he stopped breathing, his hand relaxed, and within seconds a white vapor ascended from his opening hand and disappeared. This I have been given to understand as being the release of the soul from the body and have heard of it before.

"When I was about 18, our dog Rowdy, then 13 years old, died. He simply disappeared from our home and I did not at first believe he was dead although a body looking like his had been found, and I continued for a few days to put his food out by the back door for him. Then one *evening I saw him come up* toward the food. He would not let me touch him and would not touch the food. He then walked away toward the side of the house. In a few minutes I followed him but he had disappeared. Later on a few occasions I saw him on the front lawn, where he had been accustomed to sit, and once heard him barking out there. I told my parents about it but I don't believe they ever saw him.

"This clairvoyance can be less than a blessing. When I was

about eight or nine there was a child in our neighborhood who had died of an illness, and one day about a month after his death (I knew him but he was not a friend of mine) I was with some children near his home when I saw him standing on the driveway and I said so. I was called a liar and lost at least one friend as a result of it. After that, I stopped mentioning things I saw. At the time I did not know I saw a ghost. I thought they were not telling me the truth about the boy being dead!

"I also saw another ghost in San Francisco in 1947. Until about 1961 or 1962 I did not know whom I had seen. It was *not until then* that I read about her. Her name I do not have but can find out. Her story is in a book called, I think, *American Ghosts*. It was while my roommate and I, vacationing in San Francisco, were riding on a cable car up to Nob Hill. We both saw her.

"The cable car had stopped at a cross street. There were other people on the street and she caught my attention because of her filmy white dress. It seemed inappropriate on the street. She was a young girl, not pretty, but smiling and apparently nodding to people on the street. She seemed substantial enough until she started to pass a couple of girls on the sidewalk, when her full skirt and part of her body *passed part way through one of the girls*. Just before she passed these girls the side of her gown suddenly appeared spangled with water drops or brilliants, but it seemed as if water had suddenly been sprayed on her gown. Knowing then that she was a ghost, and having caught her eye, I tried to tell her in my mind to go to heaven, but she looked frightened and disappeared. My roommate and others saw her and she has been seen many times walking along the street on Nob Hill.

"In my first letter to you I mentioned the peculiar atmosphere near our barn. There was something I forgot to mention and it did not come to my mind until about five days ago when *I heard the voice again.*

"After we had been here about six weeks or so one day I heard a child's voice say 'Hi!' very cheerfully. It seemed to come from across the yard. I did not see anyone and it was during school hours and I didn't understand it but felt, my vision being so poor at the time due to temporary eye trouble, that I had simply not seen the child. Also, one day at the clothesline, I thought I saw, directly in front of me but on the hill about 40 feet away and partly obscured by a tree, a human being, male, not very old. As I watched through my misty eyes, I saw him walk away, I thought, over the brow of the hill. Now that I can see better I know the hill doesn't slope away abruptly there. You would have to walk at least another 50 feet.

"The children and I have heard the cheery little 'Hi' a few other times but after the summer was over we did not hear it again until a few days ago when our only dog and I were home. I had just walked away from the door about six steps when I heard a cheery little 'Hi.' I turned quickly but saw no one (it sounded about six or eight feet away from me). The dog heard it too and got up—not frightened or suspicious (he is half German shepherd and quite alert), but only curious. He went around to the side of the house, apparently saw nothing and ran across the drive to the side of the hill and looked down. Not seeing anything he came back to the front of the house and lay down, unperturbed. Today, when my little daughter, aged 8, came home from school she told me her little friend that she walks home with thought he saw a boy running across the lawn when there was no one here. I have been saying rosaries for the repose of the soul of this person if that's what it is and also for a nullifying of the uncomfortable atmosphere on the road leading to the barn and the barn itself and believe this is helping. At least, the last time I was at the barn, a few days ago, it had a pleasant, peaceful country air.

"So much for my experiences."

No wonder Mrs. Hinzie sounded well educated—she was! I had not bargained for the San Francisco story and welcomed it of course, especially as I seemed to recall it in an indefinite way from James Reynolds' *Ghosts in American Houses*.

I decided to go after the story immediately, as it seemed so unusual by ghostly standards: after all, a ghost in the middle of the street seen by several people is out of the ordinary. I requested the testimony of the friend who Mrs. Hinzie claimed was with her at the time she had the experience in San Francisco. The friend, now Mrs. William Mace but at the time named Peggy O'Conner, was Gwen Hinzie's roommate for about a year and a half. Since Miss O'Conner's marriage in 1948 they had not kept up the contact, however, except for an occasional Christmas card.

"She saw the ghost and was very upset about it," Mrs. Hinzie explained. "Other people on the cable car I was in also saw the ghost, as I heard a couple of women comment on it."

Imagine riding up a hill in a cable car, looking out the window and seeing a ghost!

I suggested Mrs. Hinzie meet me in San Francisco so we could locate the exact spot where the incident took place. She readily agreed, and offered to come with her close friend Sharon Bettin, with whom she shared many interests; also, Mrs. Bettin's parents had a house at Santa Cruz, and the two ladies could stay there.

It sounded fine to me, but Mrs. Hinzie warned that there might be a hindrance. If her husband, who was the custodian at the local school, should not be able to arrange to take care of the children, she would not be able to go. As it turned out, the powers-that-be made her trip possible exactly as planned.

At the time of the incident, Mrs. Hinzie recalled, she was staying at the Fairmount Hotel, atop the hill, and the ride was no more than three or four blocks up the hill. She was reasonably sure she could find the spot again. I, of course, was going to bring Sybil Leek with me, not telling her the reasons.

The story, as reported by James Reynolds in *Ghosts in American Houses*, is quite a shocker, considering the period it occurred in. The story was, of course, unknown to Mrs. Hinzie at the time she saw the ghost.

The disappearance of Flora Sommerton a few hours before her debut was a great mystery for many years. Flora was the only child of Charles Benfow Sommerton, originally from Kansas City, Kansas, who had built a mansion on Nob Hill, San Francisco. Sommerton was rich, his wife was ambitious, and the debut of their daughter on her eighteenth birthday in 1876 was to be an affair of splendor. Moreover, Flora's parents had wedding plans for Flora. They insisted that she should marry in due course a young dissolute snob named Hugh Partridge whom she despised.

On the afternoon of the day of the debut, Mrs. Sommerton urged Flora to take a long nap in order to be fresh for the party at ten that evening. Instead Flora insisted on going out, and she disappeared. She was last seen by a grocer's delivery boy to whom she gave a written message for her mother. The boy delivered the note to the Sommerton residence, which was in a great flurry of preparations for the party; in the excitement the maid who received it promptly mislaid it.

Came early evening and no debutante. Also missing was the beautiful white gown covered with crystal beads that had been ordered from Paris for the debut. A family conference was called. A maid finally found the misplaced note. The family decided to carry off the party anyway. The domineering Mrs. Sommerton would not permit her husband to notify the police. Guests were told that Flora had had a sudden illness and had been sent to the country. In spite of all this, the ball was a great success.

In the morning Mr. Sommerton called in the police and put up a huge reward—$250,000—for the return of his daughter. That money was to lie unclaimed in a San Francisco bank for many years, even after the death of Charles Benfow Sommerton, which occurred shortly after the fire in 1906 which destroyed the Sommerton mansion.

Throughout the decades many tips and clues were offered, but Flora was elusive. Mrs. Sommerton finally called off the search although there was a little evidence that Flora was still alive. Mrs. Carrie Sommerton died in 1916.

The evidence was an undated letter written to the police by an Adele LaBlanche in Los Angeles. Miss LaBlanche was the prima donna of a touring company that was presenting *The Prince of Pilsen* in Los Angeles. But her letter referred to an incident in Chicago. Miss LaBlanche had sprained her ankle and had been obliged to call upon her understudy, Miss Jarvis. Her costume, however, did not fit the smaller Miss Jarvis. Whereupon the wardrobe mistress, described by Miss LaBlanche as "a quiet, faded, middle-aged woman," fished out a dress she said might do in this emergency. It was out of fash ion but beautiful, a creation of white tulle "sprinkled like the heavens on a starry night with crystal beads." Miss Jarvis wore it and then tried to buy it. Said the wardrobe mistress: "No, I cannot sell it. It is my only link with the past. It is Nob Hill and what I might have been." Then, Miss LaBlanche wrote, "a startled look came into her eyes, and she took her dress and fled, again leaving no trace."

The mystery was finally solved in 1926. Flora Sommerton was at last located, dead, in Butte, Montana. Here she had been known as Mrs. Butler, housekeeper for ten years in the Butte Central Hotel. Coroner's verdict: death from heart disease. But the police were skeptical about her name, Butler.

In her valise was found a nest of clippings dating back from 1876 to 1891 that referred to the search for Flora Sommerton, daughter of a multi-millionaire nabob. The clippings came from all over the United States. When Mrs. Butler died, she was dressed in a white ball gown conjectured to be of the 1880s which was entirely covered with crystal beads. Her age was given as about 57, but she must have been 68 when she was found dead in a hotel room by a housemaid.

The Reynolds account ends with a rumor.

"Now people report seeing a girl in a shimmering dress strolling in streets and gardens in the Nob Hill section of the city. She seems to be returning from a late party. The figure smiles at passers-by and moves in a leisurely manner. As in her life, Flora is still walking alone."

The time had come for me to fly to California and follow up on the story so vividly told by Reynolds, and, of course, to check up on Mrs. Hinzie's experiences. It was a warm day in May of 1966 when I met Mrs. Hinzie and her friend Mrs. Bettin at the Hilton Hotel in San Francisco.

I had decided to discuss the case once more with the ladies prior to proceeding to the spot. Present during our conversation was my good friend Lori Clerf, a social worker living in the city. Sybil Leek was to join us downstairs about an hour later, just in time for the ride. She could not overhear any of our earlier conversation.

We established once again that the cable car was the California Street line, and that the girl in the party dress had walked down one of the streets crossing California Street.

"You were looking out the window of the cable car when this happened?" I asked.

"No, there was no glass—just the open side of the cable car, where you step up."

No reflection then, on glass. That alternative explanation was out.

"When she walked through two other people, did you think it was unusual?"

"Well, she was also improperly dressed for the street—that's how I noticed her in the first place."

A woman would, of course.

"Coming home from a party in the middle of the afternoon," Mrs. Hinzie added. Even in San Francisco that might be considered unusual. "As I was looking at her, the dress seemed diaphanous, but you could not see through it. All white, no other colors. And as I was watching her it looked as if there were water suddenly sprayed on her side; it clung there, shining as water does in the sun."

There was some time still before we would meet Sybil, so I went over my previous notes and questioned Mrs. Hinzie about other psychic experiences she might have had and not told me about. For it was already plain to me that the most interesting part of the case was not the ghost but the lady who saw her. It is not often that a person observes with such wealth of detail psychic events that are later checked out and substantiated, and I wanted to make sure I had all the incidents right. Had Mrs. Hinzie told me all?

She had not. In 1941, when she was 21 years old, she had gone with her mother and sister to be house guests of W.A. Anderson, in Winnipeg, Canada.

"In January of that same year," Mrs. Hinzie began her story, "my father had passed away and in March of that year Mr. Anderson had lost his wife, so he and my mother were both widowed, and they had been friends since 1924. The house had over thirty rooms, and at the time the only people living in it were Mr. Anderson, his daughter Betty Jane, and three servants.

"The day we arrived and drove up the gravel in front of the house, I saw what I thought was someone at the window upstairs that turned out to belong to Mrs. Anderson's sewing room. But there was nobody up there at the time. We entered the big hallway, and Mr. Anderson was standing there to receive us. At this moment, my hair went up, straight. I don't know why, for I had met him a number of times before. He welcomed us and we were taken into the living room. It was a hot day and I had a headache, so I sat in a chair in the living room, facing the hall, while someone went to get an aspirin. At this moment, as I sat there, I heard a car pull up on the gravel outside, then a door slam, but I did not hear the front door open. But a moment later I heard some steps come across the hall, and a young girl crossed the hall in front of my vision, and she was wearing a white dress with silver slippers with rhinestones on them, and one of the straps was broken. I thought there was mud on her stockings and shoes, and that her skirt was torn; her hair was blown and her eyes were very pale blue. *She had a dark spot right up on the crown of her head.* That was all—she just went out of my field of vision."

"How did she get in?"

"She was just there."

"What did it all mean?"

"Well, the Andersons had a daughter who committed suicide in 1936. Her name was Martha, and she had married a man against her parents' wishes."

"Did you tell Mr. Anderson what you had witnessed?"

"Yes. I had at first thought it was his other daughter, Betty Jane. But Betty Jane only arrived later that afternoon. We were in the house for ten days, and I saw the girl several times more."

"Can you elaborate on these experiences?"

"When I got to the top of the stairs I would see her going to her bedroom, and on one occasion I was standing in the hallway just about to go into a room my mother was occupying on the second floor when I saw this girl cross by me and go into that room; but the room, which was decorated in orange and beige, seemed to be all white, white draperies all over—and she just vanished into the white draperies!"

"Anything more about the girl with the dark spot on her head?"

"Once she walked into the room and faded into the white of the draperies. Then I could see a man standing on the other side of the bed behind these curtains. She walked in and went 'Hah,' like that, and they started to talk, but I could not make out the conversation. I stood there mesmerized, just watching. Then it sounded as if someone had just broken a stick, I mean the noise I heard, and she came out from behind the curtains, with her arms up behind her head, walked about three steps, then she fell, right in front of me. Her eyes seemed crossed as if she had been hit on the head. A little trickle of blood came down her forehead. Then her eyes half-closed, and at that point I felt a terrific blow on the back of my own head—it felt as though I were being driven through the floor . . . and my sister was standing in the hallway screaming at me . . . saying, 'Bunny, Bunny' . . . which is my nickname . . . and I felt very peculiar. My mother of course insisted I had imagined the whole thing."

"Remarkable," I said. "Then you actually saw the entire traumatic scene just as it happened. You are indeed psychic."

Mrs. Hinzie nodded with a wan smile.

"The following year my mother married our host. Two years later, she came to see me in Los Angeles, and referring to the incident finally admitted—'I saw it too . . . it was horrible!'"

"What happened to the house?"

"Mr. Anderson and my mother later rented it and finally took an apartment where they lived until his death. The house is still standing but I have no idea as to who owns it now."

"What about the scene you witnessed?"

"Mother asked me never to tell Mr. Anderson and I didn't. But I had still another experience in this house, on the day we left.

"I was sleeping in Martha's bedroom—she was the daughter who died—and I slept very badly that night. I woke up early, when I heard someone working the door handle. Now I had locked the room from the inside on retiring. But a woman came in, nevertheless, and I said, 'Oh, Mother . . .' but she did not look like my mother— she wore a silken long dressing gown . . . she had her hands up over her head . . . I was still kind of sleepy . . . I must have dozed off again, and when I woke up a little later she was still in my room, only now she wore a cotton dress, and I thought it was Mother and said, 'Oh, Mother, what time is it?' But she said, 'I'm Em . . .' and I said, 'When are we leaving?' and she replied, 'Ten minutes of nine.'"

"What happened then?"

"She moved the clock on the dresser, and walked out. I got up—it was just eight o'clock—and I put on my clothes fast. I realized then who Em was. The late Mrs. Anderson."

"What about this ten minutes to nine remark? Any significance?"

"I don't know, but we actually did leave exactly at that time. Ten minutes to nine."

"Was that the last time a dead member of the Anderson family appeared to you?"

"In 1953, when my husband and I returned to Los Angeles from Omaha where we lived for a while, we stayed at the house shared by my mother and Mr. Anderson for several days. That particular night I am about to mention, a son of Mr. Anderson's by the name of Gordon and his fiancée were also staying in the house, which was at Ninth and Western Avenue. At this moment, my husband was lying down, for he was not feeling well after an operation; Mother and the fiancée were out of the room to look at some jewelry. Gordon was in the kitchen and Mr. Anderson was out of the house, so I was sitting in the living room all alone.

"I got up and walked into the adjoining dining room where I found Gordon, whom I had thought in the kitchen, mixing drinks. There was always bad blood between us, and for one reason or another he grabbed my arm. The others now came back in, just as a voice was heard seemingly from outside saying, 'Gordon, stop that!' Mr. Anderson seemed taken aback. 'Why,' he said, 'that was Em's voice.'"

"Two ghosts then," I said, "mother and daughter, but mother evidently is free to travel."

"She died naturally," Mrs. Hinzie explained. "No reason she should be earthbound."

"Quite so." I nodded and looked at my watch. It was time to meet Sybil and go to California Avenue where the ghost of the girl in the party dress might be waiting—if we were lucky.

The important point of the incident was Mrs. Hinzie's total ignorance of the story or tradition about this ghostly girl at the time she saw her. It was fifteen years later that she accidentally came across the account in James Reynolds' book in the Public Library. Thus we must rule out unconscious hallucination of a known event.

When we arrived atop Nob Hill, it was about four in the afternoon, and traffic was heavy. Lori parked her shining white car carefully—that's the only way you can park a car in San Francisco if you don't want it to roll downhill—and we walked a few steps to the street intersection of California where Mrs. Hinzie remembered the incident. What did Sybil feel at this spot? Did the noises of the onrushing traffic blot out all psychic impressions, or did she feel something other than flesh-and-blood and gasoline?

"Yes, I do," Sybil intoned immediately. "I feel fear . . . someone is afraid . . . more than one person involved . . . fear . . . someone wants to run away . . ."

How right she was!

"What sort of person is it wants to run away?" I prodded.

"A young person," she replied, while trying hard to get an impression above the din of the traffic. No medium ever worked under more trying conditions, but then the experiment was unique.

"Man or woman?"

"Young . . . feeling of panic . . . I feel cold . . . despite this hot day . . . look at the goosepimples on my arms. . . ."

"Why is this person running away?"

"I think there is a link with the house I just pointed out to you."

The house, though old, was not the house belonging to the girl's family, though the spot might have been the same site.

"It's someone who runs away from a house," Sybil continued, "she ran this way. . . ."

"She?"

"I don't know . . . but suddenly I felt 'she.' I have 1830 in my mind. '30 is very clear. Several people are involved in this . . . this chase. A hounding."

"Any unhappiness involved?"

"The girl . . . she is panic-stricken."

"Why?"

"I have a feeling of terrible disease, horror."

Later I realized that Sybil might have picked up the girl's death. She had died of heart disease.

"Is she still here?"

"Yes, definitely."

We left the crowded spot none too soon, for people began to recognize us—Sybil, in her purple dress and stockings, and me, the Ghost Hunter—from our television appearances, and I never like to answer questions on busy street corners.

Sybil had no way of "guessing" the connection of the spot we took her to with the ghostly girl. Nor could she have picked the unconscious mind of Mrs. Hinzie, who was distant from Sybil, nor mine, for I, too, let Sybil go around the area by herself.

Mrs. Hinzie had indeed impressed me with her experiences and I decided to follow up on what had originally brought us together, courtesy U.S. mail: the haunted house and barn at Newbury Park, California.

Mrs. Hinzie wanted my opinion on her "problem," but I had been so intrigued with the San Francisco case, I had put the question aside.

"I have been disappointed that you have not yet commented on our situation here," she wrote me—"the uncomfortable atmosphere around the barn and the voice I've heard saying 'Hi,' but I do have, I believe, additional information on that which we think is interesting."

"First I will tell you about our town, Newbury Park. It is on the map and up to five years ago had a population of about 5,000 or less. We now have about 11,000 people, I believe. My husband and I have lived here since June 1961 but in another part of town until last February. The town's only claim to fame is its stagecoach inn, a hostelry which, I understand from Mrs. Michael Hagopejion, the president of the Conejo Valley Historical Society, was used as a hotel and stop-over for the stagecoach travelling between Santa Barbara and Los Angeles from 1876 to 1915. The inn is now being moved from its location, the equivalent of about two city blocks from us, to another location a few hundred feet away, as the freeway overpass will pass through the original site of the inn. It is a two-story frame building of 19 rooms.

"Up to 1960, Newbury Park, except for a very small residential section, was all ranch land. These ranches were in size from hundreds to thousands of acres. Many of the owners were related to each other, and so for the past 90 years it has been a small ranching community.

"I have learned from our friend Martin Bettin that sometime in the late 1800's there was a boy staying at the inn who, probably in exploring the hilly country close by, became lost. The boy was never found. I cannot help wondering if the child's voice we have heard, and it *is* the voice of a young boy, could be the ghost of this lost child?

"Martin Bettin got his information from a fireman at the

Lake Sherwood fire station. His name is Simeon Dyke and he got the story from his father, an old-timer in the Conejo Valley.

"Another thing of interest to the barn area (which I find uncomfortable): This property, belonging to Allen Hays, our landlord, was purchased by his father sometime between 1910 and 1920, I understand. We live on about 2 1/2 acres of land, but the Hays ranch consisted of hundreds of acres and, after old Mr. Hays' death, was divided between his children, Allen Hays and Reba Jeffries.

"Through Simeon Dyke, Martin learned that in about 1920 there were a house and barn in the pasture adjacent to our present barn. They were torn down years ago. But at that time the people who lived in that house had a little girl, aged two or three, who fell into an open well or cesspool and was drowned. Could this, I wonder, have anything to do with my feeling about the barn area? Actually, however, my feeling is not around the pasture but the barn itself, outside that fenced pasture and also the road—part of it— above the barn closer to the house.

"I overheard a conversation between Martin and Sharon Bettin and Sharon's mother, Mrs. Davies, while I was at Mrs. Davies' house, and asked them about it. Apparently they didn't want to say anything in front of me, but Martin and Sharon have admitted to Mrs. Davies they have an uncomfortable feeling in our barn. I had always felt myself *like a trespasser there*, and seldom visit the barn, but Martin has about 100 rabbits there and he is there frequently. He says he feels as if someone might come around the corner at any time. He says it's almost as if you expect someone to suddenly come up from nowhere and tap you on the shoulder—and Martin isn't timid. Sharon said she felt uncomfortable there, too."

By now I thought I knew Newbury Park pretty well without ever having set foot on this little speck of land. Mrs. Hinzie had a way of describing her world that had authenticity, and I decided to let her be our guide if and when we could go there in person.

Meanwhile I asked her to report further unusual happenings to me when they took place. Mrs. Hinzie was a bit worried about my postponing our visit to the fall of 1966.

"We expect to move from here in about a year, and it is unlikely that the place will be tenanted again after that, as Mr. Hays, our landlord, wants to sell this property for commercial use and undoubtedly this little house will be torn down. It is 10 years old and made of cement blocks.

"There have been three occurrences that I have not mentioned, over the past two months. The most recent was a weird 'singing' or 'whistling' noise which I heard a few nights ago. I am reasonably sure this was not my imagination, as my son, David, has told me of hearing such a noise about two months ago while he was in the bathroom. He was frightened, but no one else heard it and I could not imagine what it could be other than a little air in the pipes. But when I heard what I assume was the same noise it was while I sat up alone in our living room-kitchen.

"The other thing that happened was the day I saw the ghost. I knew from the voice that it was a boy of about 10 or 12. But this day (in late January) while I was washing the windows, I saw through the window pane clearly standing by the fence a young boy *and you could see the fence through him!* It was in the morning and that side of the house was shaded but the yard behind it was in brilliant sunlight. I wasn't sure I could believe my eyes and when I turned around he was gone.

"Another hard-to-explain thing that happened was one evening at least a month ago—maybe more—when my husband and I were sitting in the living room and the room was fairly quiet. We both heard a sound that could only be called a whimpering near the door. I had heard this several months before but no one else had."

The experiences of young children are generally considered unworthy of belief when one investigates scientifically phenomena of this kind, and yet no one dares say that all children make up stories and that there are not keen observers among the very young.

I did not attach importance to the testimony of the Hinzie children by itself, but coming on the heels of so much *adult* evidence, it seemed to reinforce the whole case and therefore I am reporting it. Mrs. Hinzie carefully wrote down what her children reported seeing in the house.

"David told me about some misty shapes he had seen, and said the other kids also saw them some time ago in their bedroom. He said it was dark in the room and these 'things' were light.

"Near the ceiling he saw three misty shapes and they seemed to be looking down at the children. They were vague but he thought they were people. He called me and when I came in and opened the door they disappeared.

"Until June of 1965 (that is, in reference to our staying in this house), my husband, Don, worked nights (2 P.M. to 10:30 P.M.). It was during that period (between late February and mid-June) that one night there was an uproar in the bedroom and the children all called me and I rushed in, after removing books, etc., from my lap in the living room and opened the door and the kids pointed to the *ceiling* near the end of the bedroom partition and said, 'See it, mom'—'see it.' But I saw nothing.

"I turned around to turn on the light and it was gone.

"The kids said, that night, they 'saw something' in that spot. They said it was 'horrible' and could not describe it. Said it was not misty and had, according to them, no definite shape. They asked me to leave the door open, which I did after first closing it and telling them it was nonsense. But they were nearly hysterical when I closed the door, so I immediately reopened it. They settled down almost immediately after that and slept. There was no reoccurrence of that particular night.

"The children sleep in a room that is on the north side of the house and has two windows on that side. There are no windows in the east wall or the south or west wall and the two bedrooms I mentioned are really one room partitioned to within about three feet of the door.

"The 'shapeless, horrible' thing the kids saw was on my mind for a while after that, and when I saw something in there later on, I was not sure it was not subconscious suggestion on my part and never mentioned it to anyone, but it was about three weeks later that it happened. The children were insisting upon the door being left open and I allowed it for several weeks after they saw this thing.

"The night I saw *something*, the door was, therefore, open. I was sitting across from the door by the windows and looked up to see a *misty, whitish shape in the doorway* next to the partition and partly over it—above floor level some six feet, I would say. It seemed to move slightly and I really thought the kids must have seen something. I went in but all was silence. There was no odor of smoke, and the thing must have gone farther up on the wall because it seemed higher. Also, it did not move now as I looked at it. I left the door open and went back to my chair, but when I had sat down again it was no longer visible.

"At least once, after we had been in the house about a month, my son John asked me if fog could come in the house and into the bedroom. He was in bed at the time and asked me if I could see the 'fog in the room.' I told him that if fog came in (we had much rain and fog at the time) it would not be visible, as the house is warm and would make this vapor disappear. However, he insisted there was fog in the room. I could not see it.

"John, too, has been subject to nightmares in the past 5 to

6 years and I am beginning to wonder about them. He is not a particularly fearful child when awake—is, as a matter of fact, braver than our other two children and very matter-of-fact. He is highly intelligent and is always seeking answers to things. He will be 10 in June. Many times my husband or I have had to call out loudly and sharply to John during the night when he has been shouting in his sleep—sometimes sitting up—to jolt him out of his dream, as he doesn't hear you when you speak to him in a normal tone and are beside his bed while he is having one of these nightmares. I have found he is not as bad lately but have also found touching him or being by his side will often frighten him greatly even with the light on. I sometimes find, though, that calling out to him only half awakens him, and I have to go into the room, turn on the light and go up to his bed talking all the time before he knows who spoke to him. Then he settles down. But children do have nightmares, and I did not give it really serious thought until about Christmas time last year (1965) when one night, after I had gone to bed and all the family was asleep, I heard John start talking as if he were awake, making comments and talking (apparently) to David.

"Then I thought I heard a patient voice answering him *and* calling him by name saying to the effect 'no, John,' then John began to get excited and I, thinking it was David, heard finally an irritable 'Oh, John, go to sleep, shut up!' There was just a moment or two of silence and then John started very excitedly: 'What? *What?* Who's there? Who *are* you?' I called to John, 'It's Dave,' and then went into the bedroom and turned on the light. John was as close to hysterics as I've ever seen him, huddled in his bed, alternately covering his head and pulling out. He began to relax when he saw me, and Dave was sprawled out on the bed looking very much asleep—and I'm sure he was, as he was face up and made no effort to shield his eyes from the light when I came in. I went up to John's bed and said to him, 'John, you're dreaming,' but am sure he was not asleep because he looked at me, *seeing me*, and said he wasn't. He said he thought someone was asking him questions but he didn't know who it was. I told him it must have been Dave, but he said it didn't sound like Dave and I must admit it really didn't—the voice was somewhat slurred at times and different from Dave's. John insisted there was someone else in the room, but I told him this could not be. He was sure it was a boy.

"There hasn't been much else happening around here recently other than my hearing outdoors, apparently on the hill behind the clothes line, a whimpering sound, quite loud, that lasted for several minutes at a time.

"Also, yesterday afternoon, my daughter and I were sitting on the patio and we both heard distinctly two car doors slam on the other side of the house. She went to see if the truck doors had slammed shut, but they were both open and there were no cars out there. On many occasions, particularly after we had lived here only about a month or so, when I was here alone in the afternoon, I would hear a car stop on the gravel by the carport and a door slam shut—not very loud but distinct—and not so loudly as we heard them outside yesterday. Yesterday, however, I heard no crunching of gravel.

"At first, when I heard the car pull up and the door slam I would get up and go look out the kids' bedroom window, but I never saw anything.

"I forgot to mention that one day, three months after we had moved in here, I was sitting at the table in the living room-dining room-kitchen area and *saw the door open*. The handle was turned gently. I heard a little sound and it opened—about six inches. I went and closed it and that was all."

The incidents in the little house at Newbury Park seemed to point out some pretty curious things: for one thing, the white form was seen well above ground level, near the ceiling, as it were. After we looked over the house in person, I realized *why*. The house had been built onto the hillside, artificially terracing it, so that the ceiling level coincided with what was formerly the ground level. Any ghosts appearing at the ceiling were really walking on what was *to them*, at least, still ground level!

I had not yet been to the house when the children's report was sent to me by Mrs. Hinzie, although we had met in San Francisco. But at that time I specifically asked Mrs. Hinzie not to talk of the events in her house at Newbury Park so that Sybil could not "tune in" on them, and nothing pertaining to Newbury Park was discussed. When we finally did go there in October of 1966, it came as a great surprise to Sybil to meet the ghost lady from San Francisco again—in her own surroundings this time!

On May 18th, Mrs. Hinzie was further disturbed by occurrences of a paranormal nature.

"Last week I walked into the house from outdoors and closed the door behind me. There was no one in the house and no animals in the house, but I distinctly heard a few feet from me a cat hiss sharply. I looked around to be sure that no cats were in the house. This had also happened last summer.

"Twice in the past month—only a few days apart—I thought I *was touched by someone.* The first time I was washing dishes at the sink and felt, I thought, two small hands lightly on my back at the waistline. I turned around thinking John had sneaked up on me (the children were in bed) but there was no one there. A few days later I walked outside in front of the front window, to the door. There is a bench in front of the window. As I walked by the bench I distinctly felt the *back of my skirt and my slip being pulled firmly.* I reached down to touch my clothes but they were in place and the pressure immediately stopped.

"Perhaps I should have known there was something odd about this place when we moved.

"The day my husband brought me to the house to see the place I had a strange experience. Don, my husband, had just painted the house inside and it was clean and when he asked me what I thought of it, I said, 'Well, it's all right, but don't you think Mr. Hays ought to fix *that hole in the wall?'* To me it looked as if, above the stove, there was a cement block neatly removed from the wall. He said, 'Where?' and I said, 'Why, right there where that red light is coming through.' He said there wasn't one and yet I thought there was a red light glowing there, not fire but more like an electric light. It faded out and the block was, of course, in place. My family laughed at me, so I thought I had imagined it, but last week as I sat with my back to the window, facing the stove, I was watching television. For some reason I looked up and saw the calendar on the wall to the left of the stove lighted up as if someone had thrown a beam of red light on it. The curtains were opened behind the couch where I sat but no one could have stood outside and played a beam of light on the calendar. It encompassed only the calendar."

The skirt-pulling incident reminded me of similar attention-getters in other cases of hauntings, except that I felt a certain pathetic helplessness here, as we were apparently dealing with the ghost of a child, and there is nothing sadder.

On May 31, Mrs. Hinzie had further developments to report, for as so often happens, the nearer one gets to visit a haunted place, the more frantic do the restless ones become, to make sure, perhaps, that you don't overlook them!

"The last occurrence—which I had not told you about—happened within a few days of my return home from San Francisco. I walked between the dining table and the fireplace and felt small gentle tugs at the side of my skirt. There was nothing there to catch the skirt on and I was, for once, *not* alone in the room. But I didn't mention it to anyone then. *It would seem that someone wants to get my attention.*

"The night after I returned from seeing you (Tuesday, May 17) I was sitting alone in the living room and the children and my husband were all asleep in bed. I heard a *loud* slam of a door in the bedroom (there is only one leading outside) and went in. Everyone was still asleep, apparently undisturbed, and I found the door ajar—I mean by that closed but not firmly latched—a slight push would have opened it. Yet a slam as hard as I heard would surely have latched the door firmly, as there is nothing wrong with the catch.

"The last thing that happened was day before yesterday when my son John, who was reading in the bedroom, heard a car pull up on the gravel. There was no one there, but there was a distinct crunching sound as tires passed over gravel. This, strangely enough, is the only really consistent thing that happens here. I have heard a car's tires on the gravel so many times since we moved in that I usually simply ignore it. Only when it is *very* distinct (I mean really loud) do I look outside. When I hear it, I am not aware of the sound of a motor—just the sound of the tires as the car comes to a stop.

"The first time I ever noticed this house, I felt a Model T Ford car, open sedan type, coming up the front road to the house. This makes no sense as the road has been here only about four years.

"That particular day I was sitting in the car with the children at the foot of the hill, in the parking lot there, and one of the children brought the house to my attentlon. Few people notice it—although we are not isolated—possibly because you can see only the roof top from the parking lot below.

"The house was built 10 years ago. The hill was excavated to make room for the house and no one else had ever lived on the spot. There was another road, now not in use, on the other side of the house from the road now used near the front of the house, but it was closed off by part of the hill being excavated only about four years ago. The road generally used now goes through the parking lot at the foot of the hill. There is also another road connected to the road not now in use which goes to the barn."

The business about the Model T Ford puzzled me, of course. But there are cases on record where ghost cars have been observed by psychically gifted people. Anything touched by human emotions may have an etheric double, and if such a car had been part of an emotional experience, a ghost of that car might very well still be part of the atmosphere around the house!

It was plain to me that Mrs. Hinzie was able to see simultaneously into both halves of our world, and that events impressed upon the psychic ether around us were just as clear to her as events in the physical world.

On recollection, Mrs. Hinzie admitted to still another incident involving clairvoyance, which seemed to me particularly relevant because it concerned another ghost car.

"This happened about 1945 or 1946. Fremont Place is a small walled section of Los Angeles—a few blocks only in size, on the south of Olympic Boulevard opposite Los Angeles High School. It was an affluent district in the 20's and the early 30's.

"My mother and her husband, W.A. Anderson, were on a visit to Los Angeles and they had rented a house for a month on a street in the area.

"I sat in the back seat of the car—my brother-in-law drove and my sister and mother and W.A. Anderson were all present. As we drove up the street, I looked into the rear view mirror and saw behind us and gaining on us (we were going slowly) an old sedan (1920's), very high and narrow—a closed car. I could clearly see a woman sitting in the back seat. It looked a little dusty and muddy as I recall but not particularly worn out, or shiny and well-cared-for either. As my brother-in-law eased the car toward the curb, this old sedan passed us *very* closely on the left side and turned closely in front of us in to the curb. It stopped or had almost stopped—that was more my impression (there was no sound of a motor, by the way)—and the door in the rear right side opened immediately and a woman got out. Her face I did not see but she wore a black dress, the 30's hemline, rather long, and a widow's veil on her head. It was thrown back from her face in front and hung over her arms and back to about her elbows. She was walking quickly up toward a house—I think it was the house we entered—when my attention was called away from her by someone in the car. I did not see her again. As my brother-in-law rolled to a stop he hit the old car and we *felt a jar.* I told him what we had hit, but apparently *no one else had seen the car* as they all laughed.

"We then walked up to the house and opened the door. My hair, I was told, stood on end all the time we were there, which was less than 10 minutes.

"There was a large entry hall and lounge room to the right which we went into. I kept feeling as if someone were going to rush out of the butler's pantry behind the dining room to the left all the time I was there, but never really saw that part of the house so I don't even know if there *was* a pantry!

"Mother and W.A. Anderson had been there since the day before—rented the house sight unseen. They had, mother said, quarreled the night before in the house and her husband slapped her—this I think was significant—the place had such an air of tension as if suddenly a fist fight would start. I asked if it was the house in which a man had committed suicide in the 30's; he was a well-known business and society figure, as I recall."

When I was in Hollywood in October 1966, I passed through the area. It is indeed an aristocratic looking "compound," where the politically great and movie stars had made their homes. It still has an air of mystery around it.

On October 5th, shortly before our planned visit, Mrs. Hinzie had had another brush with the uncanny.

"The thing I'm about to tell you happened about 2 to 4 weeks ago. I was outside. The children were just out of school (about 3:30 P.M.) but none had come up the hill. Our dog, Penny, was with me. I heard a child's voice; it sounded like a little girl 5 to 6 years old. She called out something very clearly but I do not remember what. It sounded as if she were not exactly on the road but *above it* near the trees at the bend of the road. The dog heard it, too, and went over near the road and then came back.

"The other thing that happened was a week ago Saturday about 6 P.M. I was standing at the sink fixing something for dinner. The kids were down at the school and Don, my husband, was at the barn. The bedroom and bathroom doors were open but the front door was closed. I heard the front door close—*not open*—not loudly but not stealthily—and saw from the corner of my eye a child, *a boy wearing a white shirt,* go from the direction of the door toward the bedrooms or bathroom. I was so certain I had seen and heard someone I went in search of him because I knew it was not one of my boys. They don't ever wear white shirts, except on Sunday. But there was no one there. That same night I saw a streak of light on our bedroom partition—about two feet long and about four inches at one end, two inches at the other—a pointed thing like an arrow.

"It was very white and low on the wall—about three and one-half feet up—I don't know where it could have come from; it was quickly gone."

Finally, the great day arrived. Everything had been prepared for our coming by Mrs. Hinzie—by everything I mean not only her own house and "case," but two other hauntings not far away which she had brought to my attention and which we intended to look into on the same day prior to returning to Los Angeles.

347

It was an unusually warm day in October 1966 when we started out from Sybil Leek's apartment near Western Avenue. My wife, Catherine, was driving, I was doing the piloting with a map, and Sybil was snoozing in the back seat, tired out from an avalanche of radio and TV appearances in connection with her latest book.

Thanks to Mrs. Hinzie's exact instructions, we made the trip over sundry freeways in about an hour, going toward Ventura and finally veering off the freeway when we reached the little town of Newbury Park. With some maneuvering we managed to find the parking lot through which we were to drive in search of the dirt road leading up to the knoll on which the house stood.

It was the kind of road perfectly suited to a Model T, and not really to a modern no-shift car, but we made it and arrived at the Hinzie house around noon, with the sun blazing down at us at something like 95 degrees Fahrenheit. Our hostess came out to greet us, and we quickly entered the neatly kept little house. The children were still at school and only Mrs. Hinzie and her friend Mrs. Bettin were in the house. Sybil took a chair near the window and I started to work with her almost immediately.

As always, I first asked Sybil if she had any feelings about the house as she came upon it for the first time.

"Not about the house," Sybil replied, "but about the ground . . . the side of the house. I don't think it is a road now. The land is more important than any building here. There is a spot outside the house. . . ."

She did not feel particularly restless *inside* the house, however.

"Outside, there must have been a great deal of coming and going," Sybil continued. "More than one person is connected with it, a communal feeling. This, I am sure, was a meeting place."

She felt that the spot went back three hundred years, and that more than a single restless personality was in evidence. With that, she began to relax and her state of trance became more pronounced.

"Two different periods," Sybil mumbled now. "Sixty years ago, beginning of the century, and then . . . two different nationalities. . . ."

"Who is present here now?"

"Daniel . . . Walker . . ."

For a few minutes there was heavy breathing, and then another personality appeared to be in command of Sybil's lips. At first, the voice was faint, and I had to strain to hear at all, but gradually, as we paid attention, it became stronger until it was heard clearly for all of us to understand—except that it was in Spanish, a language Sybil did not speak fluently; she knows only a few phrases and words, about as much as a tourist might pick up on a casual visit to Spain.

It was a man's voice that came through her now.

"*No gusta,*" it said, and repeated, as if to impress us with the fact that there was something he did not like, "*no gusta.*"

"What is your name?"

"Rafael."

"What?"

"Rafe. . . ."

"Why are you here?"

"Wait."

"Whom are you waiting for?"

"Man . . . Pietro . . . *frater.* . . ."

"What is your brother's name?"

"My—brother—Darshee—Darshin——"

"Where does he live?"

"Valley. . . ." He pronounced it "*Valle,*" the Spanish way.

Then he seemed to become cognizant of my presence.

"Who are you?"

"I'm a friend," I replied softly, "who would like to help you."

"I shall kill you. Go away quickly!"

"Is this your property?"

"Mine."

"How long have you been here?"

"Don't know."

"What year is this?"

"Eighteen-eighty-two," he said haltingly.

"What day?"

"Day?"

"What is your birthday?"

"June . . . birthday. . . ."

"What is your father's name?"

"Daschee." I could not be sure if he said Darshee, Dashee, Dasche, or something sounding like it.

"First name?"

"Dashee Hermanos." Did he perhaps mean "Taje" pronounced in the Spanish way?

"Your mother's name?"

"Maria Garcia . . . Graciella."

"Where did you go to school?"

"School . . . *escuela*. . . ."

"Do you understand English? What I am asking you?"

A moment of silence.

"No . . . I am married . . . Melita. . . ."

"What was her maiden name before she married you?"

"Doran."

"Where was she from?"

"*Escuela. . . hablo . . . escula. . . .*"

I decided to try to get the information, which had been very confusing up to now, by using what Spanish I knew.

"Do you understand English?" I said in Spanish.

No reaction.

"*?Estan Vd. Espanol?*" I tried.

"Si . . ."

"*Por que razòn està Vd. acqui?*" I inquired again. (Why was he here?)

"*Me . . . hermano . . . muerte . . .*"

How old was his brother who died? "Ten," he said in Spanish, becoming very emotional now.

What was his brother's name? "Dan . . . Dana . . . Dajo. . . ."

What could we do to help? "Where is my son?"

Evidently he was looking for his son. I asked where he would like to go now.

"*No gusta,*" he repeated, and we were back where we started, not much wiser.

"*?Que desira Vd. ?*"

"*Mi hijo,*" he pleaded, "I want my son."

The son, it seemed, was only two years old.

I asked him now what was his profession, what did he do. But I did not get an answer. He slipped away before I could get him to tell me, and Sybil returned to her own body—and senses. But before she was entirely "out," I sent her back, this time to observe while entranced, and to describe to me, still in trance, what she saw in the nonphysical world around her.

"Four people . . . child and two men . . . little child, not baby, died suddenly here . . . two men are digging . . . for the child is dead . . . also a woman . . . she is watching me . . . disturbance here . . children play . . . I don't think she likes the men . . . very uneasy feeling between the people here . . . children playing will disturb the little one . . . this is a bad spot for children . . . child can't move . . . hot, no water . . . spirits in the mountains . . . spirits protect this ground, this is not for people to live on . . . should respect the land . . . this land belongs to the spirits . . . sacred to the great . . . from the mountain. . . ."

"Are the four people still here?"

"Feathers and food . . . for spirits . . . lot of people here . . .

dancing quietly . . . dark hair . . . nothing at the top and trousers
. . . Homayo is the name . . . spirit . . . from the mountains to
this spot . . . Homayo the great one . . . eagle feathers. . . ."

I promised we would "sacrifice" in their honor.

"No animals here . . ." Sybil continued, "this is Homayo's
place. Do not disturb. Children should not be here."

I assured the Indian spirit that his memory would be
respected and then I recalled Sybil to the year 1966. But Sybil
stayed "with it" awhile longer, it appeared.

Homayo was still on her mind. Nothing would grow here,
she felt. There was a plague here, and the child was a victim of it.

"The child is buried under the tree," she now said. The
only tree, we later found, was in back of the house, an ancient
tree indeed.

"By the little road," the entranced Sybil added. That, too,
was correct. The little road in back of the house did go by the
tree. There was a house there once which no longer exists.

What did the parents want done about their child?

"Don't disturb it," Sybil reported, "leave the tree."

"What are they looking for in the house?"

"Digging. . . ."

"What was here before?"

"Wooden house. Child died here. No water."

The men were fighting over the land, she added. "Too
many people coming here, Homayo strikes them down.
Thirst."

"What does the child look like?"

"Thin, brown child."

"Male or female?"

"Can't tell. Perhaps ten, nine, ten. Walking, riding. Has a
cloth over it. On the ground. Long hair."

"What is its name?"

"Raffi. . . ."

Evidently the two layers confused Sybil, for she was not

sure which was which—the Indians or the later settlers.

Finally, Sybil came back to her own self. While she rested up from all that had come through her the past hour, I turned to Gwen Hinzie and asked for her comments concerning the material that had now been added to our knowledge of the case.

"Well, of course, we've seen a ten-year-old boy several times here, and yesterday I saw a man, too, outside this window, in his middle fifties, with kind of a humped back—and there were Spanish-speaking settlers here and it is a fact that the Chumash Indians lived here . . . also, there was a house behind the school over there, where people lived until about 1920. They had a child, a little girl, who fell into a well and died. There certainly were people out here in 1882, and many of them spoke Spanish."

"What about the name Daniel that was mentioned early in the session?"

Mrs. Hinzie nodded.

"A family named Borchardt owned much of the land here for many years . . . and Daniel was Mr. Borchardt's first name, I think. But I'm not sure."

"What about the child being buried under the tree?"

"Well, there is this big tree behind the house, and I did see a child—a ghost child, that is, about a year and a half ago, behind that tree."

"Was it male or female?"

"Male, but it looked older than the one I had seen on the lawn at the house. I thought at first it had gone down the hill, but it could not have disappeared from view at that spot—unless it had sunk into the ground. There just is no way to go."

I agreed that this would have been impossible, after inspecting the spot.

"About those Indians," Mrs. Hinzie said, as an afterthought, "it sounds like a ceremonial ground rather than a burial ground. Women would never do in a ceremonial area."

Mr. Hinzie, who had come in at the onset of the trance session and had sat quietly watching it all, now spoke up.

"There is an Indian burial ground being excavated right now nearby."

I then talked to the three children, ranging in age from 9 to 12, and they reiterated their stories substantially as told to me by their mother. They seemed like bright, normal youngsters, no more imaginative than ordinary children and not too eager to talk about it all.

When they pointed to the ceiling of their room as the haunted spot, Sybil, who had stepped into the room now, nodded assent.

"That would be the original land level," she remarked, "and *they* would walk on that level."

We then went outside, as Sybil felt an urge to "putter around" despite the great heat.

Sybil insisted that there was an Indian trail leading from the hills to the sea directly through the house—in fact, over the spot where the children had seen the apparitions. Mr. Hinzie confirmed that there was such a trail although he did not know its exact location.

We returned to the car now, as Mrs. Hinzie had other points of psychic interest in store for us.

Since then, Mrs. Hinzie has tried to check up on some of the Native American doings in the area. In nearby Agoura, in the San Fernando Valley, archaeologists from the University of California were busy digging up a Chumash Native American burial ground. These Indians, Mrs. Hinzie discovered, had been converted to Christianity by Spanish Franciscan priests. This area was within the ground covered by the mission at San Buenaventura, now Ventura. The Native Americans had disappeared and there is but one survivor living in Newbury Park now who is half Chumash and half Mexican.

I haven't heard anything further about any disturbances at

the Hinzie house since our return from California. With so many layers of psychic consciousness in the spot, it seems a little difficult to sort out the ghosts. But the fact remained that Mrs. Gwen Hinzie has a prolific talent for seeing and hearing them, and our own Sybil was able to give information that dovetails with the earlier testimony. Native American ceremonial grounds are a little hard to pin down, as there is no written literature among the Indians, but the little lost boy, between two states of being, as it were, must surely be guided across the threshold. Perhaps as the flesh-and-blood children in the Hinzie house grow older and their available energies cannot be drawn upon any longer for some of these psychic manifestations, the ghost of the boy will also fade away into the "land of the great spirit" where red or white skins no longer matter.

A few days before, as we were flying toward Los Angeles, Sybil had suddenly turned to me with a puzzled expression.

"What a strange occupation," she said, "to be a worm rancher!"

I was nonplused. What had brought on that remark? Sybil was not sure. It had just entered her mind.

I dismissed the strange thought, but when we met Mr. Hinzie, he took us to the back of the house where the barn stood.

"I've got a little business on the side going in there," he explained lightly. *"I'm a worm rancher!"*

I had never heard of anyone raising worms for fishermen, but apparently this occupation was not unique, though admittedly rare.

Sybil evidently had a premonition of all this. It makes me feel that our mission to Newbury Park was indeed "in the cards" long before we set foot there.

Mrs. Hinzie kept looking for possible confirmations of

some of the things that had come through in trance. For one thing, the business about Indians at her house wanted further elucidation.

In January of 1967, Mrs. Hinzie was able to send excerpts from proper sources on the local Indians, the tribes Sybil had referred to in trance.

"I have researched the Chumash Indians out here to some extent and have found out a little bit bearing out Sybil's description of religious rites, which I'll quote here. This information comes from a book called *San Buenaventura, The Mission by the Sea*, by Father Zephyrin Engelhardt, O.F.M., printed in 1930 for the author by the Schauer Printing Studio, Inc., Santa Barbara, California.

"The following (pp. 33–40) was written by Father José Senan between 1812 and 1823 during his term of office as Presidente at Mission San Buenaventura, in Ventura. It was in answer to a list of questions proposed by the Spanish Government and sent to the priests at each mission with regard to the Indians of their area who lived and worked at the particular mission. They were called *neophytes* and all were of the Chumash tribe. The quotes are numbered apparently as they were in Fr. Seilan's *Requesta* (reply).

"'12. No inclination to idolatry is observed in our neophytes; nor can it be said that in savagery they practiced any formal idolatry. In the vicinity of their rancherias (small villages) *and on the mountain*, they used to have some places which they kept very clean, swept, and adorned *with beautiful plumage* put on poles. To these places they would go as to their sacred places. Here they would *assemble* in time of need and conduct a sort of pilgrimage. One of their number, in the name of all the rest, who observed profound silence would pray for rain, offering an abundance of acorns, seeds, and wild fruits which constituted their daily sustenance. They would catch fish or kill deer in order that no bear might catch them or the bite of a rattlesnake might not afflict them. They would pray also for health and other good things. At the end of the supplication, they would in their simplicity and crude veneration offer beads, acorns and various seeds, in order that they might be regarded with favor by the invisible one, whom they pictured to themselves according to their rude notions as the author and giver of rains, seeds, fruits, and other good things. The first part of this petition was always uniform. It was preceded by a salutation which in our language (Spanish) means as much as "Grand Captain or Captain of Captains, behold us and hear what we say."

" '19. The gentiles (pagans) of this vicinity have not adored the sun nor the moon.

" '28. They never offered human sacrifices to gods.

" '33. . . . in paganism they used only a flute-like thing made of elderwood, as also a bone *whistle*, with which the players produce a shriek and violent trill, at the same time making strange and ridiculous contortions of the body. Their songs are weird, more adapted to arouse sadness than gladness.

" '36. The dress of the male neophytes consists of a short overall, called cotón, or a breechcloth, in place of breeches, and of a blanket. All this clothing is made at the mission. The pagans know nothing of dress, except that women wear the hide of a deer or fringes of grass to meet the demands of natural decency.'

"This, above, is shown to have been written August 11, 1816, at Mission San Buenaventura, by Father José Senan."

"As to our own house, all is peaceful and serene, except that twice in the past month I've heard someone humming (kind of tunelessly) outside the door or at least close to it. It is the voice of either a child or a woman. We have no more lights or opening of doors and cars arriving on the gravel or slamming of car doors.

"There is no longer the feeling of little cat feet on our bed.

My husband used to feel a cat walk across his feet whether he was sleeping on his lunch hour or at night. I had always felt it walking up toward me on my side of the bed but until he told me he felt the little feet I really thought it must be my imagination. It never walked ON me, just beside me. This was true almost from the time we moved in here. It is a very light step, almost weightless but not quite."

To sum it all up: Sybil, a stranger to those parts, had correctly described the ghost of a young child, the presence of Indians on the very spot where I had taken her, and a number of small but significant details, such as the ridiculous bit of information concerning Mr. Hinzie's worm-ranching activities. More important even, Mrs. Gwen Hinzie's own place in our psychically oriented world of study and knowledge seems pretty secure to me. She is, to borrow from Gilbert and Sullivan, the very model of a modern amateur medium!

In July 1967 Mrs. Hinzie contacted me again. All had been serene at the house for several months, except for a couple of gentle reminders that perhaps one of the ghosts, the child, had not yet left, even though the father had gone on.

A door opened by itself on one occasion; then a small white cloud appeared next to Mrs. Hinzie's bed which she at first mistook for cigarette smoke, until she convinced herself that the ashtray was cold. But the clincher came a few days after, when she was awakened in bed by the touch of a hand taking hers! The unseen hand felt soft and warm, but very firm. When it clasped Mrs. Hinzie's own hand, she naturally tried to withdraw it. The ghost hand tightened, and at the same time Mrs. Hinzie felt a strong pain in her armpits, as if fingers were pressing there.

In desperation, Mrs. Hinzie moved her own hand, with the ghost hand holding on to it, to her face and *bit into it*.

"It felt as though I had bitten into foam rubber," she said, but the ghost hand let go now and soon sleep returned to the "ghost lady of Newbury Park."

I advised Mrs. Hinzie to speak to the little ghost, should it ever return, as a mother would—to have the little one join his father out there in the great beyond. But then some children, even ghostly ones, are notoriously bad at taking orders.

THE HAUNTED BARN

$\mathcal{M}$rs. Hinzie had really done some useful spadework for us. There were two sites where uncanny goings-on had been reported and she wanted us to see them firsthand. In a place like California, where so much violence has taken place not only during the 19th century pioneer days but in comparatively recent times, psychic occurrences are not at all unlikely, and I only asked that there be some specific "complaint" in these cases. There was.

Our first stop was the Stagecoach Inn, a handsome mid-19th century building originally erected as a way station when this spot was a major factor in the stagecoach route to and from California. Later, it had deteriorated into an inn, the kind that takes on all comers and does not ask too many questions just so long as they can pay their bills.

According to Guy Runnion, editor of the *Conejo News*, who is the unofficial historian of this landmark, there had been killings here, and as far back as the 1930s, reports of hauntings at the Inn were prevalent.

A Mr. Dyke of nearby Thousand Oaks confirmed that his own father, a well-driller during those years, had spoken to him of such goings-on.

At this time, the Inn was a museum, and it had just been moved on its foundations to a new location a few yards farther back from the original site to allow the freeway to pass. Whether the alleged ghost or ghosts would resent the move, or move out themselves, was a moot point—for me to find out.

The historical society in the person of Dr. Cyril Anderson was in charge of the buildings then.

From 1952 to 1965, however, it had been used as a gift-shop by a couple named McIntyre who spoke of a female ghost there; however, when questioned, Mrs. McIntyre passed the matter off as "just a story" without substance.

When Gwen Hinzie was doing newspaper work in the area in 1962, she had occasion to visit the Inn frequently since it was only a few blocks away from the Hinzie house, and the land, in fact, is really one and the same parcel, connected with both the hill on which the Hinzie house now stood and the entire Hays family holdings around it. That this was of some significance we were to learn a little later.

But when Mrs. Hinzie first entered the 19-room mansion, Mrs. McIntyre remarked how odd it was that Mrs. Hinzie's hair should suddenly stand on end. Evidently hair raising is to Mrs. Hinzie what goose pimples are to Sybil Leek: an indicator of pyschic energies in the area.

At this moment, Mrs. Hinzie heard a crash upstairs, but she was assured by the proprietor of the giftshop that there was nobody above stairs. But her curiosity was aroused and she next talked to Donna Fargo, of the famous Wells Fargo family, regarding the Inn. Bandits, it seems, were roving in this area during stagecoach days, and only twenty miles away at Colahasas, things were truly "the wild west."

The Inn had been built in the expectancy of a great deal of business because of the Butterfield mail route which was supposed to have gone through the Conejo Valley on the way to St. Louis; and there was already a post office at Newbury Park in 1875. But the Civil War interfered and the Butterfield line declined in importance, and the main route went through the Santa Clara Valley instead.

We arrived at the house while the sun was blazing, and the coolness of the inside was a welcome relief from its unremitting rays. The work of restoration was in full progress, but one could see that the house had had some stature at one time; it reminded one of the typical Western gambling inn movie set, complete with stairway leading to the rooms upstairs.

Sybil had started to "putter around" and I took great care to point out the various pitfalls where she might have landed in the basement without benefit of stairs. But Sybil is agile, and her five senses, not to mention her sixth, kept her out of trouble. I found her in a room to the left of the stairs, a room that undoubtedly was once a guest room when the Inn was a hotel.

"This room interests me," Sybil explained, "more than the rest of the house. Before we arrived I had a feeling of something very unstable. Well, it is. The foundations are not ready. The house has been moved. Also, I feel a connection with the other place as if this were in line with it."

I realized that the land was of one piece. Was Sybil picking up the Indian trail again?

"What sort of place do you feel this is?" As always, I had not told Sybil anything about the place we were in at the moment. It could be a private house, a manor, anything; there was nothing to indicate that it was an inn, especially a stage-coach inn. And yet Sybil got the scent.

"A meeting place . . . not just a residence. Too many people come and go and leave disturbances . . . a food and drink place. . . ."

Meanwhile, Leighton Field, a photographer with the Historical Society, and Kathy Berg, a young lady reporter from the *News-Chronicle*, had arrived and followed us around in the hope of catching, if not a ghost, at least some interesting conversation.

"I'm very depressed," Sybil now said, "especially in this room . . . tragedy . . . perhaps the room above also. . . ."

We entered the upstairs room and Sybil picked up something stronger now.

"Think of the name Pierre Devon," Sybil suggested, "that is the name that is there . . . 1882 to 1889 . . . violent headache . . . right hand side of head . . . died here . . . still present in this part of the house . . . short, dirty, not a farmer, mountains . . . passing through . . . passing through before Los Angeles . . . *hidalgo* . . . what does it mean?"

"That means gentleman," said the curator, who had come up to us. "The house was built in in 1876, so it was here in 1882."

But despite a careful search of the fragmentary records still extant about the period in question, no Pierre Devon could be pinned down. If this man was merely a transient passenger, spending a night here en route to Los Angeles, there hardly would be any. And if some local murderers had relieved him of his gold, there would be even less reason to let the world know.

Thus it appeared that Pierre Devon, whoever he was, had taken the secret of his demise with him. I only hoped that seeing Sybil, and being briefly aware of the outside world through her, would have sufficiently shaken him to allow him to leave the place of his death. And, since the Inn had been moved back from the original site, he really had no reason to stay on. Who ever heard of a ghost sitting on the freeway? He'd get himself killed all over again!

Our main objective that afternoon, however, was a *haunted barn* not far away in Thousand Oaks. What I had gathered through Mrs. Hinzie was that at that time, there were two local theaters: an old one no longer used as such, and a new one that had just opened, and that both, strangely enough, were haunted. As we were in direct line to the new playhouse first, I decided to have a look at the Conejo Valley players' spanking new theatre and talk to those who had experienced the uncanny.

The new theatre turned out to be a tastefully constructed auditorium with modern stage facilities, seats graduated for excellent viewing, and an overall feeling of newness belying anything ghostly. I had been told by Mrs. Hinzie that the original site of the haunting was the "old theatre," a barn at Thousand Oaks which had been turned into a Baptist Church, but that somehow the ghost had travelled with the actors and taken up residence in the new house. This I had to see, for ghosts, to my mind, do not leave the spot of their passing.

To greet us, several members of the community theatre— an amateur endeavor, of course—were on hand. The auditorium, I noticed, was built into the hillside, very much like Mrs. Hinzie's house. In fact, it partook of the same piece of land as the Hinzie house and the Stagecoach Inn; thus I would not have been surprised, I thought, if Sybil felt Native American influences here, too. She was walking around somewhat restlessly, examining her feelings in the place. But she felt nothing here.

I turned to Mrs. Beverly Adams, one of the principals of the Conejo players, who had experienced some of the phenomena connected with this theatre.

"The first time anything happened," she began, "was when my husband and Herman Detering were here with me after rehearsals, one night about a year ago. We were closing up and we were all standing in the control booth, and I walked to the doors looking into the auditorium, on to the stage, and I heard voices and walking around in the back dressing room. I mentioned it, saying, evidently everyone isn't out of the theatre yet, so my husband and Mr. Detering went backstage to get them out—but they found nobody there. They, too, had heard the footsteps and voices. The dressing rooms are to the left of the stage and I was in back of the theatre, but I heard it. It sounded like a couple of people talking back there. A man and a woman."

"Could there have been someone there who left before you got to the dressing room?"

"Impossible. We would have seen them leave. The rear door is locked. That was around 11:00 at night."

"Only once?"

"No, I have heard unexplained noises around here two or three times. One night I was sitting in the first row watching rehearsals of *Finian's Rainbow* when I heard someone at the door trying to get in. The doorknob was rattling, so I went over, for we keep the door locked so you can't open it from the outside, but only from the inside. There was nobody there. I sat down again when I heard footsteps going up onto the stage from the other side, and I thought, well, they must have gone through the other door. Then it dawned on me that the steps outside were concrete and that the steps I heard being walked on were wooden! Then I heard walking back and forth in the wings, so I asked Laverne Kaufman, who was sitting next to me, and she had heard it too."

"Have you had any psychic impressions here other than the noises you heard?"

"Yes," Mrs. Adams replied, "I've had cold, clammy feelings both here and in the old place, here in the first row where we are now and backstage in the wings also, at various times."

"How old is this theatre—was there anything here before?"

"Two years and there was nothing here before."

I turned to dark-haired Laverne Kaufman, who had now joined us, and asked what she had experienced here during the time she had been active in the community theatre.

"As my friend has told you, when we were watching the

rehearsal of *Finian's Rainbow*, I, too felt the cold—strangely enough she felt it on her left leg, and I on my right leg; she got up to leave and get some coffee, and the sensation left me—but when she returned, the chill was back. At one time I have heard the piano give off a run which I recognized as a piece of music from a show. My son also heard it and it went through twice, yet there was nobody at the piano at that moment!"

I'm sure the musicians' union would not have liked this.

At this point Sybil reported that the left-hand side of the stage was a haunted area.

"Let us now find out what occurred in the *old theatre*, the one that is now a Baptist Church," I said, and turned to Mrs. Adams. "What happened to you there?"

"Shortly after I entered the theatre for the first time— that's the old barn—I was helping on the sets for one of the plays when I heard directly above us some footsteps. *Someone was pacing back and forth above us in the loft!*"

"A man?"

"A man's footsteps, heavy, long strides. This was about three years ago. I was with another player, a gentleman, and I turned to him, saying, 'I thought we were alone here—who's up there?' Instead of an answer, he took me outside the building. The only entrance to the loft was from outside the building. The loft was much too low for a man to stand, much less to walk back and forth in. Moreover the door was locked, and the lock looked as if it had been in place for quite a while. We unlocked the padlock and entered the loft. There was nobody to be seen. We looked in every nook and corner but the loft was empty. So we locked it up again and went downstairs to resume work. No sooner had we done so, when the pacing above started up again. I've heard this same pacing many times since, sometimes during the day, sometimes at night, even during performances. And there is never anyone there— visible, that is."

"Didn't the audiences notice it?"

"If they did, they must have thought it part of the performance, or crew."

"But you knew?"

"Yes, we knew the difference. We had the key and the loft was securely locked at all times. We never found out about any tragedy in this place, but I, being somehow psychic, have always felt a tragedy there—a triangle involving two men and a woman."

"You say you are psychic—have you had other impressions?"

"On one occasion I was in the theatre and commented on my belief that a murder had been committed as part of a triangle, and at this point I had a cold, clammy feeling surrounding me—and I felt this one man was trying to get through to me and that his name was something like Byron."

"Byron?"

"Yes. I started to check up on the name, but every time I was in the theatre I had this horribly oppressive feeling so that I became afraid to check any further."

"Have you had any psychic experiences before the ones at the theatre?"

"I've always been able to sense if there was going to be a death in the family . . . or trouble . . . even as a child, but people made fun of me. . . ."

"Is there any similarity between the ghostly noises heard by you at the haunted barn and at the new theatre?"

"Yes, I seem to sense that this Byron is at the other theatre also. He always liked music at the barn and does so here, too. One night we were rehearsing *A Thurber Carnival* over at the barn, and when we played some taped music and then stopped it to go home, we heard four loud bangs on the ceiling as if to tell us to continue. When we sang the same song, to see if 'he' would react, we instantly heard the ghost pacing above us. I've even had someone pull my covers *at home*, scratch the under-side of my pillow and pull at my mattress, so I am wondering if he isn't following me home, too!"

"More human than ghostly!" I interjected.

"I guess he wanted my attention at home, to keep him company," Mrs. Adams replied, "or something . . . I would hear pebbles hit the roof, bumps against the wall—and I have the same cold, clammy feeling here as I had in the old theatre. I think he's attached himself to me because I'm sympathetic."

"Did you ever have any visual impression of what your friend looked like?" I asked. Evidently this was not an ordinary ghost but a lost soul looking for an explanation to his confusion.

"At the time I sensed the name Byron," Mrs. Adams recalled, "I had the impression of this man standing at my left, about five ten, a husky man, like a construction worker or log-ger, wearing jeans, boots, and a pale blue plaid shirt, sleeves rolled up to his elbows."

"And his face?"

"Heavy features. . . ."

"Did you feel any unfinished business around him?"

"Yes . . . he was trying to tell me about some tragedy, something he wanted to have found out—he was almost beg-ging me to check further into that location, that area—*things that happened there at the old barn.*"

"Then it is there that we may find a solution," I conjec-tured, hoping that Sybil might pick up a clue where the tragedy originated.

"One time here at the new theatre, after we had heard him make noises, I said, 'Goodnight, Byron, we will see you again'; and as we were riding home in the car—I felt him sitting in the backseat. It felt so cold and clammy I was greatly relieved to get out of the car when we arrived at my house. I put my purse down in the bedroom and walked back into the living room and sat down to read; and all of a sudden that same cold, clammy feeling was with me, and my dog started to set up a howl and bark frantically, just sitting at my feet staring into the hallway!"

"Was that the last time the ghost tried to reach you?"

"Yes, I moved shortly after."

Herman Detering, one of the men active in the running of this community theatre, seemed like a quiet, soft-spoken realist to me, not the sort of flamboyant actor one might conceivably accuse of imagining things. I questioned him about his own experiences.

"Nothing special here in the new theatre, but at the old barn, I recall one early morning, I was working alone in the control booth when I heard footsteps overhead and got the distinct impression of someone looking over my shoulder, to see what I was doing. I was recording some music at the time. I shone the light on the loft, which had been locked, but there was nothing in the area where I had heard the footsteps except so many seats stacked that nobody could possibly have walked there."

"What did you do?"

"I locked the door and went home."

"Could anyone have walked in the area of the loft where you heard the steps?"

"Impossible. It is only three feet high, not counting the seats stacked there. Nothing of flesh and blood could walk there."

We proceeded to the church now called the Missionary Baptist Church which stood on a bluff overlooking the freeway access road. We had been told that our visit was not welcome when Mrs. Hinzie had requested permission from the minister, one Elder Wayne Ivett, to have a quiet sitting in the church that would not interfere with worship. He intimated that the Bible (his version, anyway) said there were no ghosts, and if there were any in his church, they'd be the work of the devil, and nobody in his congregation believed in ghosts.

Under the circumstances I decided not to bedevil the poor man, and to have a look at the outside of the building and see if Sybil would pick something up by being close to it. Since the minister did not own the public road, that would be legitimate.

Well, the church looked exactly like an old dairy barn, which it was originally, when a Mr. Goebel owned it. However, none of the current flock were around, so we approached and looked at it through windows. There was a big padlock on the door, so if the devil was inside, he must have gotten in through the rear entrance. Since I was not about to have any ol' devil best us, we walked around that way, too, which was not easy as the road around the barn was more fit for small animal traffic than human feet.

Sybil abruptly halted when we passed the entrance to the loft, which was a small wooden door atop three small steps. It, too, was locked.

"Someone is escaping . . . running away . . . thirty, forty years ago . . . a man is escaping after committing some crime . . . an element of violence. . . ."

"Do you feel he is still here?" I asked. The others had grouped themselves around us now, hanging on Sybil's lips.

"Yes," Sybil replied emphatically, "because he did not escape in his real life. I *think he was stabbed.* But *his* crime was not stabbing somebody else. Perhaps theft. . . ."

Mrs. Beverly Adams reacted at this moment as if something of importance had just struck her.

"That's what I felt all along," she said excitedly, "and I had the impression that the man who was stabbed was the lover of the wife of the man who did the stabbing."

As we passed the rear of the building, one of the party noticed that the back door was open. I hesitated to enter, for the welcome mat was certainly not out for us; on the other hand, any tourist visiting the area would have walked in and not have committed a sin, for a church is the house of God and should be open to all, no matter who they are.

We decided to have a quick look at the inside of the barn church, since fate had obviously so arranged it. The inside was plain and uninspiring. A small room to the right of the stage and a washroom were all that the building contained in addition to the stage, on which the pulpit stood, and the seventy-five seats. But then faith does not require fancy trappings.

I turned to Sybil for her impressions.

"Same thing here . . . the man trying to escape . . . I think he was connected with some crime connected with the earth . . . stealing . . . he was killed upstairs. . . ."

We went outside again, for the atmosphere suddenly seemed very heavy.

"I wonder if any of the congregation has heard the footsteps," I wondered out loud, and Gwen Hinzie took me up on that.

"When we were here in August—just two months ago—a lady and her 14-year-old daughter, members of this church, came in while we were here, looking at the church. I questioned them about the phenomena and the girl looked at her mother and said—'Shall I tell them?'

"It seems that she and a young friend had clearly heard footsteps overhead especially while music was being played. On one occasion the two girls were alone in the barn church, and one of them tried the piano.

"Suddenly, both of them heard footsteps in the loft over their heads. They were quite alone in the building, or so they thought, and they went to check the door to the loft. It was tightly locked."

"In other words," I said, "the haunted barn is still *active?*"

Mrs. Hinzie nodded. "I'm afraid so."

I asked both Sybil Leek and Beverly Adams to send mental messages to the unfortunate young man who thought he had to stay on because of his tragic death, that he need not do so, but that, in effect, all was well for him now.

He seemed to have found a measure of joy in watching the theatricals underneath his self-imposed prison. When the barn ceased to be a theatre and became a church, he stayed on. Perhaps he does not even know the difference. That's how it is sometimes with ghosts.